FEAR WORDPERFECT FOR WINDOWS™ NO MORE

Danny Goodman

with
Katherine Murray

Fear WordPerfect for Windows No More

///|Brady

New York   London   Toronto   Sydney   Tokyo   Singapore

Brady Publishing

A Division of Prentice Hall Computer Publishing
15 Columbus Circle
New York, NY 10023

ISBN: 1-56686-111-x
Library of Congress Catalog No.: 93-21158

Printing Code: The rightmost double-digit number is the year of the book's printing; the rightmost single-digit number is the number of the book's printing. For example, 93-1 shows that the first printing of the book occurred in 1993.

96 95 94 93   4 3 2 1

Manufactured in the United States of America

Dedication

To my very loud and very wonderful family.

Credits

Publisher
Michael Violano

Acquisitions Director
Jono Hardjowirogo

Managing Editor
Kelly D. Dobbs

Production Editor
Bettina A. Versaci

Editorial Assistants
Lisa Rose
Yana Strutin

Book Designer
Kevin Spear

Cover Designer
Jay Corpus

Imprint Manager
Scott Cook

Production Analyst
Mary Beth Wakefield

Indexers
Jeanne Clark, Michael Hughes,
Joy Dean Lee, Craig Small

Production Team
Diana Bigham, Katy
Bodenmiller, Brad Chinn,
Tim Cox, Meshell Dinn,
Mark Enochs, Howard Jones,
Beth Rago, Carrie Roth,
Greg Simsic, Marc Shecter

Marketing Director
Lonny Stein

Marketing Coordinator
Laura Cadorette

Acknowledgments

Gremlin battling is an exhausting process. Special thanks to the exterminating efforts of the following people:

KiDDo Dobbs, Managing Editor at Brady, who is a truly amazing person capable of Great Things (a great secret weapon for any publisher lucky enough to have her), and one heck of a lot of fun.

Jono Hardjowirogo, Brady Acquisitions Manager, for giving me the opportunity to participate in another Fear No More project. I love these things.

Danny Goodman, series author, for his vision and thoughtful creation of this series. Also, on this title in particular, for his vote of confidence and support. Thanks for letting me help.

John Gieg, the Creature Guy, for creating the perfect little monsters that are tamed in the pages of this book, but who will, I hope, continue to live on. (Maybe a line of stuffed animals, John? Or T-shirts, Jono? Somebody call marketing...)

My agent, Claudette Moore, of Moore Literary Agency, for being so darned good at everything. She's the best advocate an author could have—much smarter than the Average Bear.

My kids, Kelly, Christopher, and baby Cameron, who are on summer vacation and have to put up with a mom who isn't.

My husband, Doug, who helps more than I could ever say, and is the Best Daddy Ever.

About the Author

Writing computer books is a habit that Katherine Murray has learned to deal with. She was born in a small shack in Silicon Valley and left to be raised by a pair of PCs. Sure, they did the best they could, providing her with an 8088 education, but as technology increased, their mode of parenting became outdated. Today, Katherine is the author of 30 computer books and the mother of one desktop, one laptop, and one notebook computer.

Contents at a Glance

Contents

Introduction

Oh no. Not *WordPerfect*. Your friends have warned you about it. The people in the next office over had to hire a trainer just to help the staff open the package. The people downstairs had to build a storage closet just to hold the documentation. You're supposed to learn this program and get *good* at it?

Who are they kidding?

We've all heard the WordPerfect horror stories. Well, take a deep breath and relax—most of them are not true. Yes, WordPerfect offers a gazillion features, but you learn them one at a time. In *Fear WordPerfect for Windows No More*, you'll take on those one-at-a-time tasks and master the little beasties. Just think of the satisfaction you'll have next time you run into a WordPerfect-phobic person at the Coke machine.

It *is* true that WordPerfect is one of the most feature-laden word processing programs of our time. It has everything from spelling checkers to grammar checkers to legal dictionaries to macros to tips for getting along with your mother-in-law. And, as a WordPerfect for Windows user, you're in luck: your version of WordPerfect is prettier to look at than its DOS cousin. Although the number of buttons and tools on the screen may frighten you at first, you'll find that clicking buttons is a lot more fun than choosing boring-old commands from boring-old menus.

You may never need to venture out into the deepest WordPerfect waters; depending on the job you do, you may be able to just wade in up to your ankles. We'll even hold your hand as you do it (and swat at those little critters that come up out of the sand looking for unguarded toes.) Let's leave the drop-off for the people with the scuba equipment.

Confronting Your Fears

You may not want to admit it—most people don't—but your single biggest stumbling block is... really... *you*. Oh, we can blame WordPerfect for being so incredibly complicated or gripe about the number of features or the disk space it takes, but when it comes right down to it, learning a new program like this one is a scary experience. It's hard to believe that someday—perhaps months from now—you'll be sitting at your desk typing away like you've done it all your life (or, at least, for a month).

The biggest something that gets in our way is fear. And this type of fear comes in five flavors:

- Fear of messing up
- Fear of looking stoopid
- Fear of the unknown
- Fear of change
- Fear of fear

You know the fear of messing up: we've all felt it. Whether it's a Big One or a small one, those screw-ups scream "Amateur!" People peek over cubicle walls when they hear that embarrassing computer beep. Your office mates get tired of telling you how to add a footer time after time after time. When your boss sees you running frantically from your desk to the printer and back again, she rolls her eyes.

You know what they're thinking. Will you *never* learn? (That's what you're afraid of!)

And that leads right into looking stupid, doesn't it? People are watching you and you're floundering like hooked bluegill. How in the world will you ever figure out how to set margins? You can't ask anyone—you don't want to admit that you don't know how. And what are fonts, anyway, besides those faceless things that chase you through your nightmares.

It's okay. Calm down.

Fear of the unknown is a big one. What if you never figure out how to set margins? What if all your reports are written in Courier when your cohorts are passing out printouts with all sorts of fancy type? What if you're still using the Glue Stick to paste on colorful graphs when other managers are including them printed right in their documents?

And then there's the fear of change. You'll recognize this one easily—it's characterized by those sudden intense pangs of loneliness for the old Smith-Corona typewriter. You find yourself rummaging through the supply closet, overcome with the urge to find the thing and hug it. Oh, life seemed so much simpler then. You typed a letter, signed it, folded it, and put it in the envelope. There. It's done. So what if you had to do the same thing—same letter, same signature—day after day after day? At least it was easy and you understood what was expected of you.

The last one—the fear of fear—is the little gremlin that paints a picture in your brain of you, six months from now, still as panicked as you are today. You haven't learned anything. Your computer still beeps. Margins still elude you. And everything you print—from memos to annual reports—are printed in that nightmarish Courier.

Take a deep breath and relax. Then invite all those little fear monsters to come on out and have a cup of coffee. Through the course of this book, you'll learn that those little devils that seem so scary right this minute are no more than figments of your imagination.

What You'll Find in Fear WordPerfect for Windows No More

In this book, you'll find a unique approach to dealing with your WordPerfect for Windows intimidation. The best weapon against fear in any form is education, and we've packed all the basics between the covers of this book. Specifically, you'll find that the following elements come together to make learning WordPerfect for Windows nonthreatening and (dare we say it?) perhaps even fun:

- A set of encounters, each helping you learn a new WordPerfect for Windows skill and dispel a demon or two

- A goal statement clearly defining what you'll accomplish in each session

- A What-You-Will-Need section that tells you, up front, the elements you need for a successful encounter

- Terms of Enfearment, which highlight the WordPerfect buzzwords you'll master

- The briefing, in which the main explanation of the encounter takes place, showing Things As They Should Be

- They're Out To Get Us, a section detailing what might happen when Things *Aren't* As They Should Be

- Demon-strations, which allow you to practice hands-on examples of the encounter topic

- Summary, which gives you a broad brush overview of the topics introduced in the encounter, and

- Exorcises, a set of fill-in-the-blank, matching, multiple-choice, and true/false questions that allow you to test what you've learned and make sure that you've rid yourself of that particular encounter's gremlin.

Throughout the book, you'll see screen shots when you need them, and illustrations of those buggy little monsters pop up all over the place. Tables are also used, as needed, to highlight information. Additionally, you'll find numbered steps and bulleted lists in passages where extra emphasis is given to steps in a tutorial section or to items in a series.

What You Won't Find in Fear WordPerfect for Windows No More

The best books don't try to be all things to all people. You won't find a bunch of things in this book:

- No super-technical explanations

- No programming code (ugh)

- No esoteric references to procedures you'll never use in a million years

- No brain-melting macros

- No tricks that require you to drink a glass of water upside-down (which, by the way, is the only *real* cure for hiccups)

- No tacky references to other Brady books you can buy for more in-depth coverage of WordPerfect for Windows (although if you *really* want to know—)

In a bold attempt to give you only what you need to slay your WordPerfect dragons and get on the road to word processing wizardry, *Fear WordPerfect for Windows No More* helps you learn the basics—just what you need to get going—and then gets out of your way. No unnecessary hand-holding, verbose descriptions, or long-winded explanations (Whew! I'm out of breath!)

Who's Afraid of a Little Program?

Hunh. Well, if you've seen the WordPerfect for Windows documentation package, you already know that this is no *little* program. If you've seen the way it eats the storage space in your hard drive, you'd call it something other than small.

But, mass and memory considerations aside, why should you be scared of learning a new program? Because it's there. Because it's new. Because your job—or, at least, your ego—may depend on it. Most of us teeter on the brink of learning a new program until something or someone shoves us over the edge. We usually don't pick up a few disks and think "Hmmmm. I've got a few hours to spare. I think I'll learn this new program!" If we've got extra time, we do things we want to do, like laundry or leg waxing or skeet shooting. Not word processing. Not *WordPerfect*.

Specifically, you can use this book to squash your WordPerfect for Windows gremlins if you fall into one of the following categories (figuratively speaking):

- You are being forced to learn WordPerfect for Windows against your will

- Your boss has told you that you can never go to lunch again until you master the basics of WordPerfect for Windows

- You begrudgingly admit that having a word processing program and being able to publish your own materials would help your business

- Your employees have already learned WordPerfect for Windows and are making fun of you because you can't even write a memo

- The newest junior manager knows WordPerfect for Windows inside and out and creates eye-popping reports that get everyone's attention (and you want to hang on until retirement)

- You just want to write a letter to your aunt and WordPerfect for Windows is the only program on this blasted computer

- Your friend said "Buy WordPerfect for Windows" and you did. Why? You're still not sure...

We don't want to paint too rosy of a picture for you (you wouldn't believe us anyway), but if you're working with WordPerfect for Windows, you've got an easier road than you might expect. If you're familiar with Windows, expect the same basic tools—but more of them. Buttons will surround you in your first attempts to create something legible, but take heart: you'll be clicking like a pro in no time.

Whether the tasks you'll take on with WordPerfect are simple or complex, whether the number of gremlins that plague you are few or many, *Fear WordPerfect for Windows No More* will help you take those first few shaky steps into the Wonderful World of Word Processing.

Now, if you're ready, think a Happy Thought, and let's go...

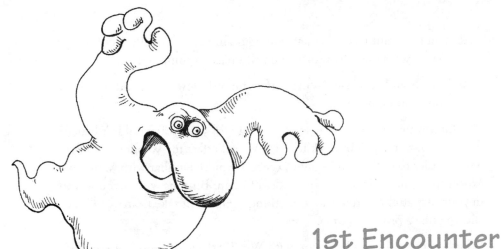

What Is WordPerfect for Windows and Why Do I Have To Use It?

Goal

To help you come to terms with the fact that yes, you *do* have to learn WordPerfect for Windows (don't blame us), and yes, you *can* do it in this lifetime.

What You Will Need

A morbid curiosity to see what's coming. (You probably watch out the window for approaching funnel clouds, too, don't you?)

Terms of Enfearment

word processing	ribbon
commands	Outline Bar
pull-down menus	scroll bars

Briefing

You know the sensation: your palms are sweating, your heart is hammering in your chest. The top of your head tingles like you're on the verge of passing out. You guessed it—WordPerfect panic. The only thing you can do to lasso those magnified fears is shed a little light on them (they scatter like roaches at 3:00 am). That's what this section is all about (dispelling fears—not roaches).

What WordPerfect Is

Even if you've just come in on the boat from some un-electricized, unpopulated, thoroughly unmodern island (sounds nice, doesn't it?), you can figure out from the name that WordPerfect is about words. Making words perfect? Well, *that* may be pushing it.

WordPerfect is an incredibly popular progam that enables you to write memos, letters, reports, brochures, books, gum wrappers, and almost anything else you would ever want to type on your average-joe typewriter. And not only can you write with WordPerfect, you can arrange the words you write, putting them in columns, pushing them up against the right margin, left margin... you get the idea. You can also change the look of the type to create different effects—professional or artsy, serious or light, humorous or post-humorous.

WordPerfect for Windows is one step up on the evolution chain from its DOS relative (depending on how you look at it). The Windows version gives you the choice of falling back on your Windows expertise (what? you don't *have* Windows expertise?) so that you're on some familiar ground as you learn word processing tasks. If you've used Windows before, you'll like the fact that everything works the same, and commands and buttons act like they are supposed to. If you haven't used Windows before... oh well, let's pretend you have.

Although sooner or later, you'll grow to like WordPerfect for Windows (really you will), learning Windows and WordPerfect at the same time is a real double-whammy. But hey—would we leave you dangling out there all alone? See Danny's *Fear Windows No More* to help you sort out and tame Windows beasties.

What Will I Do with It?

That depends—what do you want to do with it? (No fair saying "Nothing.") WordPerfect for Windows makes it possible for you to do any number of tasks—simple or complex—that require wordsmithing. Here are a few examples:

- Writing letters to send to clients
- Pounding out a quick memo
- Composing the documentation for a huge, over-budget, research project (aren't they all?)
- Creating and laying out a brochure to advertise your company
- Writing a computer book (Hey! There's an idea!)
- Designing, writing, and publishing a newsletter
- Writing, fine-tuning, and printing a corporate report

But I Hate to Write!

Oh, don't let Mrs. Moser, your seventh grade English teacher, hear you say that. She'll have you practicing on the board faster than you can say *I didn't mean it!*—topic sentence, three supporting sentences, and concluding sentence—over and over again.

WordPerfect, however, loves people who hate to write. Think you're no good at putting words together? Let WordPerfect for Windows check your grammar for you. Can't think of a specific word? Use the Thesaurus. Can't spell werth a durn? There's a whopper of a spelling checker built into the writing tools, just waiting for your eager keypress.

You still may not enjoy the process (it's something like childbirth. And if you haven't experienced childbirth... oh, never mind), but at least WordPerfect for Windows can put expert tools at your fingertips so your thoughts are presented in as polished a manner as possible.

Generational WordPerfect

WordPerfect, like many of today's popular programs, has been around through several incarnations. In fact, there are two very different versions popular today—WordPerfect 6.0 for DOS and WordPerfect 6.0 for Windows.

What's the difference? Obviously, one WordPerfect you use with DOS, and one you use with Microsoft Windows.

What's DOS? Oh boy. That's a whole nother book.

The primary difference you'll experience between WordPerfect for DOS and WordPerfect for Windows is the way it looks on the screen. WordPerfect for DOS doesn't have the cool buttons and popup boxes that WordPerfect for Windows has. And if you are using other Windows products, having your word processors right there in Windows alongside your other programs is a big benefit. (Or it will be after you learn how to use it.)

In the beginning, there was WordPerfect for DOS. Although early word processing enthusiasts proclaimed it Good, the program took some flak because of a hard-to-decipher screen; users just didn't know how to select commands (which you use to make things happen) or how to call up the menus (which are the little apartment buildings the commands live in).

Other miscellaneous things you don't need to know about WordPerfect 6.0's ancestors are that just a few generations back, WordPerfect for DOS didn't allow mice (no pets allowed) and one of the methods of selecting commands required that you push numbers—yes, numbers—to select commands. Talk about a brain-split.

WordPerfect for Windows is a cool program. You may not be happy about using it, and you may not think it looks real friendly, smiling at you from between all those buttons, but, overall, you'll be glad you've got the WordPerfect you've got. It's the bestest, fastest, and it comes with a free set of ginsu knives.

Y'Know, It's Got That Look

Right from the moment you start WordPerfect for Windows, your eyes are greeted with special effects (see fig. 1.1). The opening logo is a graphic that shows you the type of artwork you could (if you were so inclined) add to your document. When the screen appears, you see all these neat little pictures in little squares stretching across the screen. (That's not all that's there—they just catch your attention first.) See? Already you're entertained.

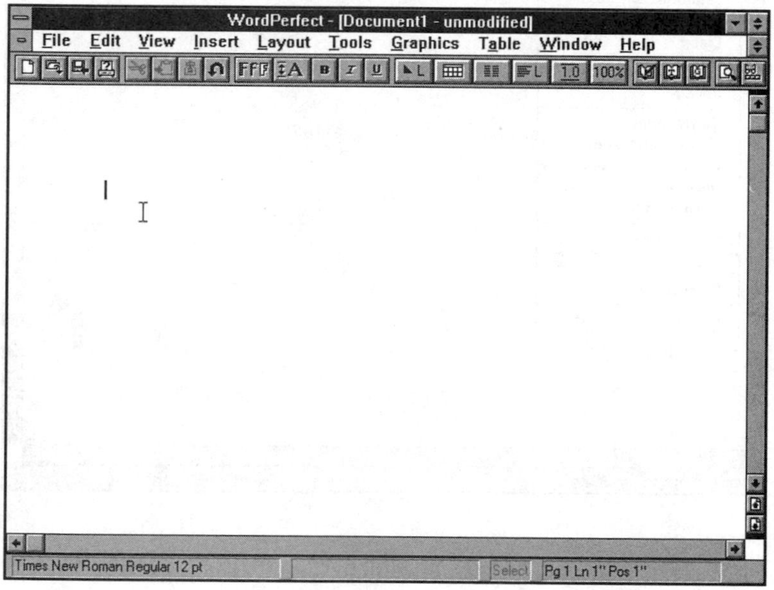

Figure 1.1
The opening WordPerfect for Windows screen.

So what are these things? At the top is the familiar Windows title bar telling you that you're using WordPerfect. (When you move the pointer to the tool buttons, this line also displays information about various tools—but we'll get to that later.)

Next down is the menu bar. If you've used Windows before, this line is no big suprise. Windows programs have menus just like this, stretching across the screen, usually in the same basic order (File first, Edit second, etc.). You can think of the menu bar like a long row of apartment buildings, each housing a different menu with different commands.

The commands in each menu have something to do with the menu name (which, hopefully, helps you locate what you want more easily). For example, the File menu includes the commands you'll use to work with files (see fig. 1.2). Logical, huh? (And you thought you needed a computer science degree to understand this stuff.)

Figure 1.2

The File menu: Exposed!

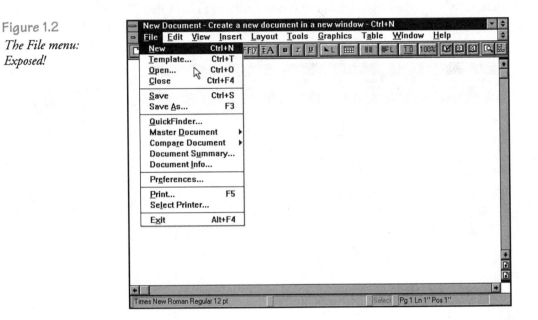

Below the menu bar is a row of buttons, which WordPerfect for Windows (rather obnoxiously) calls the Power Bar. These buttons let you do things—like print your document, add a table, or check spelling—with a simple mouse click.

At the bottom of the screen, the status line gives you oh-so-important information about your file—so important, in fact, that you may never use it. If you're into things like knowing the exact cursor coordinates or caring what page you're on, the status line may help you feel At One With Your Application—the supreme state of computer consciousness. Otherwise, it's no big deal.

When you first load up WordPerfect (which we'll get to in the next encounter—don't panic), what you're looking at is called text mode. WordPerfect also offers a graphics mode—for guess what?—and a page mode, which displays the full page layout. You don't need either of these views yet, however, so forget I said anything.

Choice versus Overload

Some people whine that WordPerfect has too many features. This makes it hard for new users to find their way around and get comfortable with the program. Some people go into a state of shock when they figure out enough about WordPerfect to open the menus but then aren't sure what to do with All Those Commands. Rumor has it that there have been several near-fatalities.

WordPerfect for Windows users have double pressure. Not only are they trying to learn a humongous new program, but they are looked on as The Lucky Ones. "Oh, you've got WordPerfect for *Windows*?" people around the water cooler will ask. "You'll learn that in no time. Windows programs are so much *easier*."

If you feel that WordPerfect lump rising in your throat when you begin looking through the menus and scanning the Power Bar, remember that the whole idea behind giving you that many different choices was that you would be able to—someday, not today—find the method of using WordPerfect that suits you best.

Right now, as you're learning, you'll try anything that works. (Oh, admit it—you know you will.) But later, when you've got some WordPerfect practice and are feeling a little cocky, you'll start experimenting with different key combinations, looking through menus you never use, clicking Power Bar buttons just for the heck of it, or playing around with stuff that's Not Necessary (like drawing lines and making boxes or using funky fonts).

Then, you'll be glad that you've got this many choices.

WordPerfect for Windows lets you use either the mouse or the keyboard, whichever you're most comfortable with. Most users do both. For basic Windows tasks, like starting the program, choosing files, opening menus, etc., most people use the mouse. The keyboard comes in handy for—uh—typing (I've yet to see a mouse that types as well as a human) and other things you can do more quickly by pressing a couple of keys.

Jargon alert: Key combination has become an accepted term for the action of pressing two or more keys together in order to carry out a certain procedure. For example, the key combination in WordPerfect for Windows for opening a file you've already saved appears in the File menu as Ctrl+O, which means press and hold the Ctrl key as you are pressing the letter O.

Changing the Look

You don't have to leave the WordPerfect for Windows screen displayed the way it is. You can add other items, such as a Button Bar for often-used commands and a Ruler Bar for measuring stuff. You can also display an Outline bar to help you make sure you've got all your Bright Ideas in the right order.

All this hodge-podge of visual information is enough to make your head swim (see fig. 1.3). Don't expect any of this to make sense to you now.

Felt your pulse go up a little, didn't you? Yes, the screen in figure 1.3 looks complicated. No, we don't expect you to know what all that nonsense means. Just for future reference, though, you might want to tuck away the knowledge that you can change the way your WordPerfect screen looks (once you know what you're doing—and care) by using the commands in the View menu (see fig.1.4). You can tell which features are turned "on" by the asterisks that appear beside the command.

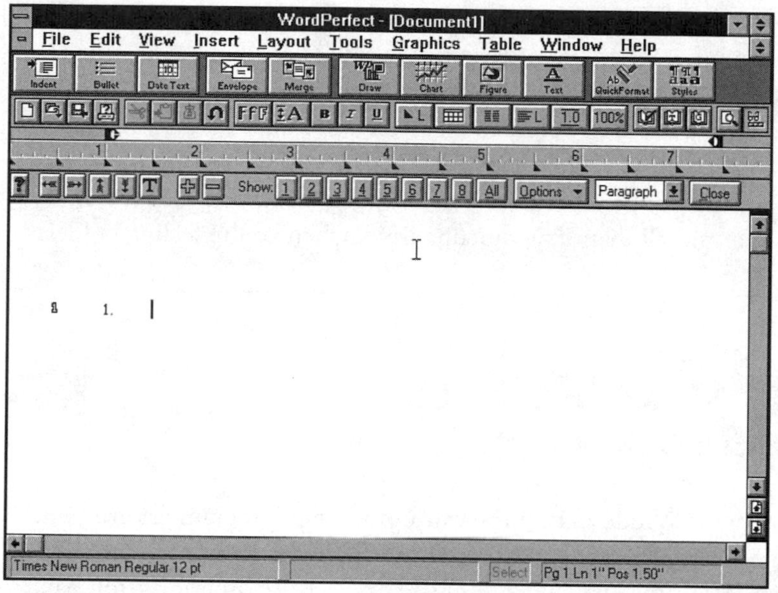

Figure 1.3

There's no place like home, there's no place like home...

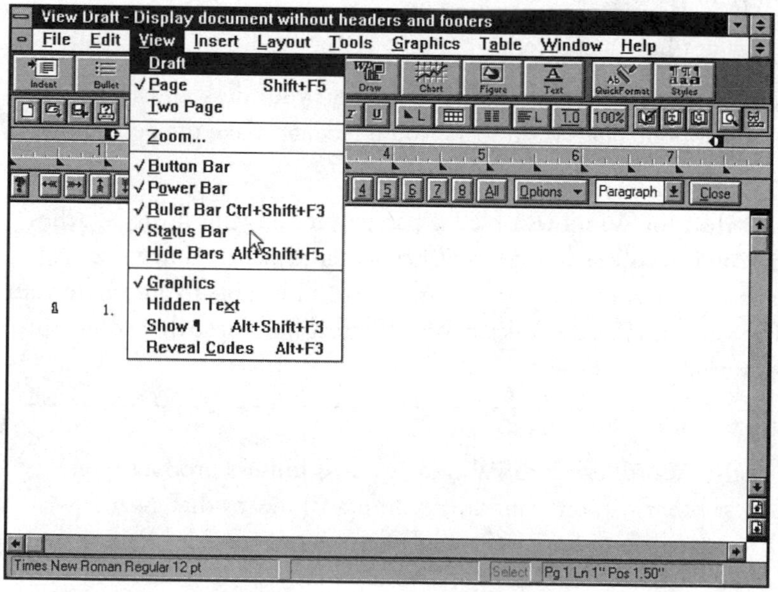

Figure 1.4

Changing the face of the WordPerfect screen.

You can wipe away everything except the scroll bars in one fell swoop (what, exactly, is a fell swoop?) by opening the View menu and choosing the Hide Bars command. A screen pops up, telling you which bars you're about to disable. To return the bars to the screen, just press Esc. Some people prefer to have a wide open space when they write— blank slate and all that. Experiment a little, when you're feeling bolder.

What WordPerfect for Windows Isn't

WordPerfect for Windows isn't the word processing program for everyone. You may not like the slew of features. You may not want mouse support. Pull-down menus may irritate you (must be a past-life thing). Button bars might give you hives.

You also may not have a choice.

If someone has put WordPerfect for Windows on your desk and said— perhaps not real politely—"learn this," you'll have to make the best of the situation.

But WordPerfect for Windows isn't the panacea for all your business aches and pains. You can solve a lot of headaches—merge printing, newsletters, forms, letters, memos, reports, etc.—but you won't be able to automate your entire office with it. (But the folks at WordPerfect have probably come up with a sister product that can.)

The fact that WordPerfect for Windows is a Windows product (you just can't say that without sounding redundant) means that even though you might not find every single feature you need for Every- thing in Life, chances are that WordPerfect will work with another Windows product that can give you what you need.

And WordPerfect isn't easy on the checkbook. We're talking several hundred dollars here—not the $129 special that comes with a 35-word spell checker and has a little cartoon mouse on the front. And anything over that $200 cut-off point becomes more than a software program—it's a commitment. By signing that check, you promise to write, edit, and print, for richer and poorer, till upgrade do you part.

They're Out To Get Us

Oh, come on. What can go wrong when you're just starting out learning about WordPerfect?

Perhaps the worst thing that can happen is someone Important walking up and saying "Here's a new program. I need the annual report by Friday." Depending on how big the capital I in Important is, you may be in trouble. Learning WordPerfect is scary enough without also being under the gun.

If you're in this situation, try any of the following things:

1. Take a deep breath, let your eyes roll up in your head, and chant "Oommm."

2. Read through Encounters 2, 3, and 4 to learn the basics fast.

3. Look at the Important person and say "Oh, sorry—Friday is the day I shave my cat."

4. If you don't have enough time to try item #2, just do the Demon-Strations in Encounters 2, 3, and 4.

5. After you read Encounter 2 and figure out how to start WordPerfect, take the tutorial (in the Help menu) to get a quick, albeit boring, introduction to the program.

6. Pretend you didn't hear him and start singing your favorite Aretha Franklin song at the top of your lungs.

Demon-Strations

Offensive WordPerfect

The best defense, as they say, is a good offense. So in order for you to get the jump on WordPerfect for Windows (before it jumps all over you), you need to think about the ways you can put the program to good use.

How? Read on—

1. Start with a blank piece of paper.

2. Make three columns: **Task**, **By Hand**, and **WordPerfect/Win**.

3. In the Task column, write everything you do that involves words.

4. Once your list is complete, read through each item. If it is something you currently do by hand, put a checkmark in the By Hand column. If it's something you could do with WordPerfect, put a star in the WordPerfect/Win column.

Your list might look something like this:

Task	By Hand	WordPerfect/Win
Write memo to Danny	√	*
Begin work on newsletter		*
Make grocery list	√	*Why?*

This list can help you identify the kinds of things you'd like to do with WordPerfect/Win, once you figure out which end is up.

Ready, Set, Go!

If you're working in an office environment and are learning about electronic word processing for the first time, you are used to doing everything manually. Insert the paper. Turn the typewriter on. Press Tab to move the typewriter ball to the correct place on the page for the greeting. And on and on and on.

But, hey—you're used to it. You probably don't even think about the millions of little tasks that comprise the bulk of your work day. Now's your chance to call attention to those little things that go overlooked (at least until review time).

1. Again, start with a blank page. (In just a few encounters, you'll be able to do this on the screen.)

2. Write down all the steps involved in doing your least favorite typing task. Be sure to catch everything (including White Out pauses and paper adjustment breaks).

	1. Get the typewriter out of the closet.
O	2. Plug it in.
	3. Get out the company stationary.
	4. Find a piece of stationary that's not folded at the corner.
	5. Insert the paper in the typewriter.
	6. Take the paper out, and reinsert it straight.
O	7. Press Tab as many times as necessary to move the typeball to the place you want it.
	8. Type your letter. (Remember to press the Carriage Return at the end of each line.)
	9. When you're finished, take the letter out and read it over.
	10. Typos? Can you use correction fluid? If not, start over at Step 1.
O	

3. Put your list away for future reference. Someday soon you'll see how much time and trouble WordPerfect for Windows can save you. Promise.

Summary

Discovering and facing what you're in for is half the battle in fear-conquering. This encounter introduced you—in broad terms—to the WordPerfect for Windows word processing program. You found out about a few of the ways WordPerfect is used and learned a little about the overall program basics. The next encounter lights a flame under you by showing you how to start the program and begin warm-ups for your own little documents.

Exorcises

1. The current version of WordPerfect for Windows is version _____.

2. Commands are stored in _____.

3. True or false: You must have a mouse in order to use WordPerfect for Windows.

4. You can change the way WordPerfect for Windows looks by _____.

   a. Standing on your head

   b. Running the setup program

   c. Using the Hide Bars command

   d. You can't.

5. Name three common uses of WordPerfect.

Time To Face the Music: Starting WordPerfect for Windows

Goal

To show you—oh, goody—how to start WordPerfect for Windows for the first time.

What You Will Need

Obviously, a computer. And WordPerfect for Windows (preferably already installed). And electrical power.

Terms of Enfearment

startup	cold boot
Windows	warm boot
DOS	installation
Program Manager	group window

Briefing

We fondly call this tender moment—the contemplative silence just before powerup—the Reflective Pause. This is the second in which you are surviving just fine, thank you very much, without the help of the electronic animal sitting on your desk. (Your computer, not the Garfield phone.) After you flip that power switch, you're going to hear whirring and clunking and then finally, a hum that fades into the back of your consciousness and you don't notice again until you turn the system off. Enjoy the silence while you can.

Turn That Puppy On!

It should come as no surprise that you can't run WordPerfect for Windows until you turn your computer on. If your computer is completely, doornail-dead, you'll need to flip the power switch. In Electrode Land, we call this the *cold boot*, this rather violent jolt of electricity that shoots through the sleeping system. Poor thing.

The Coldest Boot

If this is the first time you've started your system—ever, check the following things before you flip the switch:

- Make sure that the system is plugged in. You'll have at least one and perhaps as many as three power cords (one from the back of the system unit, one from the back of the monitor, and one from the printer).

- Plug everything in to a power surge protector, if you've got one handy. (And if you don't, call down to the supply room and order one. Everyone needs protection from wandering surges. You don't know where they've been.)

- Make sure all the cables connecting the parts of your system are tight—plugged in all the way and otherwise attached tightly. You'll find cables all over—a mouse cable, a keyboard cable, a cable between the monitor and the system unit, between the printer and the system unit—just make sure they are plugged in where they are supposed to go. (Or course, if they're not, you'll find out when you try to use them.)

■ Have your computer manuals handy, just in case ...

■ Have your office mate standing by with a bucket of cold water ...

When you've made sure that everything is ready to go, there's only one step involved in jolting that puppy into life: Find the power switch (it could be on the front, side, or back) and flip it to the On position.

> Not all computers come right out and say On/Off somewhere in the general proximity of the power switch. Some, instead, show a l and a 0 (zero means Off and l means On). One way or another, you'll figure it out.

Warming Boots

A warm boot happens when you restart a computer that was already started in the first place. When might you want to do this? After you install a program (not likely here, is it?); after your computer completely locks up and won't let you do anything else (*there's* a pleasant thought); or when your boss is walking by and you want to impress her by looking at your phone and saying "See, Garfield? This is called a *warm boot*."

> A friend tried warming (or, really, drying) her boots after a walk in the slushy Indiana snow by putting them in the oven at 300 degrees for a few minutes. Two hours later, the firemen didn't think it was very funny. Neither did her apartment neighbors, who had a heck of a time getting that odd rubber smell out of their curtains and carpet. Don't try this at home.
>
> The moral? Warm boot only when really necessary and be careful.

You can do a warm boot two different ways:

■ You can press the reset button on the front of your computer (it's that little button that says Reset).

■ You can press the Ctrl, Alt, and Del keys all together and then release them. (Actually, you're supposed to press and hold Ctrl; then press and hold Alt; then press and hold Del (see fig. 2.1). The end result is that you're holding down all three keys and when you let them up, the computer says "Reboot!"—not audibly.)

Figure 2.1

Warm your boots— only when absolutely necessary—by pressing Ctrl-Alt- Del.

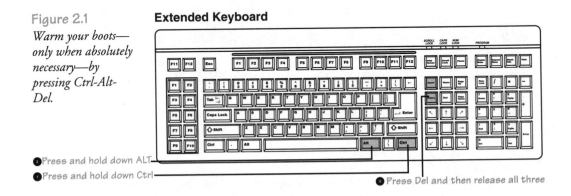

Extended Keyboard

❷ Press and hold down ALT
❶ Press and hold down Ctrl

❸ Press Del and then release all three

Now What?

Okay, you've got the computer turned on. Some of what you see depends on who's been messing with your computer. And some of it has to do with how you use DOS.

> **DOS of the Damned.** Never seen the word DOS before? Really? It's the secret code word that computer neophytes whisper to each other at a gravesite initiation ceremony. It's also an acronym for Disk Operating System, the software that makes it possible for your computer to run.

What You Might See

Most of us see a pretty cold-looking DOS prompt with a little flashing underscore beside it. The prompt (another verb turned into a noun, thanks to the computer industry) probably looks like this:

```
C:\>
```

What You Need To Do About It

Obviously, you know that WordPerfect for Windows is a Windows product. This sounds great if you're writing marketing copy, but if you're a squeaky-new computer user, what docs that mean to you?

It means you've got to start Windows before you can start WordPerfect.

Oh, okay. That's not so hard.

First, you may (or you may not) need to change to the place on your hard disk where Windows is stored before you can start Windows. (Some computers will let you type WIN from anywhere; others insist you move to the WINDOWS directory before you type WIN. If you're not sure what your computer expects of you, try typing WIN at any old DOS prompt. If you get the error Bad command or file name, DOS wants you to move to the WINDOWS directory.)

Jargon alert: The computerese word for "the place where your files are stored" is *directory*. You store similar files in a directory and create many different directories on your hard disk. You might have, for example, one directory for Windows, for example, one for Excel, and one for PowerPoint. Then, within those directories, you'd have more directories, which are called *subdirectories*.

To move to the WINDOWS directory, type:

```
CD WINDOWS
```

And then press Enter. Your prompt changes to:

```
C:\WINDOWS>
```

Now you can start Windows—start the fanfare—by typing WIN and pressing Enter. After a couple of seconds, you'll see the Microsoft Windows screen, followed by the Program Manager (see fig. 2.2).

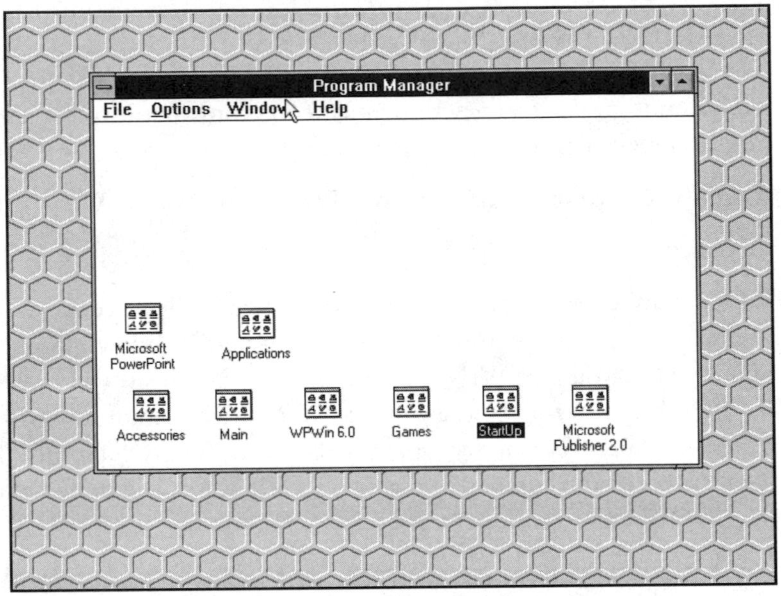

Figure 2.2
*So far, so good. The
Windows Program
Manager.*

Is all this whizzing by too quickly for you to soak it all in? For some extra Windows hand-holding, see *Fear Windows No More*, by fear-dispeller Danny Goodman.

Somebody Open a Window, Will Ya?

Thankfully, Windows basics are pretty basic. Each of the programs you've got setup to run in Windows should have its own little picture in the Program Manager. These pictures are called group window icons.

A group window contains a group of files related to a particular program. The WordPerfect for Windows group window icon shown in figure 2.2 is the one that says WPWin6.0.

To open a group window, you simply position the mouse pointer on the icon and double-click (which means to click twice fast). The WPWin6.0 window opens, revealing its vulnerable side (see fig. 2.3).

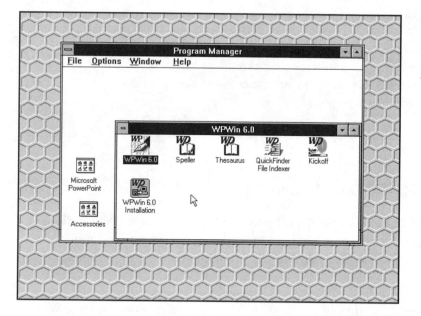

Figure 2.3
You're getting closer to starting this program.

There are several different WP pictures in the WPWIN6.0 window. You've got separate pictures for the Speller, Thesaurus, and other miscellaneous (not that they're not important) features. Don't worry about 'em.

You'll tackle the Big Kahuna in a minute.

Waking Up WordPerfect

Now that you've opened the necessary window, the next step is to start the program. Nervous? Awww—it's simple.

Position the mouse pointer on the WPWIN6.0 icon (it's the one in the upper left corner of the WPWIN6.0 group window).

Double-click.

What happened? The pointer changes to an hourglass; then the eye-popping WordPerfect for Windows screen appears. Then, like magic, without you doing anything at all, the WordPerfect for Windows work area appears.

If you know a technical person who owes you a favor, you can have them rig your computer so Windows—and even WordPerfect for Windows—comes up on your screen automatically. Don't try it yourself however; it's a DNA thing.

What You'll See

Ta-Da! There is it—the WordPerfect for Windows screen. What style—what color (unless you're using a monochrome monitor). How much friendlier than that standoffish DOS prompt everyone else complains about.

Okay. Enough baloney.

What in the world will you do with this screen? Where do you type? What are those words at the top? What are the pictures stretched across the screen? And what language is that at the bottom? Figure 2.4 shows you what you'll be dealing with. And the next section explains how to decipher it.

Figure 2.4
You've made it this far...stay tuna.

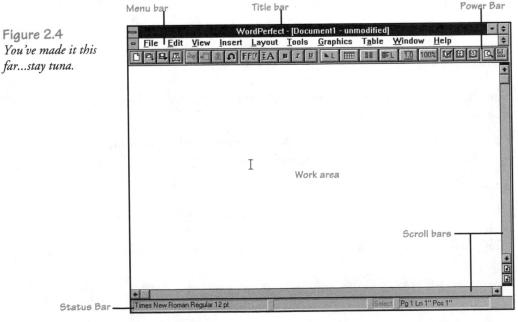

What It Means

What you're looking at is WordPerfect's default display. You've got all the basics you need to get started writing purple prose. (Although initially, you'll see white characters on a blue background.)

Seeing Bars before Your Eyes?

Jeez—WordPerfect for Windows has a bar for everything (not a bad approach, some people might think). There's a *title bar*, your run-of-the-mill Windows feature. Then there's the *menu bar,* where all the commands live. Then there's the (ahem) *Power Bar* (it makes me smile just to say that) that offers you buttons to click in case opening menus and choosing commands is too much trouble. Then there are the *scroll bars*, which let you look through longer (and wider?) documents, and finally, there's the *status bar*, telling you where-oh-where your cursor has gone and what kind of text it's dropping.

That's a lot of bars. Who's the designated driver?

Using the Menus

At the top of the screen, you see a line with ten words. These words are the names of menus, which house commands related to the menu topic. For example, commands that let you work with files are stored in the File menu. Commands that affect your view of the world are tucked neatly away in the View menu.

One letter in each of the words is underlined. You can display the menu you want by pressing and holding the Alt key and then also pressing the underlined character. For example, to open the Layout menu, you press Alt+L (see fig. 2.5). To open the Font menu, you press Alt+O. Get it?

A quicker, easier, and more sensible way to open menus involves using the mouse. Just point at the menu you want and shoot...uh, click, that is. The menu opens and hangs there until you want to put it away (which you can do by clicking off the menu or pressing Esc). More about these hands-on kinds of things in Encounter 3.

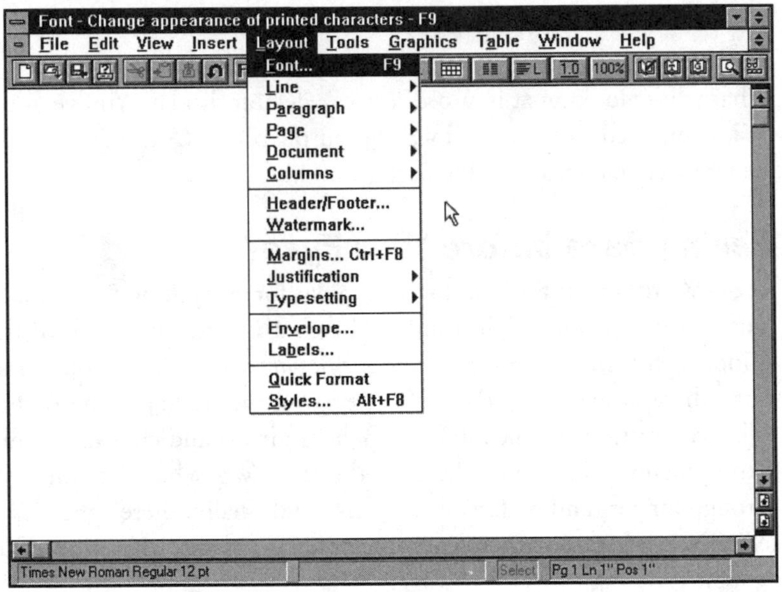

Figure 2.5

Press Alt and the letter and open sesame.

Supercharged: The Power Bar

Mouse-happy users are going to love the Power Bar that's built into WordPerfect for Windows. Now you can save that file, print that document, align text, change spacing, spell check... oh stop, I'm getting dizzy... right from the work area.

No menus, no commands.

Just point and click. Such poetry.

The Power Bar, once you figure out what all the little pictures mean, can save you quite a bit of time and hassle in your word processing workout.

Now go have some orange juice. And don't forget to check your pulse.

Deciphering the Status Line

Initially, the only other somewhat confusing thing that appears on the WordPerfect screen is the status line. At first glance, it's pretty hard to imagine what those chicken-scratchings mean. It could be calling you something rude.

Let's take it a piece at a time.

Pg 1 means—you guessed it—Page 1. Easy enough.

Ln 1" tells you the exact position of the cursor and its relation to the top edge of the page. In other words, the character you type at the cursor position is one inch down from the page edge.

Pos 1" explains the cursor's position in relation to the left side of the page.

As you type, the information in the status line is updated to reflect the cursor's current position. Seems a little like overkill, but you may be glad you have it someday. It's always there—just in case.

Why It Concerns You

Maybe it doesn't. Maybe you're ready to dive in and start batting words around on-screen. Well, be my guest.

But just think about what you've learned already. You know where WordPerfect for Windows lives, how to get there, and how to start the program. After the program starts, you know what the opening screen means and what it will tell you as you work. Pretty good for a beginner, huh?

Remember that what you see when you first start WordPerfect for Windows is the basic screen. You can do other things to make your WordPerfect time more prosperous (or more confusing, depending on how you look at it). Other items and displays are available, too. Experiment as your experience with WordPerfect for Windows grows and find the look that's best for you. (And no, the turned-off look doesn't count.)

They're Out To Get Us

There aren't too many horrible things that can happen to you when you're finding and starting WordPerfect. But there are those straggly few.

Nothing Happens

This is a general, across-the-board, we're-in-trouble problem: the computer won't start. Well, you're not going to run WordPerfect for Windows if the blasted computer is broken. If you push the power button or flip the switch and nothing—absolutely nothing—happens, check to make sure the computer is plugged in.

If the computer is plugged into a surge protector, make sure the protector strip is plugged into the wall.

If it's plugged in and still nothing is happening, see if the surge protector has its own On/Off switch. Is it turned on?

If it is and STILL nothing's happening, make sure the power cord is plugged tight into both the protector strip and your machine.

It is? Okay, check the outlet. Plug in something else electric and see whether it works. If not, perhaps you've blown a fuse.

Oh. It works?

Hmmm. Time to call the technical support guy.

Wake Up, WordPerfect, *Please*?

Here's another one. You double-click the WPWin6.0 icon and... nothing. Oh, go head, get up and do that I've-got-to-hit-something dance you do so well. Then, after a couple of deep breaths (repeat after me "I *can* deal with this. I *can* deal with this. I *can* deal with this."), ask yourself the following questions:

1. Are you sure you're sitting at the right computer?

2. Has WordPerfect for Windows been installed? Well, the only way to install WordPerfect for Windows is to use the Run command in Windows' File menu, and once WordPerfect for Windows has been installed, it shows up as an icon in the Program Manager.

3. Who's bright idea was it to buy WordPerfect for Windows, anyway?

Demon-Strations

Movin' On Up

George and Weezie would be proud; you've learned to move through the directories of your hard disk without even knowing you did it. Remember?

1. When the computer is turned on and the DOS prompt is displayed, type the following line:

   `CD WINDOWS`

2. Press Enter.

DOS changes to the WINDOWS directory (now displaying C:\WINDOWS> as the prompt) so that you can easily start Windows and then WordPerfect for Windows.

Pull the Rip Cord!

This is so easy it's almost silly to write it. Remember?

1. Type **WIN**

2. Press Enter.

So what were you expecting, the winning lottery numbers? Windows powers up and you see the Program Manager. Now you can start WordPerfect for Windows like this:

1. Move the mouse pointer to the WPWin6.0 icon.

2. Double-click the mouse button. (That's click-click.)

That's all there is to it. You're ready to rock.

Summary

This encounter has been an important one for your WordPerfect for Windows foundation. You learned how to start your computer, climb through Windows, and get WordPerfect up and running. You also found out a little about the display that greets you once WordPerfect for Windows leaps into life. The next encounter takes you deeper into the mire by showing you how to use the keyboard and the mouse to get around in WordPerfect for Windows.

Exorcises

1. True or false: You start WordPerfect for Windows the same way on all machines.

2. Explain the difference between cold and warm boots.

3. What is Windows?

4. Name that tune in four notes.

5. Explain two ways to open a WordPerfect menu.

Move Those Fingers! Typing 101 and Mouse Wrangling

Goal

To get accustomed to the keys you'll use most often and exercise your mouse.

What You Will Need

Your computer turned on, with WordPerfect for Windows running; a keyboard; and a willing mouse (don't forget the little workout suit and the ankle weights).

Terms of Enfearment

QWERTY keys	cursor-movement keys
function keys	pointing
clicking	dragging

Briefing

Word processing would be pretty pointless if you didn't have a keyboard, wouldn't it? Those Pulitzer Prize winning thoughts rattling around in your head wouldn't be able to move from your gray matter to your computer's silicon chips without being able to force themselves out through your fingers.

The mouse, on the other hand, doesn't carry the same amount of Necessity weight as the keyboard; you can do lots of things without the mouse when it comes to word processing. When you're talking about *Windows* word processing, however, life sans mouse is unthinkable. When you're talking about Windows anything, that little rodent becomes an important—if not irreplaceable—item.

Typing 101: Keyboard Fundamentals

You already know what a keyboard looks like. If you've ever used a type-writer, your fingers won't get lost on the computer keyboard.

Know Your Four Key Groups

QWERTY keys. Like a typewriter, the keyboard has all the standard alphabetic and numeric keys, in all the same orders (see fig. 3.1). These standard typewriter-like keys are known as QWERTY keys, named for the first six letters in the top left row. (Why? Maybe because it sounds better than TYUIOP.)

Figure 3.1

*Your standard,
nothing-spectacular
keyboard.*

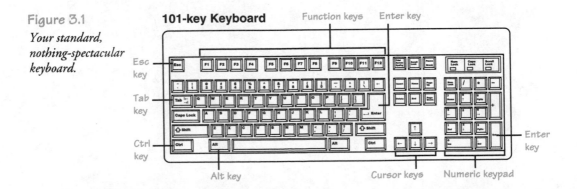

It's a safe bet that you'll be using the regular QWERTY keys more often than you will anything else on your keyboard, just due to the sheer volume of letters in a typical document. Don't kid yourself, though—there will be a certain amount of command selecting and option choosing involved. For most of those tasks, you can use either the keyboard or the mouse.

Function keys. These keys are easy enough to find—they're the numbered keys that start with F on your keyboard (F1, F2, F3, etc.). Some keyboards have ten function keys; some have twelve; some have fifteen. As a general rule, function keys are over-rated; you may use two or three of them regularly, but you wouldn't miss them that much if they were gone. WordPerfect uses the function keys as part of key combinations, such as Shift+F5.

Key combinations (the pressing of two or more keys at the same time) arc one way WordPerfect lets you bypass opening menus and selecting commands with the mouse. Instead of opening the File menu and choosing the Close command to close your file, for example, you can instead press Ctrl+F4 without taking your fingers off the keyboard.

Cursor keys. Depending on the keyboard you're using, you may also have two separate groups of cursor keys. These are located between the QWERTY keys and the numeric keypad on the far right. The top group includes keys like Ins, Del, Home, End, PgUp, and PgDn. If you're like most people, the two keys used most in this group will be PgUp and PgDn. Home and End tend to do different things in different programs, so people don't take them too seriously. The bottom group of keys shows four arrows, pointing north, east, south, and west. As you might expect, you'll use these arrow keys to move the cursor in the direction necessary for your navigational task.

Numeric keypad. To the far right, you'll find the numeric keypad. On some older keyboards, the numeric keypad doubles as a cursor movement keypad and there is no separate set of directional keys. Newer keyboards include this double function (you can see the arrows on the 8, 6, 2, and 4 keys), but they have the separate set of cursor keys as well. In order for the numeric keypad to function as a numeric keypad, the Num Lock light (in the upper right corner of the keyboard) must be on. Sound confusing? Try it: Press the Num Lock key (it's up in the top left corner of the numeric keypad.) The light goes out, right? Now, if you press one of the keys on the keypad, the cursor moves. If you press Num Lock again (and the light comes on), when you press the numbers, numbers appear.

Specialty Specialkeys

And then there are those keys that don't fit into any category. They are nonetheless as important as anything else. These keys help you get places in the program, edit stuff, and select commands and options.

Enter. This key is the Do It! key on your keyboard. When you press Enter, you're telling the computer to accept whatever settings you've entered. Also, when you're typing text in your document, pressing Enter ends a paragraph and moves the cursor to the next line. Remember this key. You'll be spending quite a bit of typing time with it.

Backspace. The backspace key doesn't say backspace anywhere on it; instead it just shows a backward-pointing arrow. It's located in the top right corner of the QWERTY section of your keyboard. No matter what you're doing, what program you're using, or what time it is (huh?), the backspace key always does the same thing—moves the cursor one space back. Whether the backspace is a destructive backspace, meaning that it deletes the last character as it takes that step back, depends on the program and the settings you've chosen. When you first start up WordPerfect for Windows, the backspace is a destructive backspace, so when you type the word *Omigosh* and press the backspace key, as shown in figure 3.2, the h disappears. (And the cursor sits there blinking innocently "Who, me? *I* didn't eat that h.")

Tab. The Tab key is an unsung hero in a lot of programs, and WordPerfect is no exception. Think of how many times in a simple memo you press the Tab key. Does it complain about always getting the pinky and never the index finger or the thumb, like more important keys? Of course not. And Tab saves you time and trouble, indenting your paragraphs, tables, and lists five spaces without you having to press the spacebar all those times. Dust off your Tab key once in a while, and let him know you appreciate him.

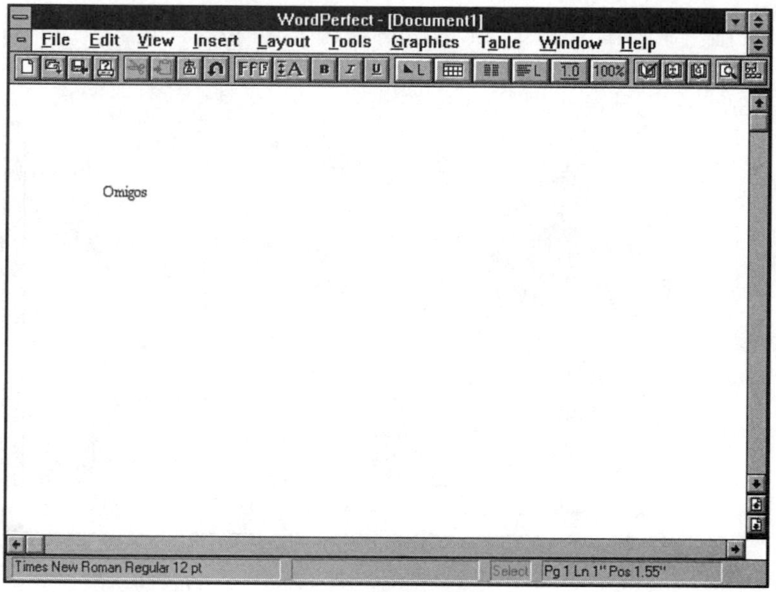

Figure 3.2
Demonstrating the destructive nature of the backspace key.

Shift. This is one of the always-been-around-so-I-hardly-notice-it keys. You had a Shift key on the old Smith Corona which you used to make capital letters out of smaller ones. Shift functions the same way on your computer keyboard, and now you have two of them. Shift is popular in WordPerfect as part of routine key combinations (for example, to open a file, you press Shift and F10).

Ctrl and Alt. These two keys are unique to the computer keyboard. In fact, there are two of each, so we're really talking about four keys. Ctrl and Alt are both used as half of a key combination (such as Ctrl+S for Save). Ctrl is most often used to select commands; Alt, when pressed along with the highlighted letter in a menu name, opens the menu and also works overtime as a command-selecting key.

Anything But Those Timed Typing Tests!

Ready to put some of this keyboard theory to work? Oh, come on.

That cursor (the flashing vertical line) should be blinking at the top of the screen as shown in figure 3.3.

Figure 3.3

Eyeing that sneaky little cursor.

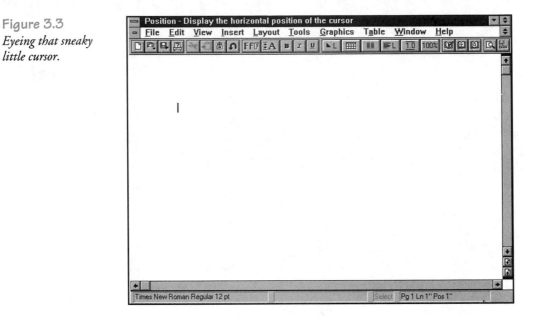

What the heck's a cursor? No one told me there'd be swearing in this program. I'm not sure I can continue to use it in good conscience. Oh, what's that? Oh, you mean that little flashing line? Well, dammit, why didn't you tell me in the first place?

If your cursor is in a different place, you've pressed a few keys (like Enter) and you didn't even ask Mother-May-I? Your penalty? Use the arrow keys to move the cursor back to the top left corner of the screen. And next time— wait for the rest of the class.

Now cut loose and do a little typing. Go ahead and be creative: type anything you want. If your creative juices need a little jump-starting, you can practice using this paragraph, if you want:

> I've never seen a stripe-ed cow. I hope I never see one. But if I see a stripe-ed cow, I'd rather see than be one.

Anything unusual happen? Hopefully not. Your letters should have gone right through the computer and popped out on the screen as fast as you typed them. WordPerfect for Windows should have moved the cursor to the next line automatically as you approached the end of it—a little bit of magic called *word-wrap* (the line break should appear right after the word *rather*). Your screen should look like figure 3.4. (That's a lot of *shoulds* in one paragraph.)

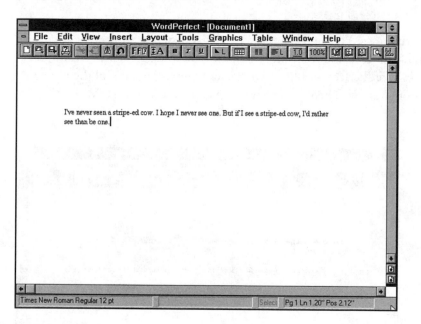

Figure 3.4
Writing about cows and udder nonsense.

Didn't we tell you it would happen? The status line, in the bottom right corner of the screen, updated itself to show the cursor position. Another thing you don't have to worry about. Isn't WordPerfect for Windows wonderful?

Ready for the next step? Take a deep breath and press Enter. The cursor jumps to the next line.

Now press Enter again. The cursor moves yet another line down. (You just left the blank line between paragraphs.)

Another step: Press Tab. What happened? (The cursor should have moved in a ways.)

Now type this pearlish prose:

> The blue moose got loose from the city zoo. He wanted to smooch a puce goose, I guess.

Congratulations. You've taken the single biggest step in working with WordPerfect for Windows: you've written something. You are—really and truly—a WordPerfect user now. Look over figure 3.5; that's all the typing we'll do right now. Then go get yourself a cup of coffee and a Milky Way. You deserve it.

Figure 3.5
Practice makes perfect.

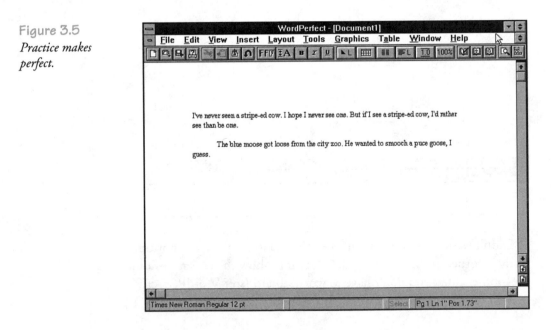

If we were logical about it, the next logical step might be using the cursor keys to move the cursor through the document. But we're not. The next section shows you some basic mouse tricks. We save the cursor-manipulation until Encounter 4.

Yippee-Ty-Yi-Ho! A Mouse Rodeo

Well, this little varmint isn't going to get by with just hanging out on the side of the keyboard while your fingers do all the work. Get out that lasso and let's get him moving.

You may be expecting a mouse definition and a few technical terms telling you what the mouse does and what different kinds of mice are available. Sorry. We figure that if you're reading this section, you've already got a mouse, so you don't need to worry about selecting one. Suffice it to say that a mouse is a little hand-held thing you use to point to stuff on the screen. You click the buttons to say "Do It!" to the computer (like the Enter key, remember?). If you want to learn more about various mice nationalities, see *Fear Computers No More*. (Oh, sorry—I said we weren't going to do that.)

Mouse Talk

When you deal with any animal (humans included), you have to know its language before you can get it to do anything for you (just ask Doctor Doolittle and the Giant Sea Snail). Here are a few important terms that you'll need to know before you can consider yourself truly mouse savvy:

Pointing. This means to position the mouse pointer on the something you're thinking about selecting. When you use the mouse to point to something, you are moving the mouse body and the mouse pointer on the screen moves right along with it. Move the mouse to the left; the pointer moves to the left. Move the mouse body up; the pointer moves up.

Clicking. This is the term used to describe a click of the mouse button. Which one? Any of the two (or three) buttons on the top of your mouse. You click a mouse button when you want to say "Do It!"; for example, when you want to open a menu, you point to that menu and click the mouse button. The menu opens.

Double-clicking. An offshoot of the click is the double-click. (*Quietly, with feeling: See Jane as she approaches the end of the paragraph. She's attempting a double-click.*) A double-click is a quick two-click action; you click once and then click again, real fast. You use double-clicking to select files, options, and words.

Dragging. The action of dragging is a lot like getting out of bed on Monday morning: You stumble off to the shower with one foot dragging, like Quasimoto (Does that mean "sort of" moto?). When you drag the mouse, you press the mouse button and hold it down while moving the mouse's body. In WordPerfect for Windows, you'll use dragging to select a phrase, a line, or a section of text.

Mouse Events

Now let's put that mousie through some of its paces by trying out the mouse theory just explained. Get your rope handy, sit tall in the saddle, and wait for the green light: Three, two, one . . . go!

Pointing. Your mother told you that it's not polite to point. And yet, here we are, years later, practicing it. Ah well. If you can get past that stumbling block (we won't tell your mother), you can learn to point the mouse way.

To point, just put your hand on the mouse and move it upward toward the menu bar. The little block mouse pointer on the screen moves right along with you. Hey—here's something interesting: As soon as you move the pointer off the work area of the screen, it changes from a vertical bar to an arrow (see fig. 3.6). Hmmm.

Here it is up here (were you looking for it?)

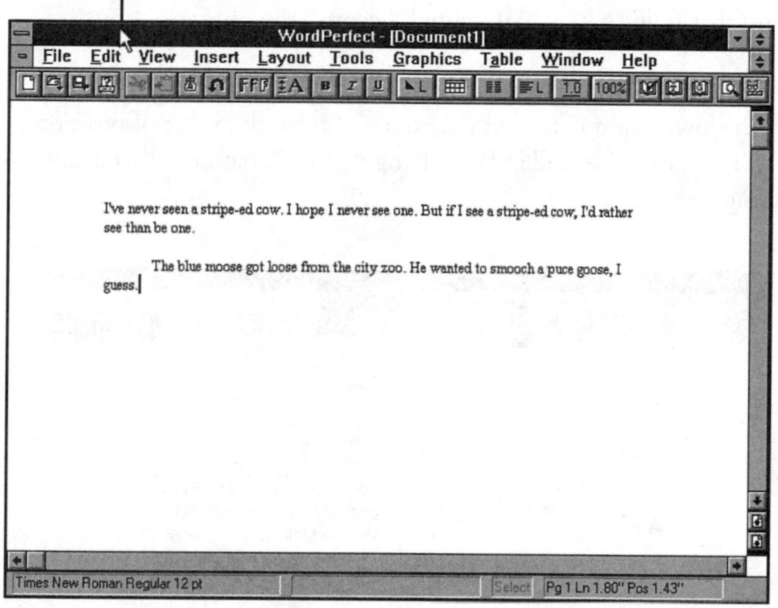

Figure 3.6
*Two pointer shapes
for the price of one!*

Clicking. This is about as simple as it gets. Push the mouse pointer over to the word Graphics in the menu bar. With your index finger (why do we call it that?), press and release the left mouse button. What happened? The Graphics menu (where you were pointing) opens (see fig. 3.7).

> Wouldn't it be awful to open a menu and not know how to close it? Here's another click procedure: Just move the mouse off the menu—anywhere—and click again. The menu closes.

Double-clicking. First we've got to get to a place on-screen where a double-click will work. Move the mouse pointer—that is, point—to the word *goose* in the last line of text. Now double-click the left mouse button by pressing and releasing the mouse button twice, fast. As figure 3.8 shows you, several things happen when you do this correctly. First, the entire word (and the punctuation that follows it) is highlighted. Second, the phrase

`Select`

appears in the lower right corner of the screen. Third, the value of position indicator in the status line (called Pos) changes also. What does this mean to you? Nothing, yet.

Figure 3.7
The result of a click?
The open menu.

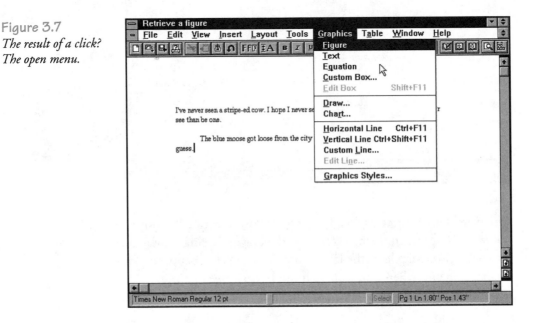

You can remove the highlighting on the word by clicking off the word (or by pressing Esc).

Dragging. Our final mouse event involves dragging. This mixes many of the tasks you learned here: pointing, clicking, and moving the mouse. First, move the mouse pointer to the *l* in the word *loose*. Then, press and hold the mouse button while moving your hand (and mouse) to the right. When you get to the space following the word *wanted*, release the mouse button. The phrase *loose from the city zoo. He wanted* is highlighted, as shown in figure 3.9.

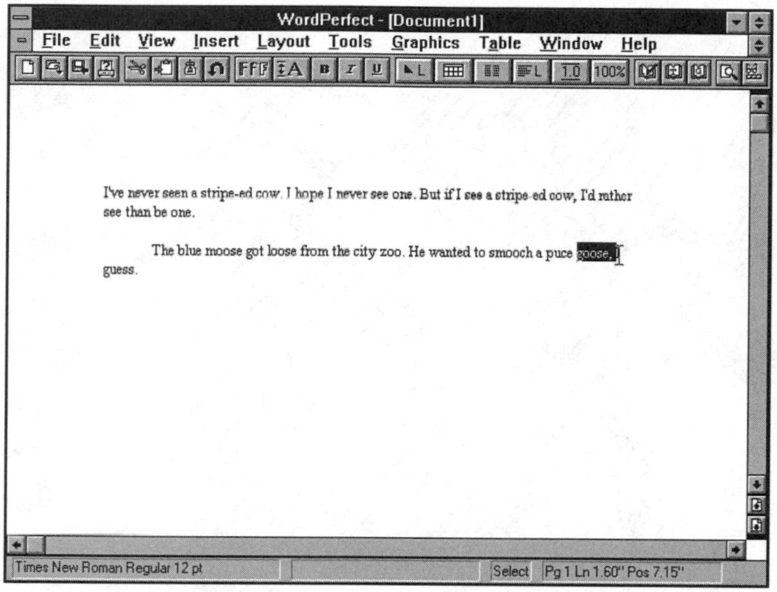

Figure 3.8
Double-clicking in action.

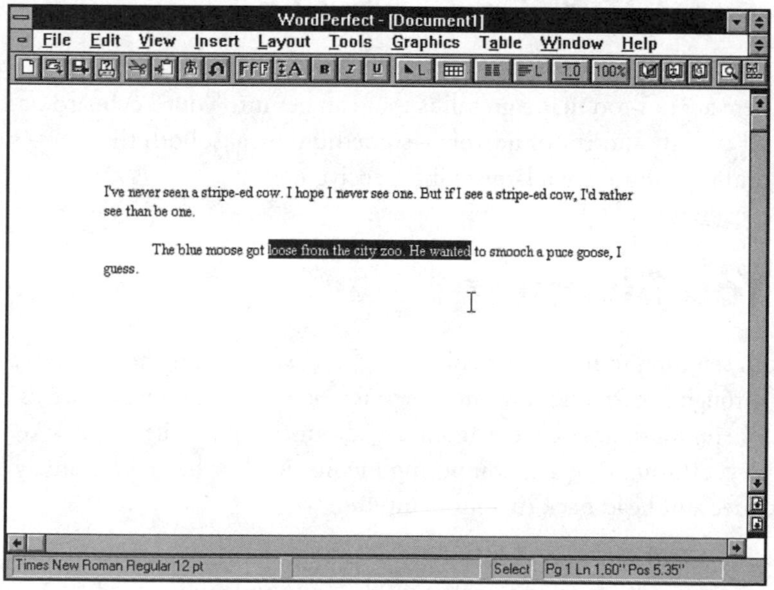

Figure 3.9
A little dragging goes a long way.

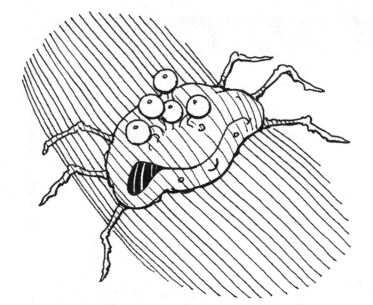

They're Out To Get Us

Luckily, there are not too many gremlins that can get into your keyboard or mouse. And even if—horror of horrors—something breaks, both the keyboard and the mouse are relatively inexpensive items.

Are You Sleeping?

You've been standing in line at the coffee machine, waiting for the hot water to trickle through brown and hot into the pyrex pot. It took forever. And as you stood there, waiting, you were agonizing about the huge pile of work you have to get through today. Composing memos in your head, you finally get your coffee and head back to your computer.

Okay, take a sip and sit down. There's the screen, gleaming blue with that flashing cursor, waiting for you to get to work. You think about the first memo you're going to write, start typing, and...

Nothing.

No beep. No characters. No nothing.

What's going on? If you haven't spilled your coffee on the keyboard (check your elbows—it does happen), you've probably got a keyboard that un-plugged itself. Make sure that the keyboard is plugged securely into the back of your computer.

Look on the keyboard and see whether any lights are on. If not, press Num Lock to see whether the light comes on. No? Your keyboard isn't getting any juice.

Try exiting WordPerfect and then Windows and start again. (You'll have to use the mouse to exit instead of the keyboard.) After you exit to DOS, turn the blasted thing off, count to fourteen-and-a-half, and turn it back on. If the keyboard is broken, your computer will tell you so.

Maniacal Mouse

Every once in a while you'll run into a strong-willed mouse with a mind of its own. You want it to go this way, and it rumbles and bumps and goes along—only begrudgingly. This, most probably, is a physical ailment and not a mouse attitude problem. Your mouse may have ball warts (which, as you can imagine, can make even the most pleasant mouse cranky).

Day in and day out that little mouse scoots along the surface of your desk, and—admit it—your desk is not the cleanest place on the face of the earth. Dust and mucky substances accumulate there. Little pieces of M&M coating get dropped and remain there unnoticed. All kinds of sticky things that can get pulled up into your mouse's delicate interior.

If your mouse is behaving erratically, turn him over. On the underside, you'll see a circle, inside which a portion of a ball shows. What may be happening is that gunk has adhered itself to that ball, making it move in a less-than-smooth fashion. You can open the mouse (don't forget the anes-thetic) by moving the circle around the mouse ball in the direction it shows. You can then peer inside and clean the mouse ball with a little alcohol-dipped cotton swab. Be gentle.

Demon-Strations

Typing Trials

1. Move the cursor to the position following the last character of the text you typed.

2. Press Enter twice. The cursor moves down two lines.

3. Type the following:

   The zebra is a funny beast

4. Press Enter.

5. Type the following lines, pressing Enter after each:

   Who lives down where it's hot.
   He's black and white straight up and down,
   But spots he has not got.

Now this, combined with the text you entered earlier, should resemble the screen shown in figure 3.10.

Figure 3.10
TFNAR: Typing For No Apparent Reason.

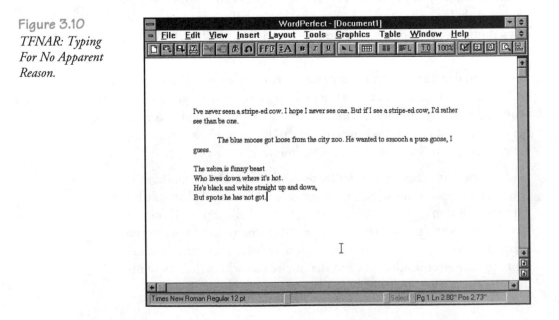

Mousercize

Ready? Okay! Everybody get your mouse and follow me:

1. Point to the word bcast (*three, four*);

2. Click on the word beast (*three, four*);

3. Point to the word straight (*four, and*);

4. Double-click the word straight (*four, and*);

5. Point to the word black (*one, two*); press and hold the mouse button (*three, four*); and drag the mouse to the word up (*one, two*); release the mouse button.

Great! You did it! Everybody do some stretching to cool down and go get some orange juice.

Summary

You've learned some important basics in this encounter. Big milestones. Monumental word processing feats. Learning the basic layout of the keyboard and experimenting with mouse procedures is an important part of feeling comfortable with WordPerfect for Windows. Right now, finding the right key and remembering the right mouse action may seem a little awkward, but soon you'll be doing all these things without thinking about them. Second nature and all that.

Exorcises

1. What are the four key groups?

2. Explain what cursor movement keys do.

3. What is word wrap?

    a. A cool street poem.

    b. Plastic covering that keeps your words fresh.

    c. An automatic feature that moves text to the next line when the current line is full.

4. What does pressing Enter say to the computer?

5. Name four mouse actions.

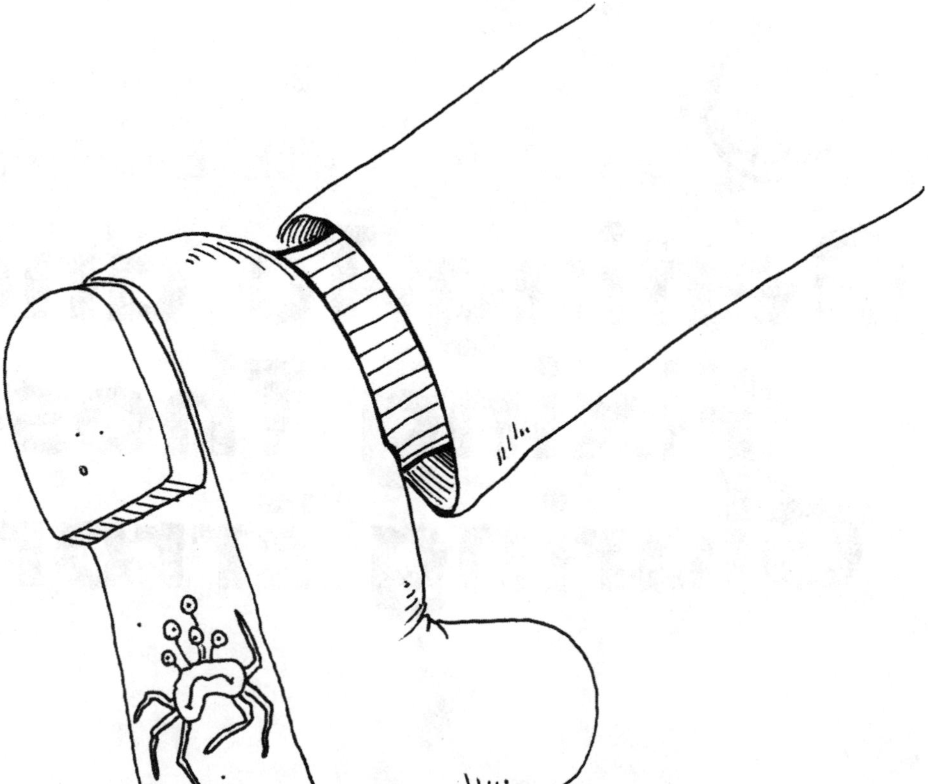

4th Encounter

Getting To and Fixing Those Glaring Errors

Goal

To show you how to hop through the text patch and weed out those thorny errors.

What You Will Need

WordPerfect up and running, and either the sample file you worked on last encounter, or a paragraph or two of your own.

Terms of Enfearment

arrow keys	PgUp
PgDn	Home
End	scroll bars
Go to	Backspace
Insert mode	Typeover mode

Briefing

The last encounter showed you around the keyboard and introduced you to the mouse. This encounter gets out a magnifying glass and takes a closer look at the simple procedures you use to get to a mistake and fix it.

Getting There Is Half the Fun

After you've learned how to enter text and then find your way through the text you've entered, you've mastered a good part of any word processing program. You already have the words in there; now you just have to process them. WordPerfect for Windows gives you several different ways to get to the places in your document that you want to reach. The method you choose, of course, depends at least in part on your document (how long is it?).

Trying to make some sense out of all this, you've lumped "moving" into the following categories:

A *small move* is when you want to move the cursor a short distance; up a few lines, over a few characters, down a couple of paragraphs.

A *medium move* is when you need to scroll through some of the text on-screen in order to find the text you need. You might have to move a screenful or two either up or down.

A *big move* is a page-to-page move. You remember a phrase you used on page 10 that you wish you hadn't; you're working on page 1 now. You need to do some serious moving in order to get to that error.

Small Moves: Words, Lines, and Paragraphs

You learned a little bit about small moves when you were working with the mouse in Encounter 3. We deferred the cursor-movement key discussion, however, to this point. (Don't worry, we'll review mouse actions here, too.)

Keyboard techniques. When you want to move the cursor a short distance, you have four basic options:

↑	up-arrow
↓	down-arrow
→	right-arrow
←	left-arrow

Each of these cursor-movement keys (also called *arrow keys*) moves the cursor one space in the desired direction. Want an example? Start with the screen in figure 4.1 (the cursor is positioned right in the center, at the beginning of the word *from*).

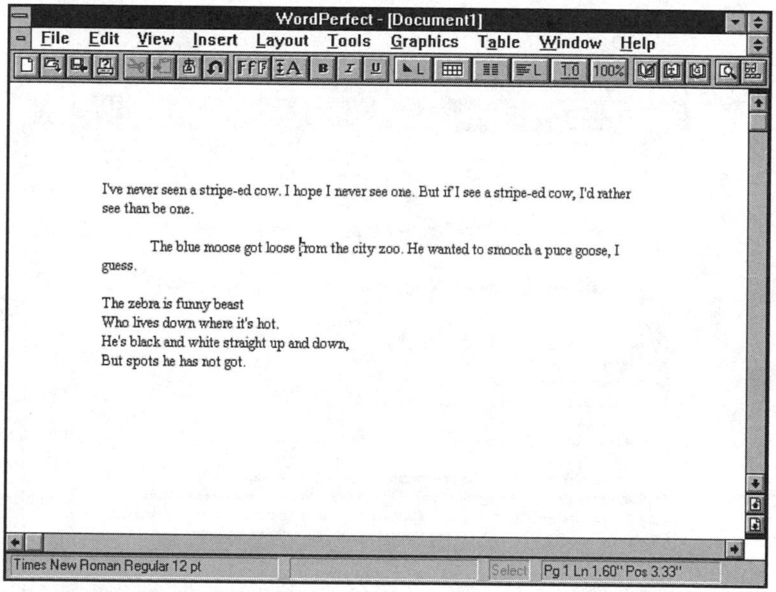

Figure 4.1
Getting ready for a little trip.

Now, if you press →, the cursor moves one character to the right, resting on the r in *from*. Press ↑, the cursor moves one line up (and goes to the left edge of the screen, because that's a blank line). Play around with the cursor-movement keys until you get the hang of it.

Mouse moving. If you're using the mouse, moving a short distance is even easier. Just point and click. Want to move somewhere else? Point and click. The cursor follows right along, your faithful friend.

Medium Moves: One Screenful at a Time

When you're working with a larger document (one that includes more text than can be shown on one screen), you need some method of displaying the unseen text. Again, you can use the keyboard or the mouse to do this.

You'll have to take a leap of faith here, in order to see medium movement illustrated. You remember the text entries we added earlier? In order to have enough text to play with, you've had to add some more (see fig. 4.2). If you want to try out PgUp and PgDn (not to mention the mouse exercises), you may want to stop now and type in some of your own pretend prose.

Figure 4.2
All right, so we added more text.

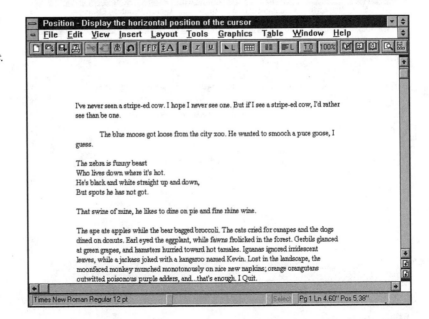

PgUp and PgDn—the Keyboard Movement Keys. When you need to see text beyond the current display, press PgDn. WordPerfect for Windows scrolls the next page down. If you don't have more than one screenful of text and you press PgDn, WordPerfect just sits there and goes "huh?" When you press PgDn and you have enough text down there to see, WordPerfect displays the next screenful so fast you can't really see the change. Figure 4.3 shows the amazing results of PgDn.

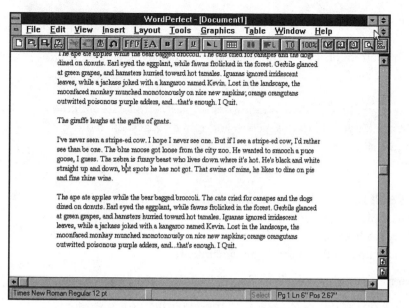

Figure 4.3
What's down there?
Using PgDn.

Obviously, you can't use PgUp until you've moved down through a document. If you press PgUp when the cursor is already at the top of the document, WordPerfect will just sit there, wondering what you're trying to do. Once you've used PgDn, use PgUp to move back up through the document.

One other key you might use when you're finding your way through a text file is the End key. When you press End, WordPerfect moves the cursor to the end of the current line of text.

Middle-Sized Mouse Moves. You may find that using the mouse is easier for almost everything when it comes to moving the cursor. Best advice for mouse cursor moving, however, is to use those scroll bars.

Oh. What's a scroll bar?

You can probably guess. A scroll bar is a bar along the edge of the screen you use for scrolling. And scrolling means to move text up or down so you can see other parts of your document. WordPerfect for Windows gives you two different scroll bars: a vertical one (on the right side of the screen) that lets you go forward and backward through the document, and a horizontal one (along the bottom of the screen) that allows you to move side to side.

> If you're an accomplished Windows enthusiast, scroll bars are no challenge for you. Skip this section and move on to some brain-straining stuff.

Using Scroll Bars. Earlier you learned that to move from point to point within a displayed screenful of text, you just point and click. Working with scroll bars is a little more complex, but not much. You use the vertical scroll bar to move up and down through a document.

You can move down through the document one of two ways:

- ▇ Click on the down-arrow at the bottom of the vertical scroll bar.

- ▇ Look for a little square box in the middle (or perhaps at one end) of the scroll bar. That's called the elevator box. Position the pointer on the box and drag it down to display the next screen. In this case, because we're working with a short document, we drag the bar to the bottom (see fig. 4.4).

The horizontal scroll bar (the on across the bottom of the screen), controls where the text is placed across the width of the page. This control is not as crucial as the vertical scroll bar, and you won't use it nearly as much. Figure 4.5 shows what happens when you drag the elevator box to the right side of the horizontal scroll bar.

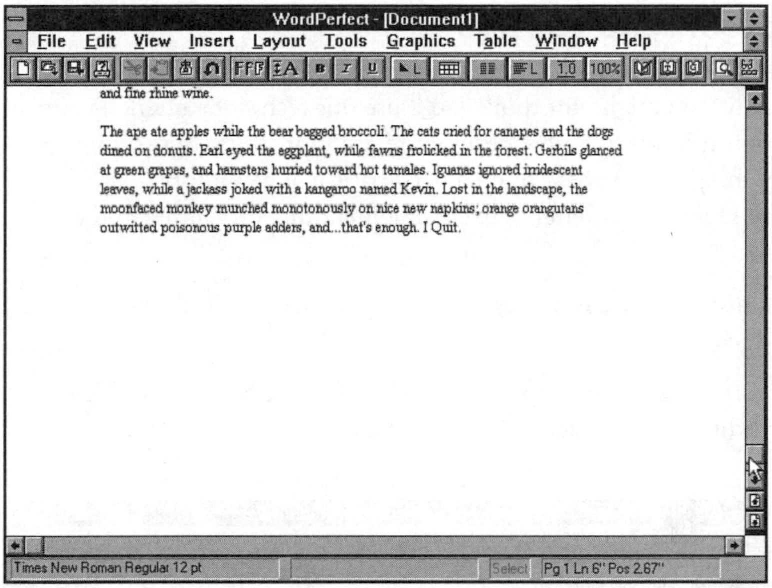

Figure 4.4
Using the vertical scroll bar to display more text.

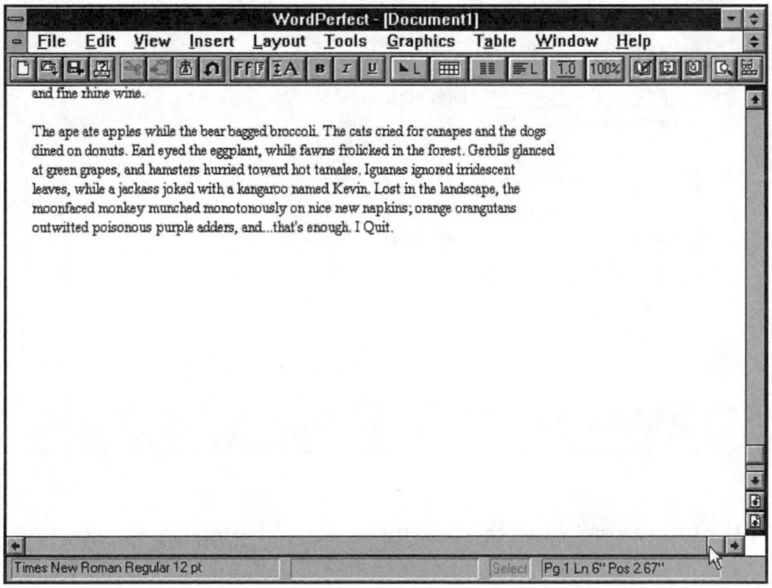

Figure 4.5
The life-changing effects of the horizontal scroll bar.

Big Moves: Page to Page

The final movement—Beethoven's 9th—involves moving from page to page. Initially, you might not think you'll use this technique often. Typing a few lines of text seems like a big deal, not to mention *pages*. But think about how many things you work with on a daily basis will be multiple-page documents: reports, newsletters, advertising literature, brochures, and on and on.

When you need to move from page to page, you'll use the Edit menu's Go to comand:

1. Open the Edit menu by pointing and clicking or by pressing Alt-E. The Edit menu appears, as shown in figure 4.6.

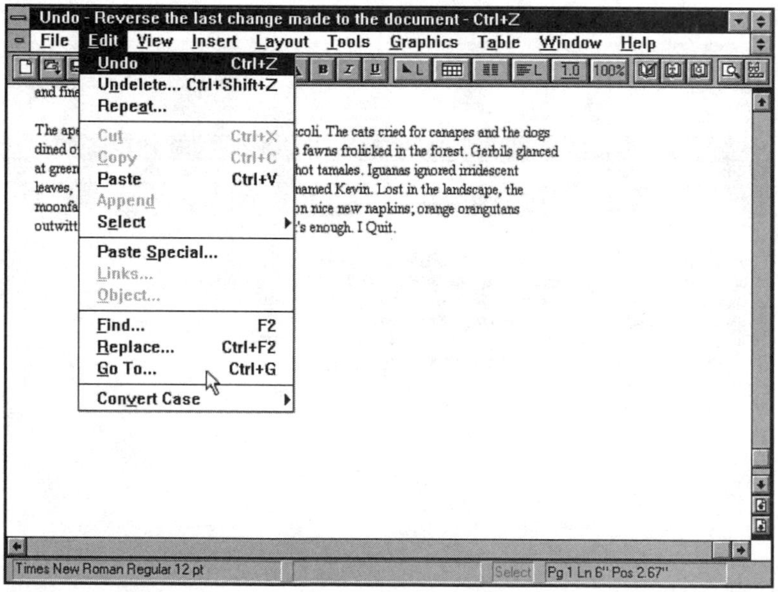

Figure 4.6
Going to Go to.

2. Select the Go to command by clicking on it or by pressing G. The Go To box dialog box appears, as shown in figure 4.7.

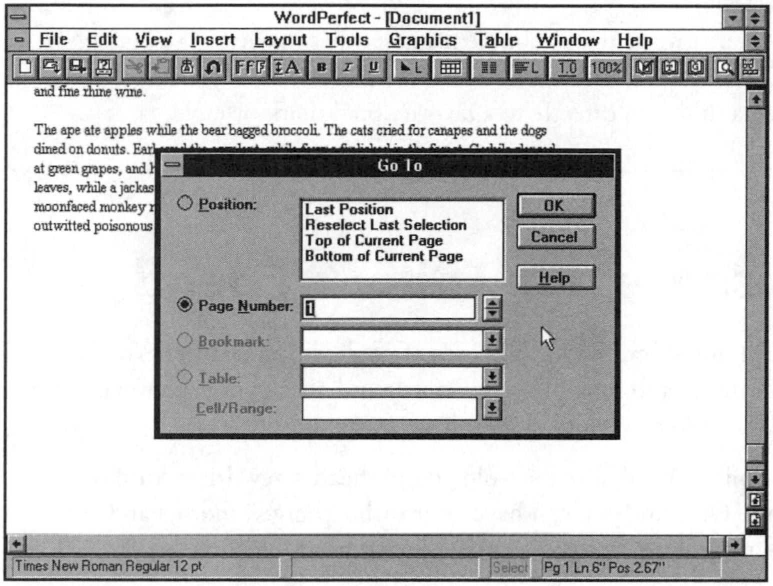

Figure 4.7
*The important
Go to box.*

3. You can select the Position you want to move to (Right Field, First Base) if you want, by clicking the Position button and making your selection. Instead, just type the number of the page you want to move to. (Who wants to take the time to think about those other things? Not me. I've got tacos to make.)

4. Click OK.

> You can use the Go to command without opening the Edit menu at all: just press and release the Ctrl and G keys at the same time.

WordPerfect then moves to the page you entered. What happens if you've only got two pages of text and you tell WordPerfect to go to page 73? WordPerfect thinks a minute and then moves the cursor to the top of the file. Joke's on you.

You can enter more than a simple page number in the Go to dialog box. Choose your position (we already said that), or, if your document has such a thing, go directly to a favorite bookmark or table.

Backspace, the Editor's Friend

WordPerfect for Windows has all kinds of cool editing features. You can spell check things and look for better words and check your grammar. And we're not going to talk about any of those cool things here.

This section is about that regular-old-straighthead-screwdriver kind of editing tool. Oh, sure, you can have your turbo-charged motors and your lightning-fast macros, but you're still going to need Old Reliable.

The backspace key.

As simple to use as the eraser on the end of your pencil, the backspace key gives you the ability to wipe away characters like they were never there. Misspell something while you're typing? Press that backspace key a couple of times and retype it. The mistake is gone, like it was never there. (If only all the mistakes we make were that easy to correct!)

But before you just climb in there and start backspacing all over the place, you need to know something about the dual—light and dark—personalities of backspace.

[Cue ominous music.]

Scoot Over—Insert Mode

When your first fire up WordPerfect for Windows, it's in a pretty forgiving mood. When you type and make a mistake, you press backspace, and—simple enough—the mistake is deleted. You can retype things correctly. This friendly mode is called *insert* mode, named because any text you type is inserted at the cursor position.

Let's try it. Move the cursor to the end of the line about the blue moose (third text line down). Click after the word *to*, press the spacebar and type

```
see Dr. Seuss
```

Then press the spacebar again. The characters after the cursor position move to the right to accomodate the text you added (see fig. 4.8). *Insert* mode. Get it?

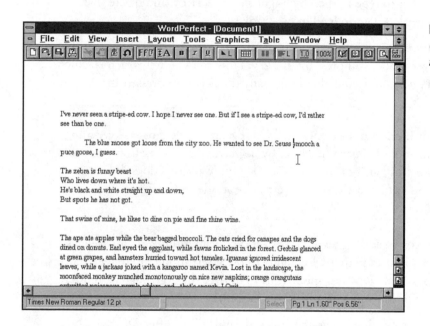

Figure 4.8

Come on in and join the fun: insert mode.

When you're using the backspace key in insert mode, you get that gentle, one-character-at-a-time deletion. Just what you'd expect from a straightforward, logical program.

The Steamroller—Typeover Mode

But there's a darker side to our friend the Backspace key. Depending on the mode of the day and whether you're working with blocks, he gets testy and swipes away whole words at a time. And the characters we type aren't benevolently welcomed into the document but are used to kill off characters that were already there.

Why, oh why did anyone ever invent typeover mode?

Most of us have trouble with this concept only once. After that, after we've lost a paragraph, or a really good phrase we just can't remember, we learn our lesson. If you're working with valuable text, make sure you work in insert mode.

Typeover mode is handy when you need to replace large portions of text and don't want to type it, then highlight the extra stuff, and delete that. Typeover lets you do it all in one stroke.

To turn on typeover mode, you simple press the Ins key. To turn off typeover mode, you press the Ins key. How can you tell which is which? Good question. Remember how many times you've pressed Ins.

> WordPerfect 6.0 for DOS tells you when you've crossed over into dangerous Typeover territory by displaying Typeover in the left side of the status bar. For some reason, WP for Windows doesn't let you know until you start eating letters by accident. Go figure.

When you're adding text in typeover mode, anything you add deletes the text that is already there. Remember how insert mode inserted characters in the text? Well, typeover mode runs right over those characters, replacing them with the ones you add. Want to see it?

If you're following along, the cursor should still be after *Dr. Seuss.* Now, place the cursor just before the apostrophe in *I'd.*

Ready? Press Ins. (Gasp!)

Now press the spacebar and type *hope his name is Fredrick.* What happened? The original line is completely gone, and this oddball phrase replaces it (see fig. 4.9). You can see how typeover can help you get things done quickly. But you also should be able to see how potentially dangerous it could be.

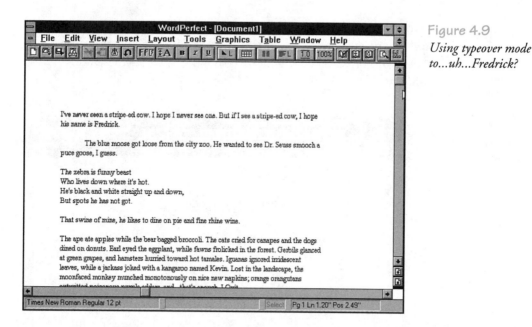

Figure 4.9
Using typeover mode to...uh...Fredrick?

If you're using the backspace key in typeover mode, you delete the character, but the space remains. Be careful if you see the sign Select in the bottom of the status bar, however, because if you press the backspace key now, all highlighted text will be deleted.

Save Me, Undo!

Luckily, WordPerfect for Windows offers a feature for those of us waiting for a caped crusader to come to our rescue. The Undo command, tucked neatly away inside the Edit menu, can return to us text we thought was lost forever.

Actually, there are two Undos. One lives in the Edit menu, and one sticks out there in the Power Bar, looking like a turned-around arrow.

What's the limit of Undo's capabilities? You can only Undo what you just did. So if you delete the word *kangaroo*, open the Edit menu, and choose Undo, the word is returned. Figure 4.10 shows you where the Undo command lives.

Figure 4.10

Saving a kangaroo with Undo.

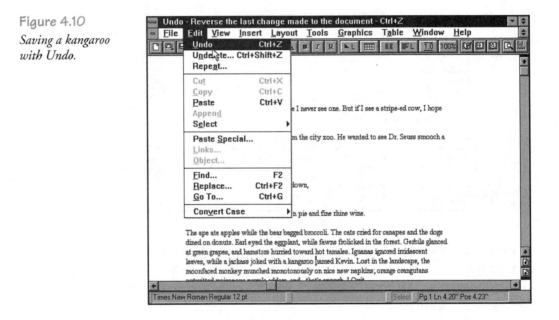

Okay, so we can save the last thing we blew away. But what if you delete *kangaroo,* and then delete *orangutans?* You're stuck, right?

Maybe not.

An extra bonus: Undelete. WordPerfect also has an Undelete command for those of us who are always throwing away things we wish we had later. Undelete can return to you the last three items you deleted; so stop and think before deleting number four.

If you deleted *kangaroo* and then *orangutans* and decide you need *kangaroo* after all, position the cursor where you wish the word was, open the Edit menu and choose Undelete. (Or, if you really want to do it quick, just press Esc.) The Undelete dialog box appears, as shown in figure 4.11.

WordPerfect - [Document1]

File   Edit   View   Insert   Layout   Tools   Graphics   Table   Window   Help

I've never seen a stripe-ed cow. I hope I never see one. But if I see a stripe-ed cow, I hope
his name is Fredrick.

The blue moose got loose from the zity zoo. He wanted to see Dr. Seuss smooch a
puce goose

Undelete

[Restore]   [Next]   [Previous]   [Cancel]   [Help]

The zebra
Who lives
He's black and white straight up and down,
But spots he has not got.

That swine of mine, he likes to dine on pie and fine rhine wine.

The ape ate apples while the bear bagged broccoli. The cats cried for canapes and the dogs
dined on donuts. Earl eyed the eggplant, while fawns frolicked in the forest. Gerbils glanced
at green grapes, and hamsters hurried toward hot tamales. Iguanas ignored irridescent
leaves, while a jackass joked with a named Kevin. Lost in the landscape, the moonfaced
monkey munched monotonously on nice new napkins; orange orangutans outwitted

Times New Roman Regular 12 pt   Select   Pg 1 Ln 4.40" Pos 6.22"

Figure 4.11
Undeleting orangu-
tans and kangaroos.

I know what you're thinking: You're supposed to see *kangaroo*, and this
crazy program returned *orangutans*. The Undelete box gives you the option
of Restore (which means to accept the word WordPerfect is plugging in the
space) or select Previous (which means WordPerfect will look at the word
you deleted the time before the displayed word). Choose the second option
by pressing P. WordPerfect then displays *kangaroo* in the space. Press R to
restore the text.

They're Out To Get Us

There aren't too many terrible mistakes you can make when you're moving the cursor around in a document. After all, you're just moving a little vertical line; you're not doing any damage to the text.

The danger comes in making corrections and confusing insert and typeover modes. You haven't learned to make any sweeping text changes (like marking blocks of text and copying them to other locations), but it is possible to start typing blindly (perhaps reading from something while you type) and overtype a slew of existing text.

Whenever you begin typing, watch carefully to make sure you're not typing over anything you need. If letters start getting chewed up by the new characters you're typing, press the Ins key to remove the message and return the program to insert mode.

Demon-Strations

Go Straight To Jail—Do Not Pass Go, Do Not Collect $200

There's always someone ready to tell us where to go, isn't there? The Go to command will help us get there.

1. Open the Edit menu.

2. Choose the Go to command. The Go to dialog box appears.

3. Type 1 to move to the top of the first page of the document. (Or, if you'd rather go somewhere else, type that document location.)

4. Press Enter or click OK. And Voilà.

Dear Diary: It's 3:00 on Friday afternoon and my boss left early. I was working on the quarterly report due Monday morning, when I was suddenly overtaken with an urge to go to the Bahamas. Without knowing what was controlling me, my hand reached for the mouse...I opened the Edit menu...selected the Go to command...and typed *Bahamas.* Here I am, listening to reggae and relaxing on the beach. Wish you were here.

Text Hide-and-Seek

Let's get that Fredrick thing out of there.

1. Use the mouse to move the cursor to the space following I in the second line of text.

2. Press Ins to turn on Typeover mode.

3. Type the following:

   I'd rather see than be one

Your screen now looks like the one shown in figure 4.12.

Hmmmm. Something's not right. We have an extra k at the end of the line. To fix it, follow these steps:

1. Press Ins to turn on insert mode.

2. Press Del. Poof! That k is history.

Figure 4.12
What's a onek?

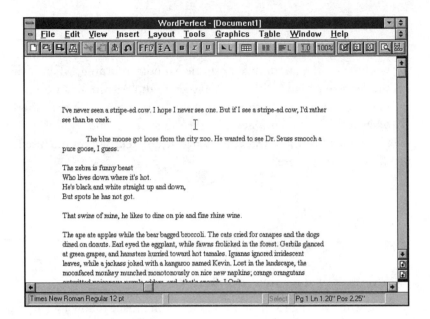

Summary

This encounter explained some of the up-close-and-personal aspects to moving around within a document. You learned that there are different techniques to use depending on how far you want to move and how long your document is. Additionally, you found out about the backspace key and the profitable and precarious nature of insert and typeover modes. The next encounter introduces you to character makeovers using fonts, sizes, and styles.

Exorcises

1. Mix and match the right terms with the right items:

   _____ Words   A. Medium movement

   _____ Pages   B. Small movement

_____ Lines   C. Big movement

_____ Paragraphs

_____ Characters

_____ Screenfuls

2. What are scroll bars and why would you use them?

3. True or false: You can search for more than page numbers with Go to.

4. In insert mode, when you enter text _____

    a. The text overwrites existing letters

    b. It goes into a separate file that you can later insert into the document.

    c. The existing text moves over to make room for the new stuff.

5. In typeover mode, when you enter text _____

    a. The characters at the cursor position are replaced.

    b. The existing text moves over to make room for the new text.

    c. Nothing happens.

    d. Dominos delivers a pizza you didn't order.

Caring for Characters: Tomfoolery about Fonts

Goal

To help you set the mood, with fonts.

What You Will Need

Same old stuff: WordPerfect up and running (sounds like a book title), a few lines of text (not necessarily what we've been working on for the last two encounters), and a willingness to follow instructions blindly to an unknown end.

Terms of Enfearment

fonts	fontanel
typeface	style
attribute	pinash

Briefing

Fonts are those things that you think you need even when you're not sure what they are. It's a kind of watermark: "How many fonts do you have?" Researchers are trying to prove that the number of fonts you have is directly related to your IQ.

Do you need fonts in order to produce text on paper? No.

Then why mess with them?

Once upon a time, we were limited only to typewriterish characters. These blocky little ugly things had no spark, no life, no personality. We wrote our memos, reports, brochures, and handouts, knowing that our text was less than exciting. But what could we do?

Enter: Fonts. Style! Pinash! Excitement! A hundred and thirty-six flavors!

Now you can shout at your audience, whisper, coo lovingly (I'd like to see that), or coerce. You can make firm statements or lighthearted puns. You can find the look for your characters that matches the feel of your message.

Funny about Fonts

You may have heard that fonts are hard to deal with. That they cause headaches and high blood pressure. That they are better left to Those With Computer Experience.

Depending on the individual experience of the person you're talking to, you may hear Fantastic Font stories or Fonts From Hell. Don't put too much stock in other people's font experiences. You've got to get out there and have your own.

What Is a Font?

A *font* is a funny word that describes text in a certain typeface, style, and size.

Huh?

Okay, so we're defining jargon with jargon. Fonts come in different families, which are called *typefaces*. One popular typeface is Times Roman. Another is Helvetica. You'll find a trillion different typefaces coexisting in the publishing world.

> The word *typeface* is used in computer and real-life typesetting. It means the same thing in both worlds. To your computer, a font is really a set of instructions that tells it to create a character in a certain way. Not all printers can print a variety of fonts (check your printer manual to be sure).

Each character has several characteristics, called *attributes*. It has a font family to belong to. It has a certain size, and it has a certain style. (Kind of like classifying children: This one belongs to the Murray family, is 42-inches tall, and is Really LOUD, God love him.)

For example, one font might be

Times Roman	(that's the typeface)
10-point	(that's the size)
Bold	(that's the style)

When you apply the font to words, it looks like this:

This is an example of Times Roman 10-point bold text.

Why Do I Care?

Pretty testy question, isn't it? You may not care about fonts if you print only memos every third Tuesday. If you don't spend a lot of time with your word processing work and don't particularly care what it looks like, don't fool with fonts. They won't help you.

If you are on the chopping block every week, however, having to come up with attention-getting reports, cool training handouts, nice quarterly reports, and so on, fonts will be an important part of your word processing experience. Fonts really do make your words look—and sometimes sound—better.

When you care about the reaction of your readers, using fonts effectively can really add to the oomph of your publication.

What Kinds Are Out There?

This is a confusing question for most of us. Remember that fonts are really software instructions, like any programming code, that tell your computer how to make the characters you want. These instructions come in two varieties: screen fonts and printer fonts.

> **Screen fonts.** Using screen fonts enables you to see more accurately what your document will look like when you print. If you're using Times Roman, for example, but the characters on your monitor are something else, your printed document will look much different from the on-screen version. To take care of this discrepancy, most word processing programs—and WordPerfect is no exception—offer a preview mode.

Jargon alert: You'll see the term WYSIWYG used to describe this on-screen-and-in-print feature. WYSIWYG is an acronym for "what-you-see-is-what-you-get." Cute, huh? Somewhere there's a program developer that's really proud of that.

> **Printer fonts**. These are the important ones. If your printer can't handle fonts (and not all printers can), you're not going to get your text to look much different. No way, no how. All printers can change the way the font looks a little bit, even the lowest of the low. For example, for rough draft and editing work, I use my trusty old Panasonic dot-matrix printer. Sure, the thing can print different fonts—a bunch of them. Dozens of flavors of Courier (see fig. 5.1). How exciting.

```
This is Courier 10-point normal.

This is Courier 10-point bold.

This is Courier 10-point italic.

This is (*yawn*) Courier 12-point normal.

This is Courier 12-point bold.

This is (*snore*) Courier 12-point
italic.

This is Courier z...z...z...z...z...
```

Figure 5.1
Oh, stop. I can't stand it.

For final drafts and publishing projects, I use a more well-endowed printer, one with Postscript capability. The QMS is capable of printing 36 different fonts in a variety of type families (see fig. 5.2). And it has its own memory, so I can use other fonts (remember, a font is really a set of computer instructions) by having the program send the description to the printer at print time.

You know **Times-Roman** and Avant Garde
And **Bookman** and Helvetica;
Palatino and *Zapf Chancery*
And **New Century Schoolbook** and Courier;
But do you recall
The most famous typeface of all?

Figure 5.2
For real variety, you need something with real font capability.

Jargon alert: Postscript is a term you'll see used in connection with any standard font discussion. Postscript is actually the name of a special language used to communicate text descriptions to the printer. Some laser printers are Postscript printers and some are PCL printers, which use a different kind of language.

Where Do They Come From?

Fonts come from the far-away land of Fontanel, where they float around in the ozone until a stork with a drinking problem grabs them in a little handkerchief... wait, wrong story.

Printers with font talent come with fonts already loaded. Postscript printers have 36 different fonts available right off the bat (Times Roman, New Century Schoolbook, Palatino, and a bunch of others you don't need to know unless you've got a Postscript printer). PCL printers also have their own variety of fonts, and depending on the age of your printer, you may have a font cartridge to insert in a special slot. (Font cartridges went out of fashion about the same time as the S&L crisis, but I don't think the two were related.)

If you are one of those lucky Windows users (and you must be or you wouldn't be reading this book), you get to set up your printer by using the Control Panel in Windows before you start WordPerfect for Windows. In the Control Panel, you add special magic things called *drivers* that tell your printer how to work. When you are ready to use WordPerfect for Windows, you use the Printer Select command (in the File menu) to choose the printer you plan to print to.

Today you can purchase fonts from almost anyone standing on a street corner. Fonts are software, remember, so most computer retailers and software mail-order outlets carry packages of different fonts. You'll see lots of buzzwords when you start investigating font capabilities: bitmapped, TrueType, Adobe, the list goes on and on. You're going to leave the high-end font juggling for the experts and just learn to use the fonts you've already got.

Font Application: The Base Coat

Okay, so assuming that you can use different fonts (meaning that your printer can print them), how do you tell WordPerfect to change the font it's using?

First find out what font WordPerfect uses as the default. If you've already installed a printer (which you—or the person who installed WordPerfect for you—did during installation), the font WordPerfect uses as a matter of course is displayed in the bottom left corner of the screen, as shown in figure 5.3.

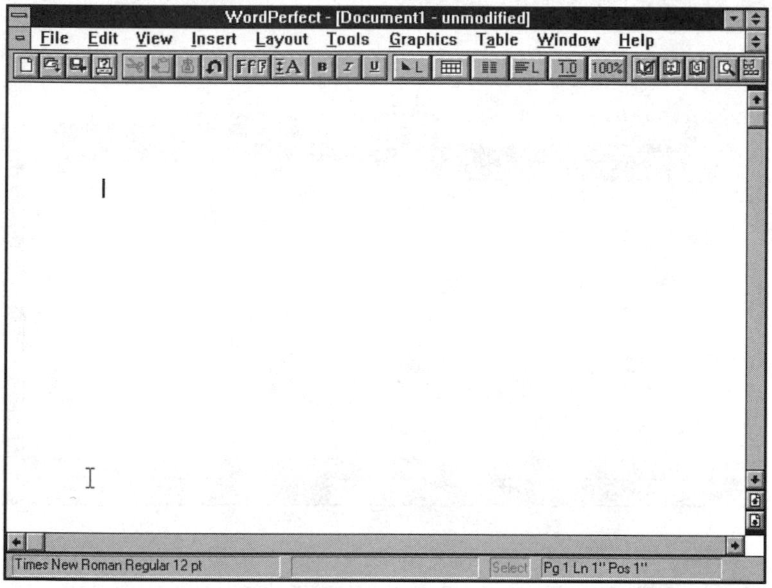

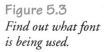

Figure 5.3
Find out what font is being used.

Here, Times New Roman Regular 12 is being used. Your screen might show something different. Don't sweat it.

You can change the font one of two ways, depending on what you're doing:

■ If you're changing text you've already entered, you need to highlight the text first and then change the font.

■ If you're changing the font of text you're about to enter, you can turn that particular font on before you type.

Changing Already-Entered Text

To change the font of text you've already typed, first select the text you need to change. To select text, position the mouse at the beginning of the text and then press and hold the mouse button while dragging the mouse to the end of the area you want to change. This marks the text block you that want to change. Figure 5.4 shows the highlighted block.

Figure 5.4
Selecting the text to change.

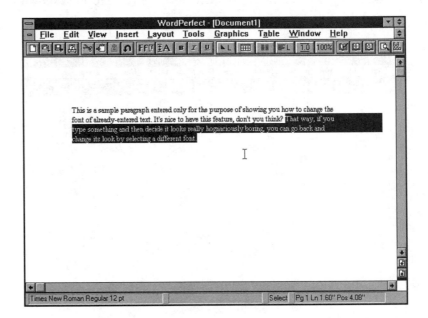

Now click the font button in the toolbar (it's the one with three Fs). An incredible list meets your eager gaze, as shown in figure 5.5. Click on the one you want and WordPerfect for Windows changes the text to the look you selected. In the example in figure 5.6, we chose Mistral, just to be difficult. Yes, it's scrunched and impossible to read in a computer book figure. But doesn't it look *artsy*?

New Text in a New Font

If you're getting ready to type a section of text and you want to change the font of the stuff you're about to enter, you can bypass all that text-selection nonsense and cut right to the chase. Just position the cursor, click the font button, and choose your font. Any text you enter from that point on is in the new font (see fig. 5.7).

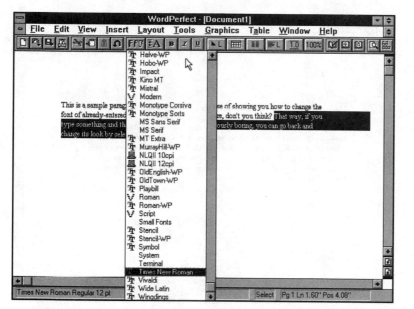

Figure 5.5
Fonts out the whazoo.

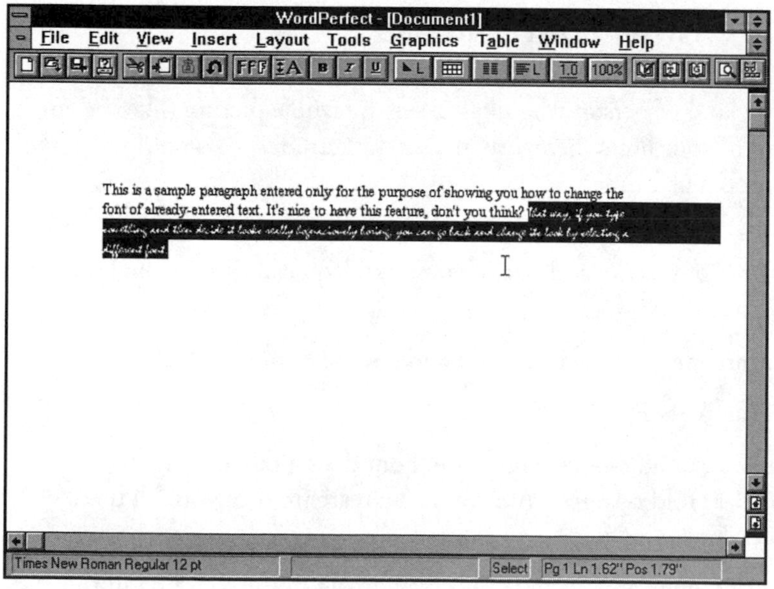

Figure 5.6
Ta-da! A new font.

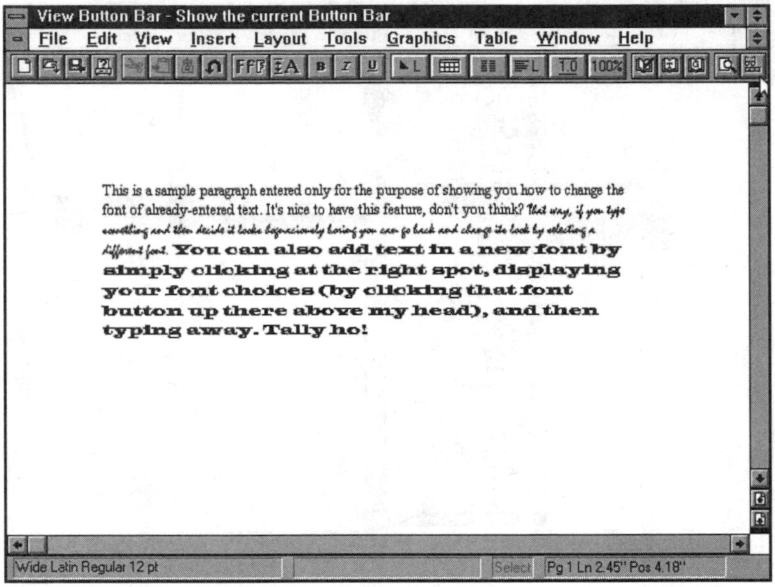

Figure 5.7

You can change the font as quick as you can click.

Blow-You-Away Font Choices

The way in which you tackle a problem says a lot about your personality. Are you the kind of person who likes to see the whole picture (like the entire foundation of your house being eaten away by termites) or would you rather find out a room at a time?

Your answer will determine whether you want to work with the Fonts dialog box to set the font, style, and size of your text. You can display the Font dialog box two ways:

- You can open the Layout menu and choose Font
- You can press F9

Either way—get ready—here comes the Font dialog box (see fig. 5.8). Whoa, Nellie! Hold on there. Are you really ready to deal with all these choices? I don't blame you.

If you want to, you can select the font by clicking in the font box in the upper left corner of the dialog box. The preview window (in the bottom left) changes to show the font you've chosen.

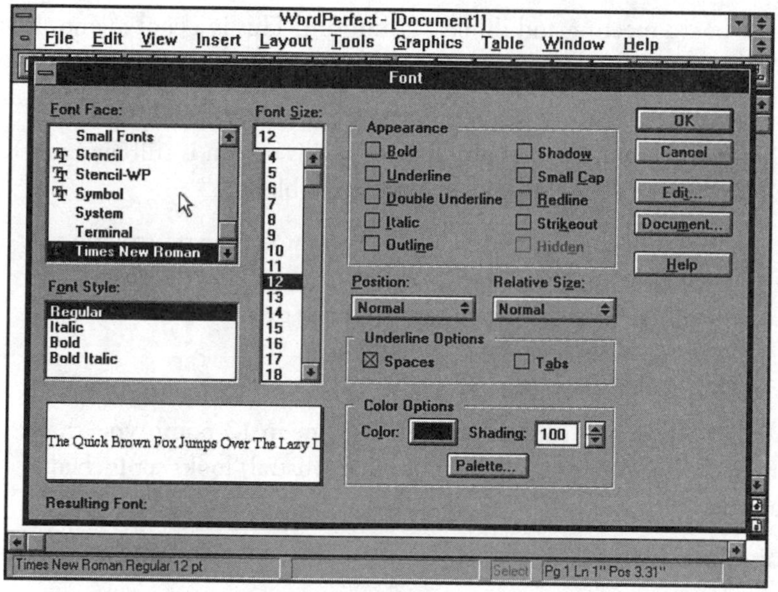

Figure 5.8
The outrageous Font dialog box.

Other possibilities this box presents include the style, size, appearance, position, and color of the text. That's a lot of wallop in one punch. (And, besides, the buttons are easier.)

Still breathing? Good. You can go one step further in the Font dialog box and set up all of the defaults for your everyday documents. By clicking the Document button, you display the Document Initial Font dialog box, in which you can choose the font typeface, style, and size used in every document (until you change it).

Getting Stylish

Whether you want to admit it or not, we all want to look good in print. If we spend minutes, hours, or days with our words, we want them to represent us well when we're not around. The boss finds your memo on her desk three days after the board meeting and thinks "Hmmmm. This is a cool memo. I can tell this person went to a lot of trouble. I think I'll dig out the bonus sheet..."

Or does she look at the memo and think "Golly, this person is still living in the Dark Ages. Maybe I should bring in some fresh blood..."

It's something to think about, anyway. Going to that little extra trouble to spruce up your documents can be well worth your time. WordPerfect gives you several different fashions in which to wrap your text.

That's About the Size of It

Have you ever noticed that some fonts look just fine in 12-point type, thank you very much, while other text (remember that Mistral) looks scrunched and unreadable?

What's going on with that?

Some fonts, because of the way the individual characters are formed, look better in smaller sizes than others. Figure 5.7 shows a mix of fonts and they all look like different sizes, too, but they're all really 12-point text. (Hey, it's a magic trick, all right?)

> **What's... gasp... a point? You've lost me!** Slow down, Maurice. Take a deep breath. A point is a favorite term batted around the coffee machine by typographers who are In The Know. For us normal people, a point is a unit of measurement for the letters we deal with. 72 points make one inch, which means that your average A in 72-point size is a one-inch tall A.

In order to change the size of your text, you can use the same basic procedure for choosing a new font:

■ Highlight the text, click the size button in the Button Bar (it's the capital A with the two-headed arrow—right beside the font button), and choose the size you want

■ Point and click that cute little text cursor, pick the size, and start typing

Want to see an example? Oh, sure you do. Take figure 5.9. Please.

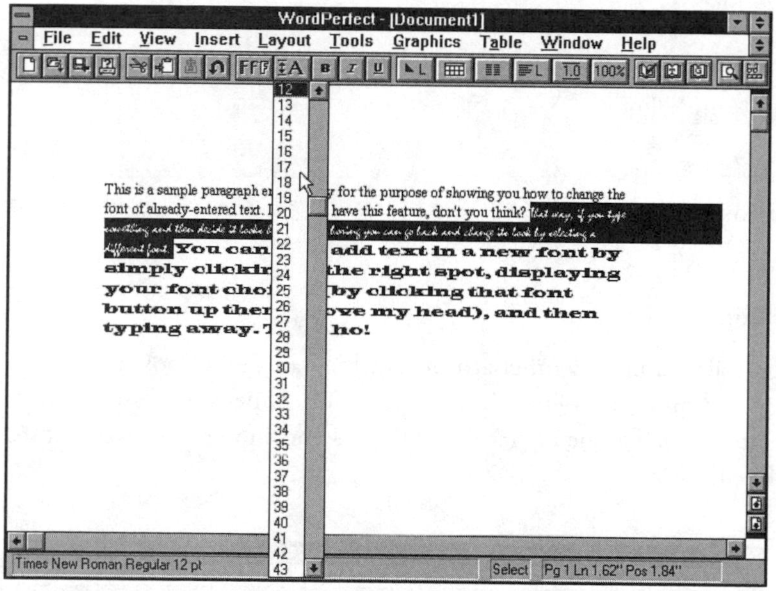

Figure 5.9
We're going to make Mistral maxi.

First we highlight the text, and then click that trusty size button and look at those cascading sizes. It's enough to make you go hog wild.

Click the size you want. We wanted to make sure that you see the full beauty of the Mistral font, so we turned the size up to 20 points. Take a look at figure 5.10 and decide what you think.

What Is a Text Style?

Unlike a font, which encompasses the typeface, style, and size of text, a text style is a single attribute that conveys the text's attitude. There are four basic styles you'll use most often in documents and others with more specialized uses. These are:

■ Normal

■ **Bold**

■ *Italic*

■ <u>Underline</u>

That's the four basic. Now for the more specialized:

■ <u>Double underline</u>

■ Outline

■ **Shadow**

■ SMALL CAPS

■ ~~Strikeout~~

Some people also lump two other attributes which are really "positions"—
Superscript and Subscript—into the Style category. Superscript causes the
characters to ride half a line higher (like H$2$0) and subscript causes text to
be half a line lower.

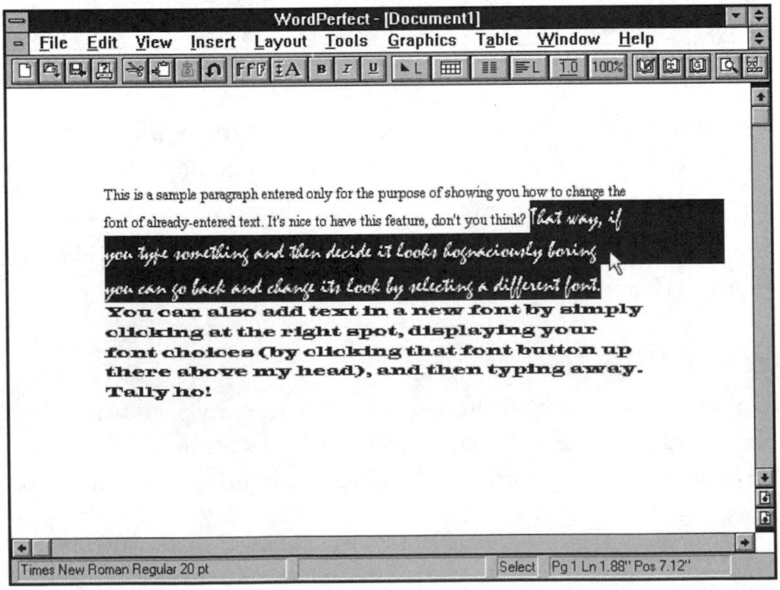

Figure 5.10
Like it?

Why Use It?

Normal, do-nothing text is your everyday paragraph. There is nothing special, no shouting, no whispering, no *emphasis*. Bold is often used to state something strongly; to call attention to a necessary term or phrase.

Italic is the standard style used when terms are defined, or when you lean on a word ("No, I *didn't* say that.")

If you are working with a printer that doesn't give you the option of choosing different fonts and using different sizes, you can still use styles to set off headings, important phrases, quotes, etc. Every printer will enable you to use boldface and italic, although not all printers can print the whole gamut of styles.

Style Application: Adding Pinash

Adding styles is simple. If you're adding a certain style to text that is already there, first highlight the text (Remember how? Hint: Use the mouse). Then you have the standard deux options:

- Press F9 to display the Font dialog box and click the style you want (in the Appearance options), or

- Click the button you want in the Button Bar (B for Bold, I for Italic, and U for Underline).

If you want to change the style of soon-to-be-entered text, click where you want to begin, click the button of the style you want, and type away. When you are done entering text in that style, remember to turn it off by clicking the button again.

After you've built up your WordPerfect tolerance, you may want to try using WordPerfect styles—these are different gremlins than font styles—to apply certain settings to your paragraphs. A style "remembers" the settings you chose, like what font, what size, what spacing, what style, and applies the settings to the paragraph or section you're working on. WordPerfect keeps track of all your settings in a container called a *stylesheet*.

They're Out To Get Us

This is an area that is so ripe for problems that we could do an entire book just on font foibles. (Get out the Pepto Bismol.) We'll cover a couple of the fixable common ones here.

Fickle Fonts

Okay, you highlighted your text, you opened the Font menu, you chose the font you wanted to use. The status line on the bottom left side of the screen said you were using the font you wanted to use.

And when you printed, your printer spit out boring, Courier, 10-point text. No eye-catching 12-point. No weenie 7.5-point. Why is WordPerfect teasing you?

First, your printer may not be able to print in different sizes. Check your printer's manual to make sure.

Second, did you install the right printer at print time? You can find out by clicking the Print button in the Button bar (that is the little picture of the printer—fourth button from the left). The Print dialog box appears, with—hopefully—your printer's name at the top (see fig. 5.11).

If a printer other than the one you are using is shown there (or if None selected appears), you need to change the printer set up to work with WordPerfect (or go out and buy the printer shown there, which isn't a real practical option). Try clicking the Select button to choose the printer you want before you take a hammer to that piggy bank.

Changing the printer setup might mean messing with Windows setup and installing printer drivers (and if you didn't do it in the first place, this is going to scare your socks off). Here is an idea: Find someone else to do it for you.

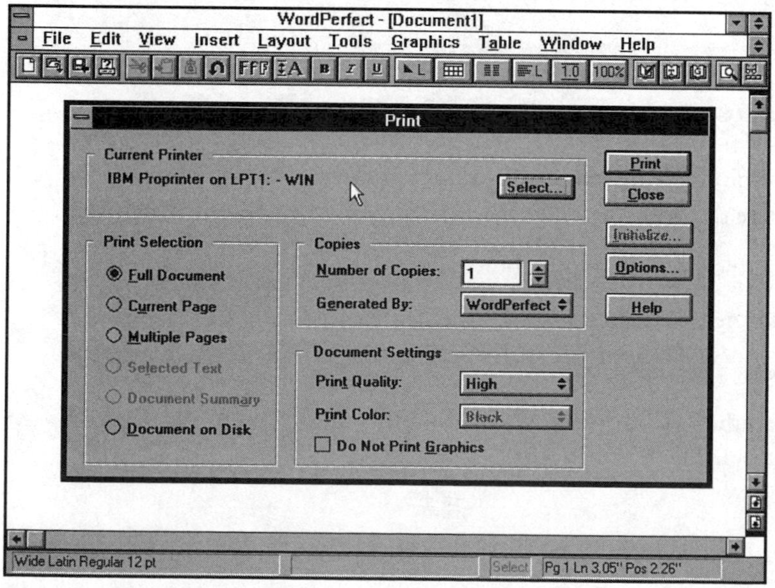

Figure 5.11
*Printer, printer,
who's got the printer?*

Nothing Works!

Oh, I know the feeling. There is great gnashing of teeth going on, isn't there? You're clutching the arms of your chair, trying to restrain yourself from beating the computer to death.

If you're trying to use fonts and everything is really screwy, you may need to do something that you probably should have done in the first place (or, at least, someone who Knows should have done it first): set up your fonts.

Some printers have fonts built right in and that's that. No mess, no fuss. But sometimes you need to set up fonts to be used with Windows, WordPerfect for Windows, and with your printer. This is not a job for the font-phobic.

Make sure you save what you're working on before you go trick someone into helping you sort out your font mess. If you're the type of person who enjoys struggling with the Rubik's cube, you'll like working with fonts. Otherwise, get out the Excedrin.

Demon-Strations

Fontasy On Screen (with apologies to Fantasy On Ice)

1. Position the cursor at the beginning of the text for which you want to change the font.

2. Press and hold the mouse button.

3. Drag the mouse to the end of the text that you want to change.

4. Release the mouse button.

5. Open the Layout menu by pointing to it and clicking the mouse button (or by pressing Alt+L).

6. Choose the Font command. The Font dialog box appears.

7. Click on the down arrow at the end of the Font box to scroll through the possible fonts.

8. Click on the font you want to use or highlight it and press Enter or click OK.

Stylish, Yet Functional, Too

1. On a blank line, click the Bold button.

2. Type *This is bold text.*

3. Click Bold again.

4. Type *This is normal text.*

5. Click the Underline button.

6. Type *This is underlined text.*

7. Click Underline again.

8. Type *This is normal text.*

9. Click the Italic button.

10. Type *This is italic text.*

11. Click Italic again.

12. Type This is normal text.

Ha! Good job. You now have settled into the rhythm of using text styles. Figure 5.12 shows you what you've just done.

Figure 5.12
Playing with text styles.

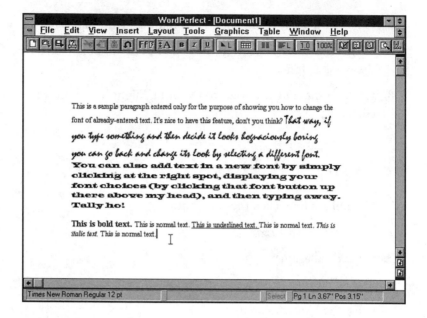

Summary

This encounter has included some of the basics for changing the look of your text. It may be something you won't want to tackle right away, or you may be juggling fonts from the start. Fonts control the overall look of the characters—typeface, style, and size. The text's style is like the text's attitude. You can make your text shout, whisper, whine, joke, or plead. (*Please, please,* let this encounter be over!)

Exorcises

1. What is a font? _____

    a. A short name for fountain.

    b. Something other people envy.

    c. A typographical term for a typeface, style, and size.

    d. A baby's soft spot.

2. Give two examples of a font.

3. What characteristics are included in a font?

4. Name four basic text styles.

5. What's the first step in changing the font or style of already entered text?

6th Encounter

This Tab's for You: Simple Formatting

Goal

To help you learn some quick-and-easy formatting techniques using our friend, the Tab key.

What You Will Need

WordPerfect (or a reasonable facsimile) and a Tab key (preferrably still attached to the keyboard).

Terms of Enfearment

Left tab   Right tab
Center tab   Decimal tab
tab stops   monospaced fonts
proportional fonts

Briefing

Tabs are not something to fear. Seemingly cryptic, ever mysterious, the tab provides an atmosphere of wonder and awe. How does the cursor know it should move that number of spaces? How do all those lines magically line up with a simple press of a single key?

The tab can make your life oh-so-much easier than it is right now. Office a mess? Push the Tab key and watch your papers file themselves in order. See your books close up and align themselves along the edge of your desk.

Sold? Let's get busy.

Do I Have To Use Tabs?

Are you whining again? No, of *course* you don't have to use tabs. In fact, you can type text into your document and try—over and over again—to use the spacebar to line everything up. (Or you can forget about trying to line everything up, but your clients won't be very impressed—and your boss will be less so.)

Perhaps you don't understand the importance of the tab stop. A little enlightenment will help. Want to know what it does?

The tab helps you align text in your documents. Suppose, for example, that you are working on a letter similar to the one shown in figure 6.1. A little text, a few numbers. If you press the spacebar, you might be able to line up the first column (although we are not recommending it).

But what happens if you want to add a second column beside the first? That second column is going to be out of alignment, unless you use a tab stop. Why? Because unless you're using a *monospaced font*—which is a font in which all the letters take up exactly the same amount of space—you're going to have unequal amounts of space given to the different letters. Thinner letters take up less room than wider letters. An "l" can slip in spaces that would be impossible for a W (without NutriSystem, anyway). These fonts, in which letters take up different amounts of space depending on their widths, are called *proportional fonts*. And because of proportional fonts your tables will look horrible if you don't use tabs.

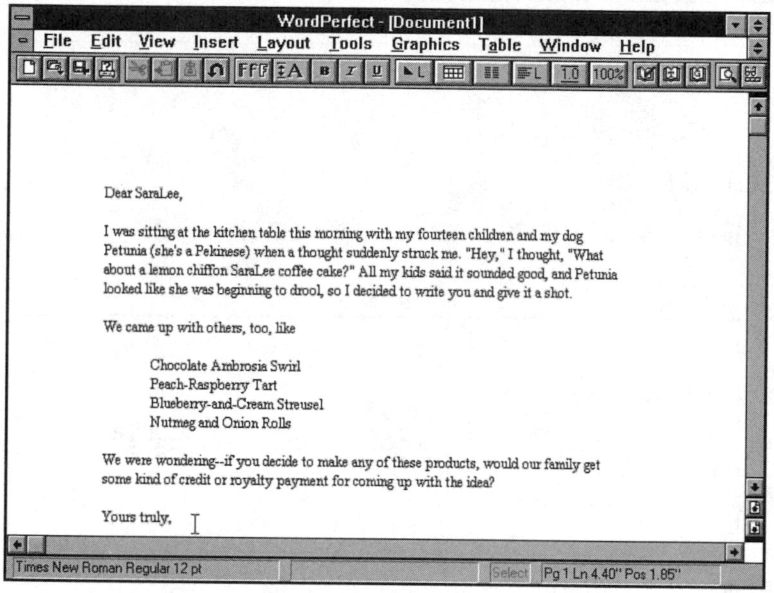

Figure 6.1
Your columns need tab stops.

Tabs and Taboos

Okay, so you know it's a no-no to use spaces when you should be using tabs. Are you clear on why? Because text that you want to look like this:

Product	Secret Recipe Code
Lemon Chiffon	B1
Choc/Ambrosia Swrl	A5
Peach/Rasp Tart	F2
Blueb/Cream Strsl	C7
Nutmeg/Onion	A3

Could wind up looking like this when you print:

Product	Secret Recipe Code
Lemon Chiffon	B1
Choc/Ambrosia Swrl	A5
Peach/Rasp Tart	F2
Blueb/Cream Strsl	C7
Nutmeg/Onion	A3

And we *know* you don't want that.

WordPerfect gives you four different types of tabs that you can use in your documents:

- Left tabs
- Right tabs
- Center tabs
- Decimal tabs

Lefties

When you stick a left tab in your document, the text lined up there lines up along the left edge. The tabbed text in figure 6.1 shows text lined up on a left tab, for example.

Left tabs are the default, meaning that when you set a tab, it's a left tab, unless you specify otherwise.

Far and away you'll use left tabs more often than anything else.

Rightwingers

You'd expect right tabs to be more conservative than their left counterparts, but not so. Right tabs are more unusual, used primarily for artistic purposes, such as when you're trying to line up text around a piece of art. When you set a right tab, text that is tabbed to that point is lined up along the right edge. (Think about it—not something you see often.)

Figure 6.2 shows how the product list looks if it is lined up along a right tab.

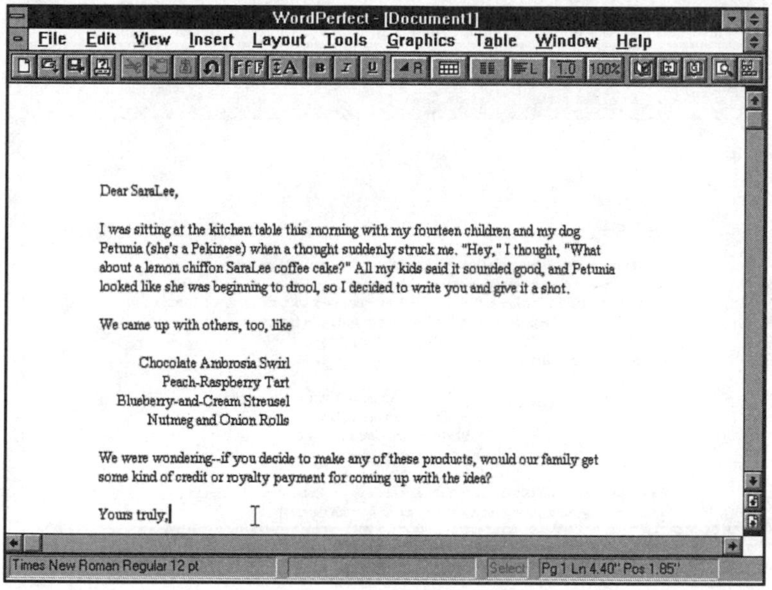

Figure 6.2
Pastry on the right.

Middle of the Road

Another kind of tab WordPerfect offers is the center tab. This guy really comes in handy when you want to center headings or create special effects (like centering all the entries on a fancy-shmancy menu).

The centered tab turns your ordinary text into Something Special, as shown in figure 6.3.

Okay, so I'm beating some flat pastry, but think about how difficult it would be to accurately center all of those different lines of text with the spacebar. You would do it once, print it, find out it's out of whack. Do it again, print it, see that you overcompensated. Do it *again*...(Come back later. I'll be here a while.)

Figure 6.3
Your words—center stage.

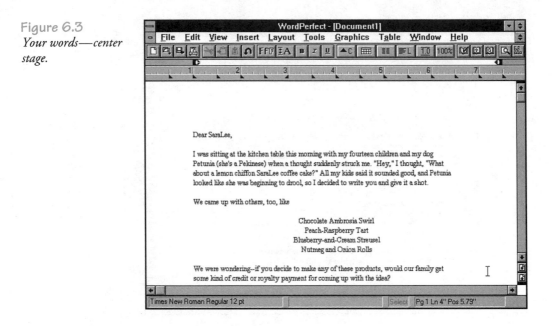

To the Point, Aren't You?

The final tab type is one that you may or may not use regularly: the decimal tab. Do you find yourself sneaking numbers into documents on a regular basis? Do you repeatedly quote financial strategems and projected sales increases? Do the numbers in your documents appear to crawl across the page all by themselves?

The decimal tab helps you line it all up. Come out of the financial closet and admit it: you are a numbers person. You like them. They make you happy.

With WordPerfect, you can use numbers in your document to your heart's content. And they never have to look less than wonderful again, all because of a little decimal tab.

To illustrate the decimal tab, we've added a second column to the sample letter (see fig. 6.4). The column, actually, means absolutely nothing and is included only to illustrate this concept (our apologies to SaraLee).

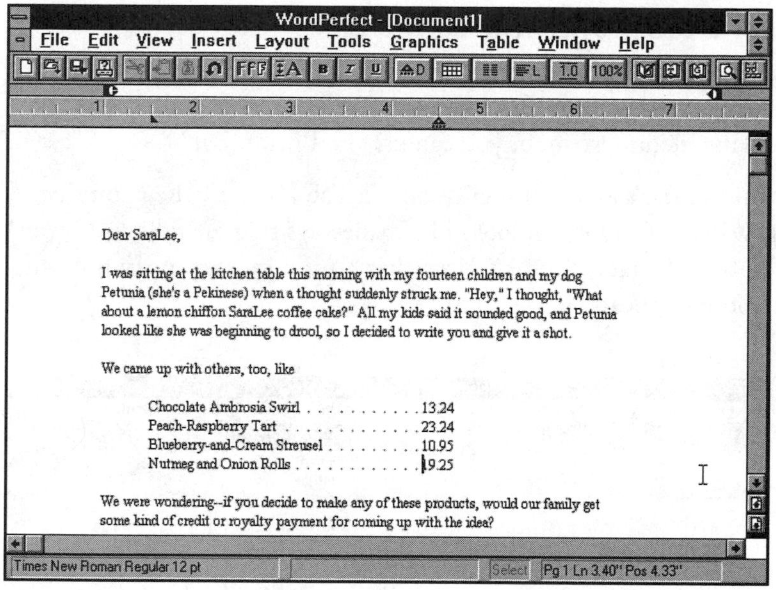

Figure 6.4
*Cross this dot—
I dare you.*

Hanging Out at the Tab Stop Cafe

Working with tabs is about as simple as anything in WordPerfect ever is. You can set tabs for text that is already there, and you can set tabs for text you haven't entered yet. You can also delete single tabs or wipe them all away. You can easily change tabs from one type to another (for example, you could change a left tab to a center tab) and include dot leaders (those little dots that stretch from the edge of your text to the number) if you chose.

WordPerfect already includes tabs—set for you—at every half-inch across the page. You may never have to mess with those tabs at all. How do you use the tabs already there? Press the Tab key! (Feel pretty silly, don't you?)

It's Time for Tab Jeopardy! The answer for $100: Press either the Backspace key or Shift+Tab. The question is "How do you move the cursor backward one tab?"

Climbing Up on the Tab Set Box

Like just about every other thing you work with in WordPerfect for Windows, you've got two options for the way you add, remove, and change tabs. You can use the menu system, or you can use the Button Bar.

Yeah, the Button Bar's easier. Just click on the Tab button (when you first start using WP for Windows, it looks like a sideways triangle followed by an L—right next to the table button). Keep that button pressed. A drop down list of tab options appears (see fig. 6.5).

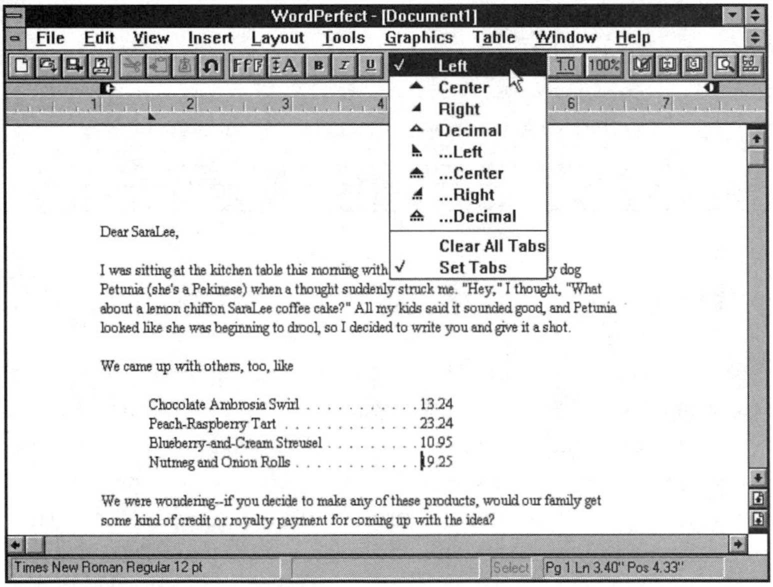

Figure 6.5
The tab stop cafe.

If you would rather, you can go about it the more leisurely way. Open the Layout menu, choose Line, and select Tab Set from the drop-down list. The Tab Set dialog box appears (see fig. 6.6).

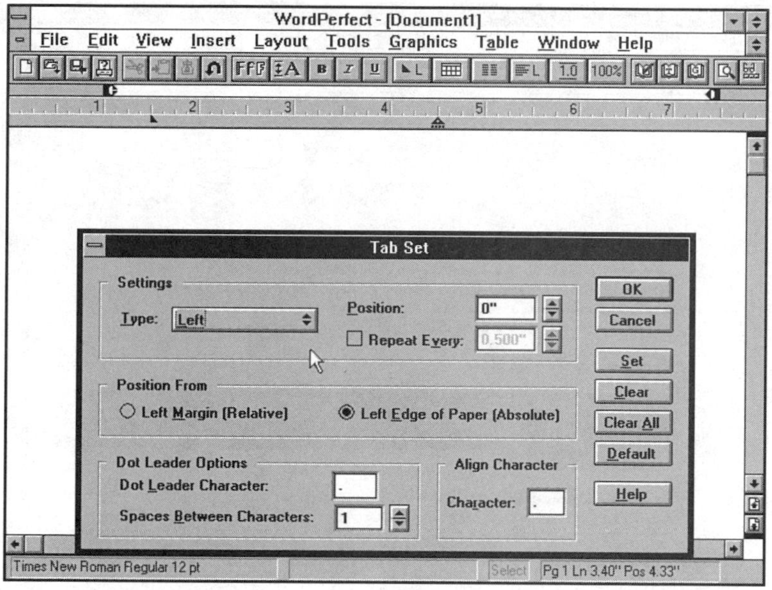

Figure 6.6
*The Tab Set
dialog box.*

Clearing Tabs

For best results, before you add your own tabs, clear the ones that are already there. (It makes working with your own less confusing.)

To clear tabs, click on the Clear All button in the right side of the Tab Set dialog box. After you click the button, WordPerfect wipes away all of the tabs and scrunches your text together (see fig. 6.6). If you're using the drop list in the Button Bar, click Clear All Tabs. Same difference.

It's Time for Tab Jeopardy! The answer for $200: Click on the Clear One button. And the question is: "How do you get rid of only one tab in the tab line?"

Figure 6.7
Hey! You call that helping?

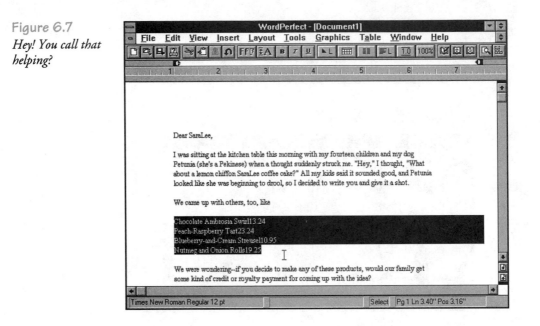

Adding Tabs

Putting tabs back in is as easy as taking them out. Let's put one back at the half-inch mark.

First click the Tab button in the Button bar and display the list. Click Set Tabs (the tab bar and the ruler bar appear at the top of your document). Now reopen the drop list and choose the kind of tab you want.

Finally, click at the point in the tab line (just below the ruler bar) where you want to add the tab. A little triangle with a line descending (to show you where the tab will line up) hangs there, waiting for you to let go of the mouse button (see fig. 6.8).

> WordPerfect for Windows adds dot leaders automatically when you use decimal tabs. If you want to get rid of the dot leaders (those little dots between text and page numbers in a table of contents), just click on the Dot Leader option in the Tab Set dialog box and backspace to remove the period—or you can use a different character, if you want to be daring. (It's *my* turn to be the dot leader! I *never* get to be the dot leader! *Mom*!)

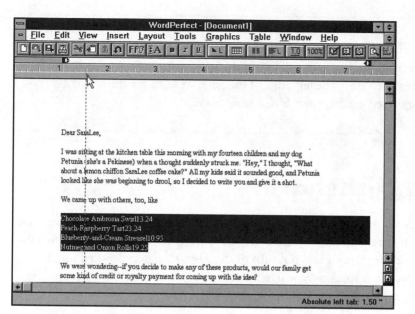

Figure 6.8
Always clean up your own mess.

They're Out To Get Us

There are lots of little subtleties and nuances involved in getting the most out of your tabs. You'll get the hang of it. Just takes a little practice.

The first time you try to format some supremely complicated table, you'll fuss and fume and swear a bit. After that, everything will start to fall into place. (Ahhh...it's all becoming clear to me now...)

> **It's Time for Final Tab Jeopardy!** The answer for the championship is: A relative tab is measured from the left margin, and an absolute tab is measured from the left edge of the page. What's the question? You have 60 seconds. *Do dee do dee do dee dooo...*

Tab Misbehavin'

Even the most guru-ish word processing extraordinaire has trouble with tabs now and then. Things may look okay on-screen, but after you enter the tabs in the Tab Set box and then return to the page, things are goofed up. The third column is stuck over where the fourth column should be—except the heading, which is in the right place.

What the heck is going on?

Sometimes it's tempting to push the old Tab key one too many times when you're working in the regular document. You might not even realize you're doing it. One word is short, so you press Tab twice so the columns line up on-screen. But then when you go to apply the Tabs, WordPerfect bumps everything over too far.

Lost? Here's an example:

WordPerfect for Windows puts tabs every half inch. Like this:

Tab	*Tab*	*Tab*	*Tab*	*Tab*
1	1	1	1	1
22	22	22	22	22
333	333	333	333	333
4444	4444	4444	4444	4444
55555	55555	55555		

See what happened? The final entry (55555) is too wide to fit in a single column, so we pressed Tab only three times. When you look at this table in the Tab Set box, all of the other rows will have the right number of entries, but the last one will have only three. The moral? Make sure you press Tab only once between each column entry. Then when you add Real Tabs, everything will line up.

Outta Whack Heads

■ Sung to the tune of Jimmy Cracked Corn (which I never understood either).

So you go to all this trouble to get the darned table lined up with its left tabs and decimal tabs, and you think you're done, when the column headings end up looking ridiculous. Oh, sure, that's professional. Nicely aligned decimal tabs, with the column headings hanging out and separated by ... (see fig. 6.9).

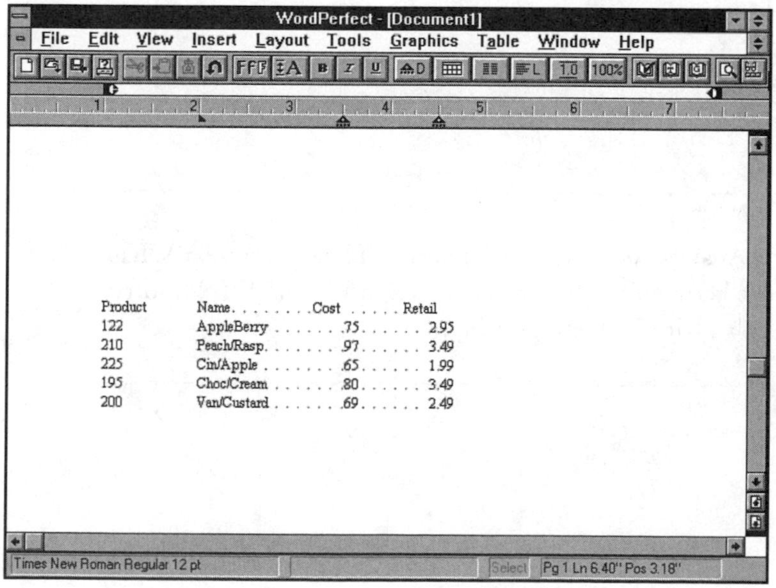

Figure 6.9

Funky column heads.

The best way to fix this is to set two different tab lines: one for the headings, and one for the meat of the table. That means highlight the heading line and set the tabs; then highlight the rest of the table and set those tabs. When you set the tab line for the headings, make the tabs at 3 and 4 inches center tabs instead of decimal tabs (see fig. 6.10). That'll fix it.

Figure 6.10

Putting heads in their place.

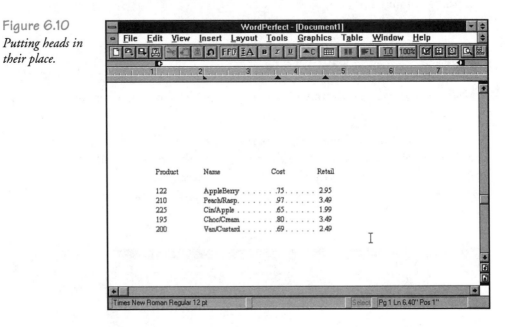

Today's Answer to Final Tab Jeopardy: The question is "What is the difference between an absolute tab and a relative tab?" (No, sorry, an uncle with a bar bill doesn't qualify.)

Demon-Strations
Swatting Tabs

Let's get rid of those extra tabs. Oh, come on—you remember how:

1. Highlight the text you want to change.

2. Open the Layout menu and choose the Line command.

3. Choose the Tab Set command.

4. In the Tab Set dialog box, click the Clear All button.

Or the quickie: Click the Tab button in the Button Bar, and select Clear All Tabs.

Grow Your Own

To add your own tabs to already entered text, follow these steps:

1. Highlight the text.

2. Open the Layout menu and select Line.

3. Choose Tab Set. (See a pattern here?)

4. Type the type of tab you want.

5. Enter the position (in inches).

6. Specify whether you want the tab to be absolute or relative, and whether you want dot leaders.

7. Click Set.

Repeat for any additional tabs, or until you've lost between three and five pounds.

Summary

This encounter has taken you face to face with one of the most hated of the formatting creatures: tabs. We've met the enemy and they is us.

Tabs really and truly make life easier, and using them in WordPerfect is no more complicated than anything else. Just practice a little; you'll get it. And if you can make your mistakes on someone *else's* file, even better.

Exorcises

1. Name the four popular tab types.

2. Explain why you might use a tab in a document. (Or if you wouldn't, why someone else might.)

3. Complete this sentence: A tab is to a document as a dog is to a _____.

4. Before you add your own tabs, you might want to _____.

   a. Turn on the computer.

   b. Remove the tabs WordPerfect for Windows set for you.

   c. Finish your coffee.

   d. Try moving one of your own.

5. True or false: Once you've set tabs for a section of text, you can't reset them.

7th Encounter

Much Ado about Printing

Goal

To help alleviate any printer anxiety you may be feeling.

What You Will Need

Your copy of WordPerfect for Windows loaded; a file that you would like to print (or a screen with a few lines of nonsense); a printer connected to the system and ready to rock.

Terms of Enfearment

preview	print options
initialization	soft fonts
print range	graphics fonts

Briefing

Whether or not you admit it, printing is truly the *coup-de-grace* of word processing. Why else would you take all that time to enter text, format it, make sure the spelling is right, and perform other brain-numbing tasks, if you never intended to print the thing?

Of course you did.

Have you heard that printing is one of those unavoidable trouble spots that you can accidentally fall into on your way to the land of Finished Documents? Some people have more trouble with printing than others. If you're trying to do a simple printout with regular paper, no fancy fonts (remember them?), and no complicated formats—in other words, you're printing a memo—you should be all right. But printing an elaborate document with columns, graphics, various fonts, lines, headers, and footers is just asking for trouble. Don't expect to get out of that print job without throbbing temples. At least the first time.

But that's the nature of all word processing programs, not WordPerfect for Windows in particular. Printing is supposed to be something like childbirth: by the time you get the document just the way you want it, you know you've done something significant. There's that feeling of accomplishment that just might not be there if things were too easy.

Well, maybe.

Remember that when you are using WordPerfect for Windows, you are actually using two programs—WordPerfect and Windows. If you're having trouble printing, are you able to print from other Windows programs? If so, something is going on with WordPerfect for Windows. Grab the nearest tech support person for a little enlightenment.

Taking a Little Look-See

Font flashback: In Encounter 6, you learned that there are monospaced fonts and proportional fonts. Monospaced fonts are fonts in which all of the characters take up the same amount of space (an l gets the same width as a w). Proportional fonts are fonts in which the letters are given space according to what they need, so the letter t would get less space than an M.

WordPerfect for Windows lets you see characters the way they will appear in print. Little letters take up a little space. Big characters take up a bigger space.

But that doesn't mean you won't want to see close-ups and panoramic views. WordPerfect for Windows lets you in for closer scrutiny or backs you up for the wider angles.

[Cue: Leave It To Beaver music.]

Ward and June Cleaver Present: Alternate Views

With the variety of views available, WordPerfect for Windows enables you to see what is coming before it hits. Avoid those shaky moments by the printer output tray. Relax in the comfort of your own office, secure in the knowledge that things are as they are supposed to be.

Alternate views. By WordPerfect.

You can display different views one of two ways:

■ You can open the File menu and choose either Two Page or Zoom commands (see fig. 7.1), or

■ You can click the Zoom button in the Button Bar and choose from the available views (see fig. 7.2).

Like Ward and June, full page displays in black and white (see fig. 7.3). That doesn't lessen the effectiveness of the display, however. Notice that you still have all of the same commands at your disposal, tucked neatly away in the Button Bar overhead.

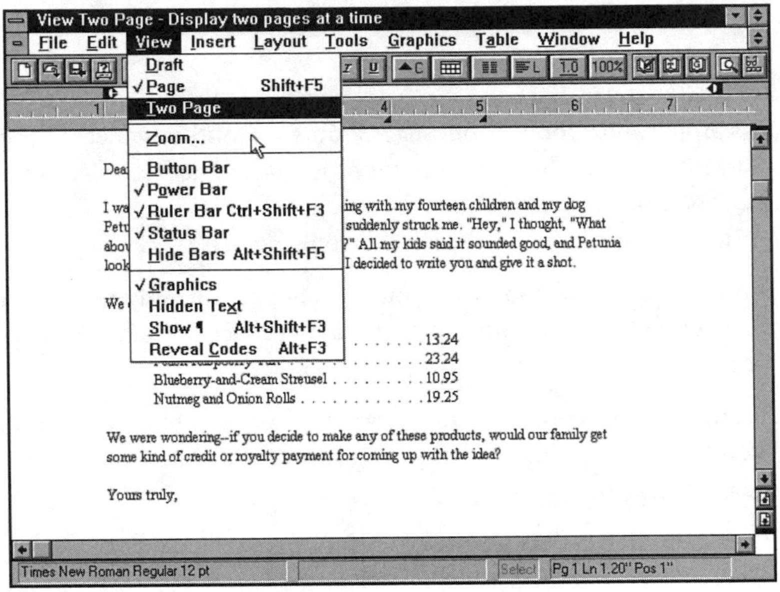

Figure 7.1
Choosing a different view.

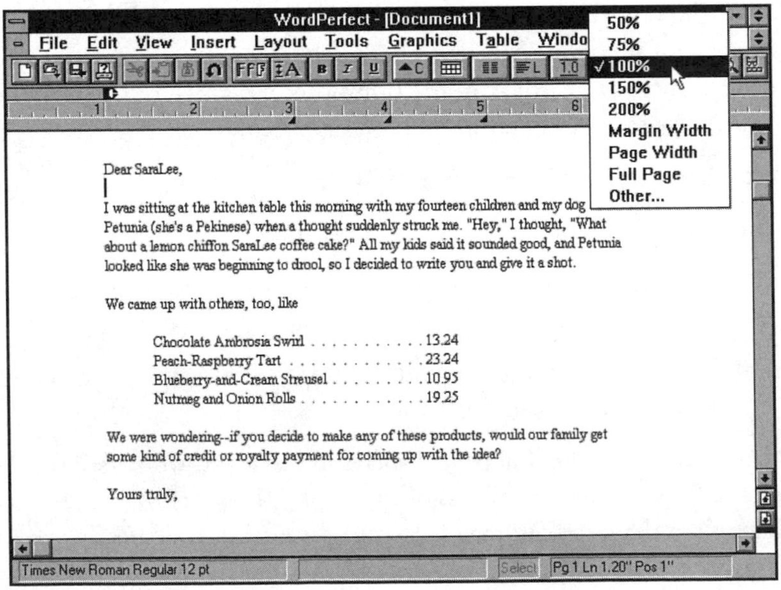

Figure 7.2
Zooming around for the heck of it.

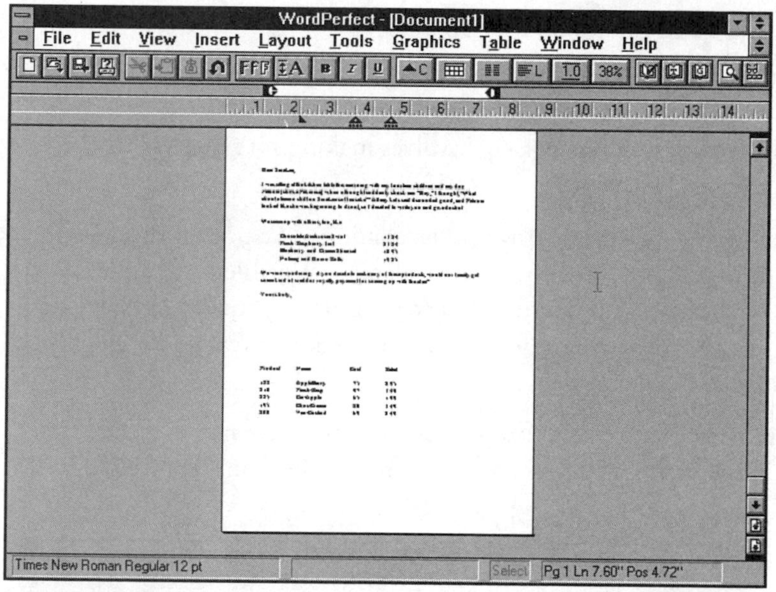

Figure 7.3
One good preview is worth a thousand bad prints.

Rules for Good Previews

Golly Gee, Wally—how're we gonna remember all this stuff?

■ Display the document you want to see before you change the view.

■ Position the cursor at the top of page 1 before printing; or, if you want to see a specific page, place the cursor on that page before zooming in. (If you forget, no big deal. You can move from page to page easily in the different views.)

■ Use the different views to check out the typeface, styles, and formatting of your words. You can choose from real-life size, magnified (two times normal view), reduced, two-page, and thumbnail views.

■ Always make sure you sit at least three feet back from the television screen.

You're the One, Babe— Selecting a Printer

Another important preprinting step involves making sure that you've selected a printer. Have you?

That usually happens during program installation. The printer that you're using needs to be "seen" in two different places—WordPerfect and Windows. If you didn't install WordPerfect for Windows yourself and have no idea whether a printer was installed, you can check by pressing F7 when you have a document open on the screen.

The Print dialog box appears. If a printer is selected, the name of the printer is shown in the Current Printer area at the top of the Print box (see fig 7.4).

Figure 7.4
Make sure the printer is selected.

This is the selected printer

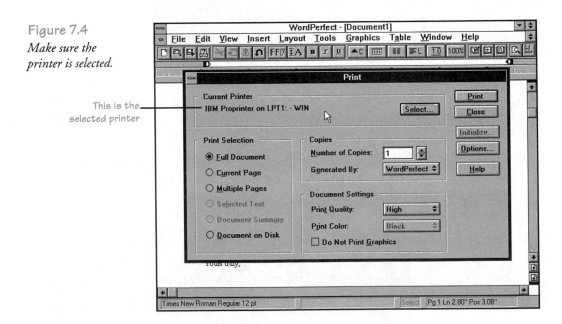

What? No printer is selected? Well, quick, before anybody notices, click the Select button. The Select Printer screen appears, showing you the possible printers you can select (see fig. 7.5).

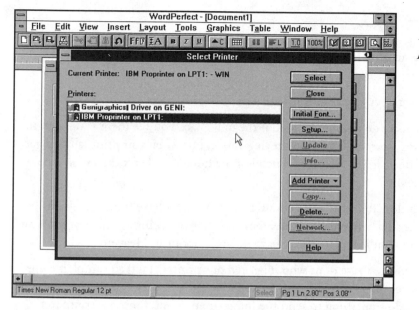

Figure 7.5
*Finding your
print-mate.*

Notice that this screen shows only two printer choices. Your department or business may have many more printers available in the Select Printers screen. To choose one of the other printers on the list, click the one you want and choose the Select button.

If you want to add a printer to the list that you don't see there, click the Add Printer button. WordPerfect for Windows will prompt you to insert the right disk (you'll need the backup copies of your original program disks) so that it can copy the necessary files to your hard disk.

Dealing with printer stuff is not an easy task. Don't expect too much your first time out. Drink plenty of liquids (but not around your keyboard) and get plenty of rest.

Font Worries

I know what you're thinking: Oh, Jeez, Edith, do we have to talk about fonts again?

Well, sorry, Archie, but fonts are part of WordPerfect life.

Fonts don't do you much good if the only place you see them is on-screen. Oh, sure, they look great in preview mode, but when you print, all you get is page after page of Courier (which is known to cause heart disease in laboratory rats).

As mentioned in the last encounter, some printers have fonts built right in. More than a convenience issue, these printers can print a variety of fonts and sizes and you just plain don't have to worry about it. Heaven.

But there are those of us who inherited our printers (and so can blame our headaches on someone else) who don't have those nifty built-in fonts and have to do something to send the fonts—remember, fonts are computer instructions—to the printer so the printer knows what the heck to do.

> *Jargon alert:* Fonts that you purchase as software and then have to send to the printer at print time are called soft fonts. Just thought you would want to know.

That something is called *downloading*. You download a font to the printer at print time, so the printer knows how to print the font you want to use. Get it?

WordPerfect will download your fonts for you, but WordPerfect wants to call it *initializing*, as in initializing the printer. To initialize the printer, display the Print dialog box (by opening the File menu and choosing Print or by pressing F5). After you set all of your options, click the Initialize button. A little pop-up box gets in your face telling you the oh-so-important rules for initializing your friend the printer. After you press Enter or click OK, the computer chugs for a moment (you can just feel those little fonts running through the print cable to the printer) and then returns you to your open document.

Could we *please* stop talkin about fonts now, Edith?

Oh, the Options of It All!

And you thought we were almost done, right? We're just getting started. You saw how many other things there were to worry about in the Print box. Let's take a look at it again, shall we? (Go ahead—look at figure 7.6.)

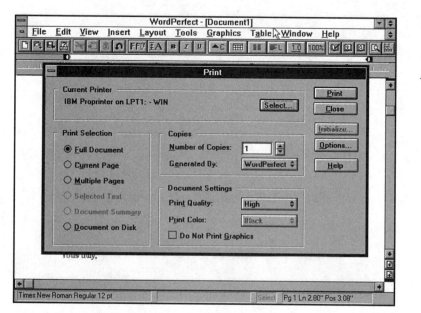

Figure 7.6
The Print dialog box—an encore presentation.

Let's just lump it all together before we lose half our audience to attention deficit disorder (or hunger pains): The rest of the printer options may concern you only once in a blue moon. You'll be lying in bed late on a Sunday night, stressing about the report that you have to print in time for the 8:30 a.m. Monday meeting. You look out the window, trying to remember which WordPerfect print options are which, and you see...sure enough...the blue moon.

In the Print Selection box on the Print dialog box, you see your typical print options. Do you want to print the whole thing? A single page? How about just a few pages, multiple pages, or a disk file?

Oh, you can choose the number of copies you need, the quality of the output, the colors for your text, and whether you want graphics to print or not (drafts print faster without graphics).

But to really get the full impact of printing options, you've got to click the Options button. (Oh, go ahead, click it.) The Print Output Options dialog box appears, as you'll see swimming before your eyes in figure 7.7. Here you can choose weird stuff like booklet printing, printing pages backwards, and printing document summaries.

Figure 7.7
Far-out options.

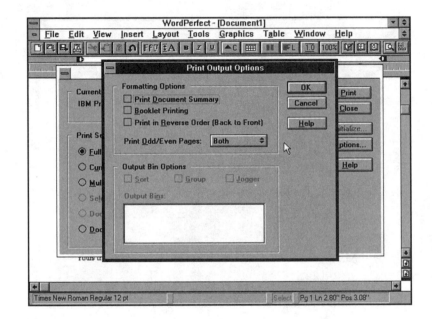

The final option, Blocked Text, is selectable only if you highlighted a section of text before you displayed the dialog box.

The Output Options box lets you set things like the number of copies you want to print and how you want your printer to behave. WordPerfect will tell your printer to sort the printed pages, collate them, or lump them together, but there is a catch: your printer must be capable of doing those things before the process will work. The printer won't just oblige you because WordPerfect told it to. One special option in this group is Print Job Graphically, which will concern you only if you're printing art images that include light items printed on top of dark ones (and how often does *that* happen?).

Just Print It!

Aren't you tired of all this hullabaloo? Let's just print the darned thing.

The Print dialog box is on the screen. You've got the right printer selected. You've chosen what you want to print. You've entered the number of copies, the Print Quality, and any other thing that might be important to you.

Finger poised?

Scoot the pointer over the Print button and click. (Whew!)

Now, keep your fingers crossed.

They're Out To Get Us

Oh, bad, bad printer. Cruel printer. You can do this to me after all the time we've spent together? After all the trouble I've gone through to keep you dusted, paper-fed, and inked up?

There are many, many things that can botch up your printing. It could even be the printer. It could be fonts. It could be the cable connection. It could be the alignment of Pluto (the planet, not the dog).

Nothing, Nada, No Way

Well, guess what happened? Nothing is a good guess. The computer thought it was printing. You heard that tell-tale chunking. But the printer sat there, dormant.

Let's whittle the possibilities down one by one:

- Is the printer turned on?
- Is the printer cable connected to your system?
- Is the printer light on, showing that the printer is on line? (That means ready to receive information.)
- Did you initialize the printer? (Although this shouldn't keep the thing from printing altogether—it just keeps the printer from printing in the right font.)
- Was your printer selected in the Print box?
- Are you sure you clicked the Print button and not the Cancel button?

Well, we had to ask.

Not an Option

Yeah, right. Selecting a printer is as easy as clicking on that Select button, huh? Well, smarty, I don't have *any* printers listed in the Select Printers box. None. Nada.

Now what?

The reason you don't see any printers is that no printers were installed during installation. In order to set up a printer to work with WordPerfect for Windows, you're going to have to get out your program disks. And that means you'll be using the Run command in the File menu (that's Program Manager's File menu) in order to update your WordPerfect for Windows installation.

Better get a cup of coffee first. And turn on your voice mail.

Demon-Strations

Coming Attractions

1. Display the document that you want to view.

2. Use the commands in the view menu or the Zoom button in the Button bar to display different views.

3. Click the view that you want.

4. Edit the document or move around as necessary. (A good stretching exercise might help right now.)

Where's the Shredder?

1. Display the document that you want to print.

2. Press F5 to display the Print box.

3. Select any necessary print options.

4. If you need to download soft fonts, select Initialize.

5. Specify the number of copies.

6. Choose the print quality and color you want.

7. Click the Print button.

Summary

Well, aren't you proud of yourself? You've learned to sneak a peak at your document before you print and hopefully—did having your fingers crossed help?—you've been able to actually print your work. Exhilarating, isn't it? The next encounter explains the ins and outs of the Save command and covers a hodge-podge of important file and program tasks.

Exorcises

1. Explain monospaced and proportional fonts. (If you have to look it up, take away two points—and shame on you.)

2. What is the primary benefit of looking at your document in different views?

    a. It tells you what movies are going to be on tomorrow night.

    b. It enables you to see how the document will look before you go to the trouble to print it.

    c. It saves paper (and innocent trees) by displaying the page on the screen.

3. What does downloading mean?

   a. Shipping feather pillows.

   b. Sending fonts to the printer.

   c. Moving the printer to a point lower than the system unit.

4. What is the benefit of displaying text in Two Page view?

5. Did you remember your vitamin this morning?

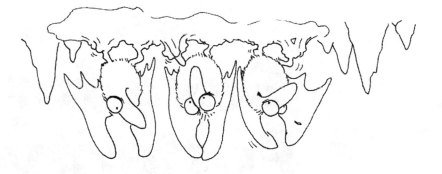

Save for Posterity and Exit, Stage Right!

Goal

To help you save those little jewels that you create, reopen them, and leave WordPerfect for Windows altogether when you've had enough. (Wait! Don't go yet!)

What You Will Need

Nothing new here: WordPerfect for Windows loaded up, some text entered in a file (any text will do), and roughly ten minutes.

Terms of Enfearment

directory	path
File Manager	Save As
autosave	

Briefing

You've already worked your way through quite a bit of the basic WordPerfect for Windows procedures (pause for back patting). You know how to create a document, edit and format it, change the font and style, and print it. We're forgetting something, though. If you don't save the file, all this fuss will have been for nothing.

Then, after you save your files, you've got to figure out how to open the files you created. WordPerfect for Windows lets you use several different features to find the files you want to work with.

Finally, knowing how to exit WordPerfect is pretty necessary information: you can't just keep WordPerfect running all the time. (Well, *possible* but not *practical.*)

Save the Files

So, you've got a file open on the screen? Good.

Chances are, your files aren't close to extinction, and they aren't in danger from oil spills or tuna nets. And yet losing that one important file—the one you needed for this afternoon's meeting—is a Really Big Deal.

Saving your files is a practical necessity. Why else would you use a word processor, if you don't want to keep your files where you can use them again easily? Saving your files also safeguards you against the accidental loss of data. Most people—just to be safe—save their current file every fifteen minutes or so.

When you save your file, WordPerfect for Windows writes the file (which at the time is being stored only in your computer's RAM, or temporary storage space) to a disk and saves it under a name you specify. The disk might be your hard disk or it might be a diskette in either drive A or B. The file lives there until you delete it, and you can reopen it, work on it, and resave it with your changes.

Nothing-Unusual Saves

Let's do a quick save. Ready?

The first time you save a file it takes a couple of seconds and keystrokes longer than subsequent saves, but it's nothing to gripe about.

First open the File menu and choose the Save command (or press Ctrl+S) as shown in figure 8.1.

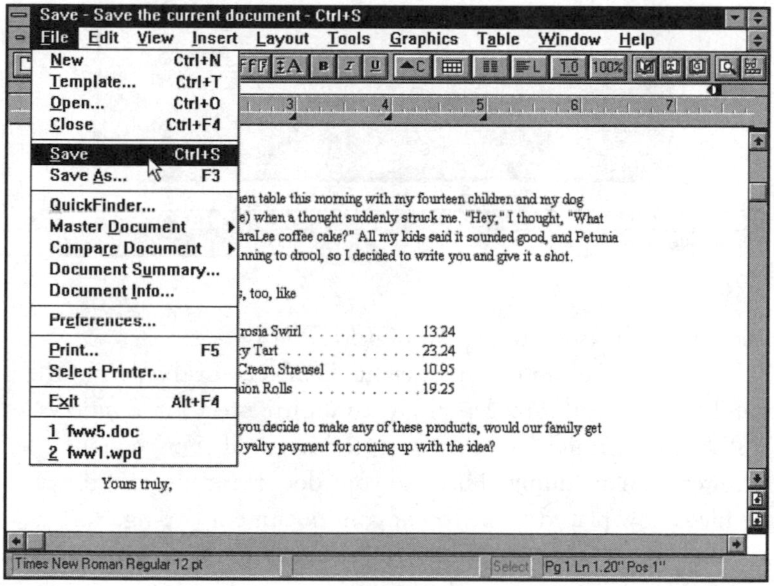

Figure 8.1
Get ready, set, save!

The Save As dialog box appears, as you'll see in figure 8.2. If you're an avid Windows fan, this box looks pretty familiar. There is the place for the name. There is the place for the directory (I'm pointing). And over *there* are the command buttons.

Ready to save the file? Don't blink, or you might miss it.

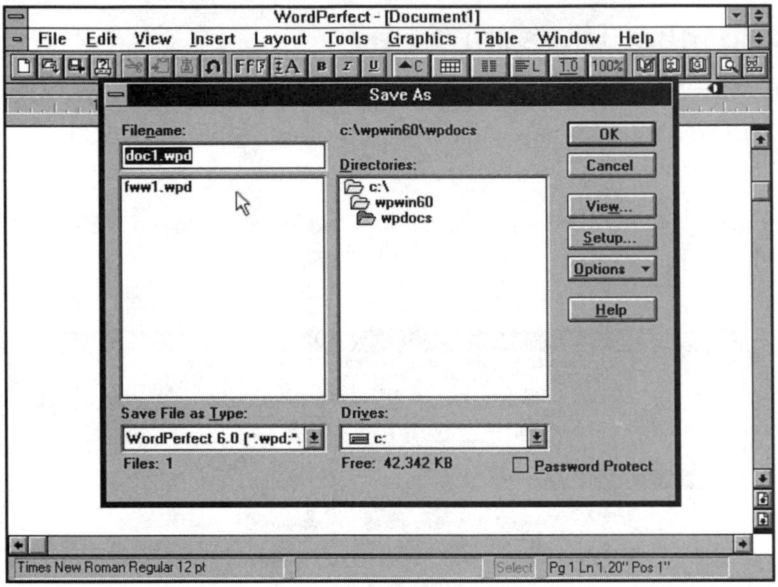

Figure 8.2
The Big Save.

Type a name for the file (something like POEM1.WPD or
COOLSTUF.WPD). You can use up to eight characters for the part of the
name before the period and three letters after. (WordPerfect for Windows
adds the WPD automatically. You may want to leave well enough alone.)
Then press Enter. You are dumped back to your document file, and the
name of the file is now placed at the top of your document (see fig. 8.3).

After you save the file the first time, you can do a quick-save by
pressing Ctrl+S. WordPerfect doesn't bother asking you for the name
or anything—it just saves the file, fast.

The Little Nuances of the Save Command

If you've got more time, you may want to investigate some of the options you have with your Save command. For example, you can do the following:

- Save the file in a format that can be used by other popular word processing programs (such as Ami Pro, Microsoft Word, and WordStar)

- Specify a different directory in which to store the file

- Add a Password so only you and Agent 99 can access the file

- Choose file display options

- Control special setup things like the default save format

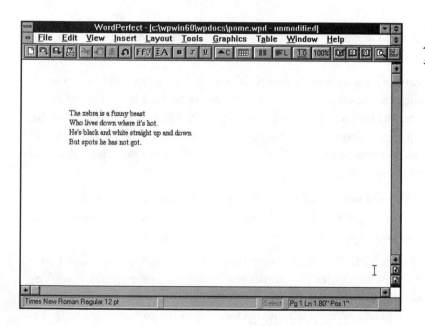

Figure 8.3
Aren't you proud? A saved file.

After you have saved the file, you can set these options by using the Save As command. And, as you'll notice, the Save As command is discussed in the next section, placed nearby for your convenience.

The Fabulous Save As Command

Hey, you know, it's not uncommon to change your mind about things. So you didn't think about where you should store the file. You forgot that your officemate is still using WordPerfect 5 and needs your files formatted for her version. No biggie.

Save As to the rescue.

When you want to Save your file As something else (pretty cool, huh?), open the File menu and choose the Save As command (or you can press F3, if you'd rather).

You see that same Save As box you saw in the initial save. This time, you'll want to set some of the options. Here is how:

> **Choosing a different format.** If you want to select a different file, click on the down-arrow at the end of the Format box. A list of possible formats is displayed (see fig. 8.4). You can scroll through the list by clicking on the arrows at either end of the scroll bar. Click on the one you want, and WordPerfect for Windows puts that selection in the Format box.

> **Setup the save.** When you click the Setup button, you can elect to choose a different default format in which all future files will be saved (unless you specify otherwise).

> **Quick, List!** Also in the Setup box, you can create a QuickList that displays directories and/or files you use often. For example, if you're always working in the BRADY subdirectory, you can add that to a QuickList and have WordPerfect display it for you automatically. You click the QuickList button or press F5 to display the QuickList box; then use the options on the right to make your changes and additions.

> **Choose File Options.** Back in the main Save As box, you can click on the Options button to display various commands for working with files: Copy, Move, Rename, Delete, Change Attributes, Print List, Create Directory, and Remove Directory are all at your disposal (see fig. 8.5).

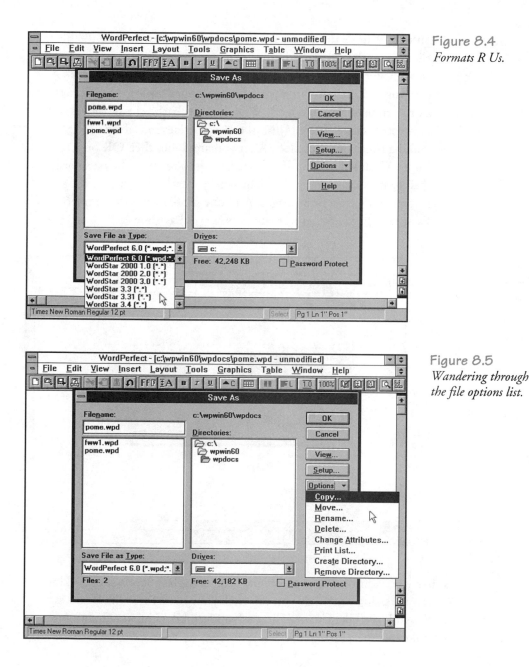

Figure 8.4
Formats R Us.

Figure 8.5
Wandering through the file options list.

Shhhh. What's the Password? You can add a password to the file by clicking on the Password button. The Password dialog box appears, in which you type the password of your choice (see fig. 8.6). Rules for passwords? Enter anything you want, in upper- or lowercase letters (it's all the same to WordPerfect). When you type, the cursor moves, but only asterisks are entered (just in case someone from the KGB is looking over your shoulder). After you are done, click OK or press Enter. What's this? WordPerfect asks you to re-enter the password (just to make sure you got it right—or to check that you are the same person you were a second ago). And one more thing: Remember That Password! If you forget it, that file is as good as gone.

Figure 8.6

The mysterious, invisible password.

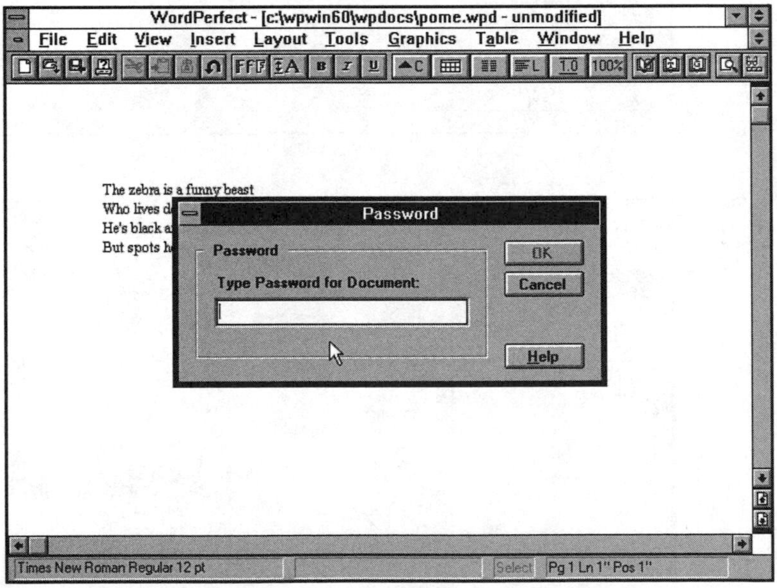

Just like the traditional Save command, you complete Save As by clicking OK or by pressing Enter. Or you can click your heels three times and say There's No Place Like Guam, There's No Place Like Guam, There's No Place Like Guam.

Goodnight, Files

Hmmmm. You saved it, but there it is, still displayed on your monitor. How do you get rid of the darned thing? Oh, sure, you could open the File menu, select New, and start a new file right on top of this one, but something just seems messy about that.

If you've saved your file and are through with it, put the file away by opening the File menu and choosing the Close command. If you've made any changes to the file since the last time you saved it, WordPerfect will ask you whether you want to save the file. Answer the question as honestly as you can, and the file will close.

Opening Files

Now you know how to save your brainchildren. After you save the files and they are tucked away safely in your WP60WIN directory (which is where all good little files go to sleep), how do you wake them up again?

WordPerfect for Windows gives you two different methods—both neatly displayed in the File menu—that will open files. This section explains them both.

Open Sesame

Well, the Open command in the File menu is a good candidate for opening files. You were going to guess that, right?

WordPerfect for Windows lets you open a file two different ways, depending on what you were doing most recently. (And did you remember to wash your hands?)

To use the Open command, just open the File menu and click Open. (Or press Ctrl+O.) The Open dialog box appears. Hmmmm. Déjà vu (see fig. 8.7).

Figure 8.7
*The Open File box
of tricks.*

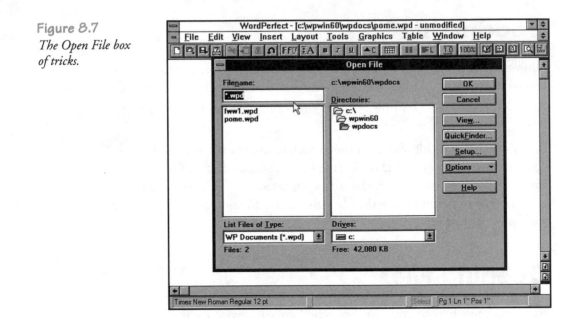

Now you can click around and find the right drive and directory that stores the file you want. When you've got it highlighted in the Filename: box, click OK.

Just a Little Click

If you've been working on the same file for a Really Long Time, you don't want to go through the Open File process every single time you open the darned thing.

WordPerfect for Windows understands.

Look in the bottom of your File menu. Ha! Isn't that nice? WordPerfect automatically keeps the last several of your favorite files close by for your convenience (see fig. 8.8). What a nice program.

Pandora's Rules for Successful Opening

The actual process for opening is simple, though. Display the File menu and choose Open. The Open File dialog box appears. Highlight the file you want and press Enter. If a password has been assigned to the file, the Password box appears, waiting for you to enter the password.

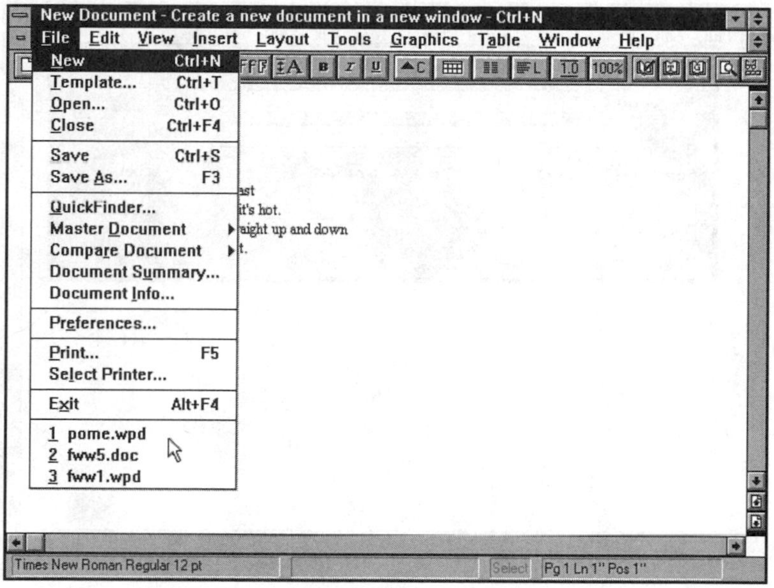

Figure 8.8
*Opening files the
quick-click way.*

Ooops!

Didn't forget it, did you? If so, you're sunk, plain and simple. Oh well. You learned a valuable lesson. Next time, name the file after something or someone you couldn't possibly forget, like Aunt Edna or your sister-in-law.

If you need to go looking for the file (it's not in the current directory), you can click the QuickFinder button. This brings up the QuickFinder dialog box which gives you a whole new gamut of options that you probably don't want to deal with (see fig. 8.9).

You can search for a specific set of words, choose search options, or specify the directory that you want to search in. For most early-on uses, however, you won't be tackling QuickFinder tasks.

Time to Quit, WordPerfect

For best results (and better gas mileage), save your files before you exit WordPerfect for Windows. Foreseeing that this isn't always remembered, the makers of WordPerfect put a little safety net in there for you.

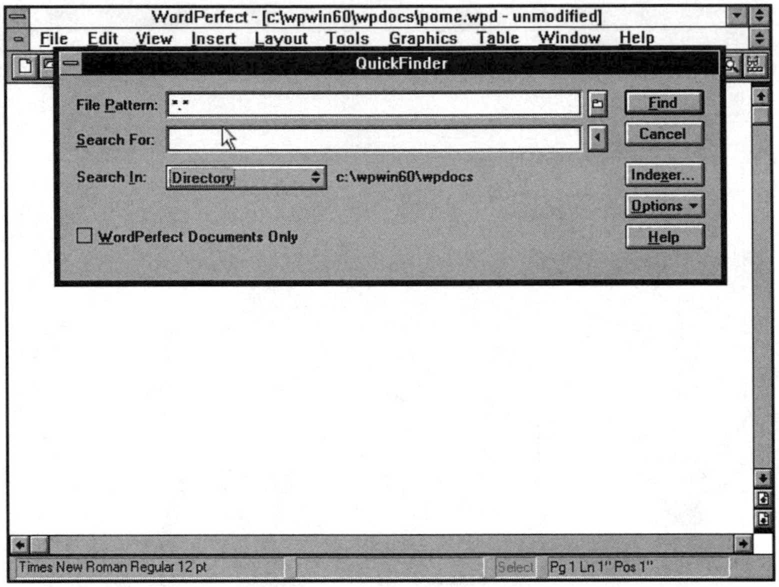

Figure 8.9
The QuickFinder box.

To exit WordPerfect for Windows, open the File menu and choose the Exit command (or press Alt+F4). The Exit WordPerfect dialog box appears, as shown in figure 8.10. If you've been working with only one open file, only one file is shown. If you hadn't saved the file, WordPerfect asks you if you want to save before exiting. If you do, click Yes.

WordPerfect then saves your file and dumps you back out to the Windows Program Manager.

Exiting Wrong

There's an Exit WordPerfect command because the programmers know better than we do what happens to a file as it's being closed. It may look like we're done with it, and we may have already saved it, but saying "Oh, I'm finished," and shutting off computer power when WordPerfect is still on the screen is a Definite No-No.

You never know what might happen. (Little green men might come in the middle of the night and uninstall the program until you're responsible enough to care for it correctly.)

WordPerfect - [c:\wpwin60\wpdocs\doc3.wpd - unmodified]

File   Edit   View   Insert   Layout   Tools   Graphics   Table   Window   Help

Elvis was a goldfish
Swimming happily around
My brother came and
Accident'lly
On the ground
Quick I scooped him u
But I was a way too la
He'd already squished
On the rock beside the

WordPerfect

? Save changes to Document2?

Yes   No   Cancel

Times New Roman Regular 12 pt   Select   Pg 1 Ln 2.60" Pos 2.96"

Figure 8.10
Mom, are we there yet?

This abominable behavior might be tolerated by the program once or twice, but sooner or later, you'll come in to work, try to load up WordPerfect for Windows, and get a Sorry Charlie error.

They're Out To Get Us

Stand in the hallway outside the office of a new user and you'll hear it, sooner or later:

"Where's my file?"

Although it seems, for the moment, that your computer has eaten the file, it is there, somewhere. Directories can be difficult things to deal with if you're unfamiliar with them.

When you save a file, WordPerfect puts it in a directory called WPDOCS automatically. You can change this directory to something else, if you want, but if you do, remember where you put the file.

When a file gets lost, there are only three possibilities:

■ You didn't really save the file.

■ You saved it in a directory different from your usual place.

■ You accidentally deleted it.

Use the Windows File Manager or the file options in the Open File dialog box to look around for the misplaced file. (If you need help using the File Manager, see Encounter 18.)

Demon-Strations

Mother-May-I Save the File?

1. Open the File menu.

2. Choose the Save command.

3. Type a filename for the file.

4. Select a format, if necessary.

5. Add a password, if you're working with sensitive stuff.

6. Click OK or press Enter.

Open Sesame

When you're ready to open a file, do the following:

1. Open the File menu.

2. Choose either Open or Retrieved.

3. Type the directory and name of the file you want.

4. You can use the File Manager to display the directories on the hard disk, if you're not sure where the file you want is stored.

5. Click OK or press Enter.

If the file you're selecting is one you've recently used, click the file name displayed in the bottom of the File menu.

So Long, WP!

1. Open the File menu.

2. Choose Exit.

3. If prompted, save any open files.

4. Click OK or press Enter.

Summary

You've learned quite a few important procedures in this encounter. Can't get by without saving. Can't get by without opening. Can't leave WordPerfect running forever. (Well, maybe...) This encounter rounds out Part I, completing the I've-Got-To-Do-This section. The next part introduces you to more specialized editing tasks—things you may or may not do as part of your daily WordPerfect for Windows routine.

Exorcises

1. What are the two different save commands? How are they different?

2. True or false: If you forget your password, you can exit to Windows, type PASSWORD, press Enter, and WordPerfect will display your password.

3. True or false: WordPerfect for Windows can use only WordPerfect files.

4. Explain the difference between using the Open command and selecting the file in the File menu.

5. True or false: You can exit WordPerfect by pressing F7.

The ABCs of Text Blocks

Goal

To help you learn how to grab the text you want to work with in what WordPerfect for Windows calls *text blocks*.

What You Will Need

You don't want to see it again: WordPerfect for Windows, a sample file, and some of those little plastic dinosaurs. (After you get your blocks assembled, you want to play with them, don't you?)

Terms of Enfearment

text blocks   marking
appending blocks   moving blocks

Briefing

In an earlier encounter, you learned the easiest of all editing techniques: the backspace key. There will be times, however, when you need to make changes on a larger scale. You need to move this paragraph over there; you need to add this sentence to that letter; you need to move this word to that sentence.

That's called block editing, which is what this encounter is all about.

New on the Block

What is a text block and why should you care? A text block can be as small as a single character, or as large as the entire document. When you mark text as a block, you're saying to WordPerfect "Here, this is what I want to move" (or copy, or delete, or print). You'll mark text as a block before you do any of the following things:

- Copy text
- Move text
- Delete text
- Print a portion of text
- Put a pizza in the oven
- Change the font of selected text
- Change the way a section of text is formatted

Marking Text as a Block

How do you mark a block of text? You have different options, depending on whether you're using the keyboard or the mouse:

■ Open the Edit menu and choose the Select command. A popup list of Select options—Sentence, Paragraph, All (or Tabular Column and Rectangle, if those items are included in your document)—appears beside the open Edit menu (see fig. 9.1). Click the one you want. The Select message appears in the lower right corner of the screen (just to the left of the cursor position indicators).

■ Use the mouse to point to the beginning of the block that you want. Press and hold the mouse button while dragging the mouse to the end of the text you want to highlight. Release the mouse button. The text is highlighted as a block (see fig. 9.2).

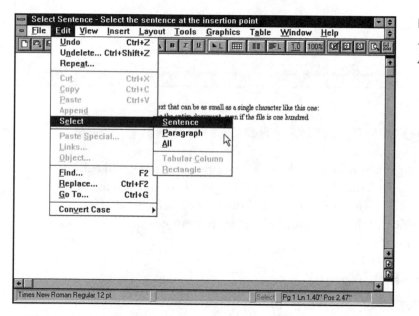

Figure 9.1
A small or large text portion today?

Figure 9.2
Blocking in progress.

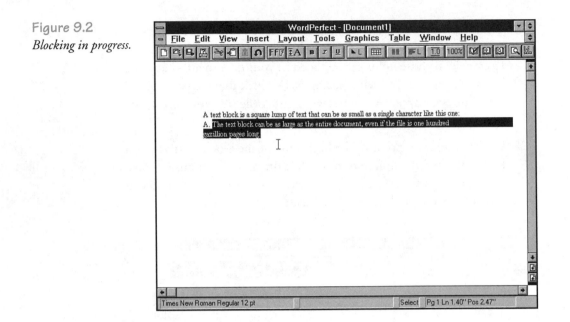

Copying and Mooo-ving Blocks

Copying and moving text blocks is a routine operation you'll perform on a fairly regular basis. If you're one of those people who writes in brain-dump fashion and then reorganizes your thoughts into some kind of logical progression (huh?), you'll like WordPerfect's easy-to-use copy and move procedures.

Say That Again?

When you want to make a copy of a section of text, start by marking the text you want to copy (remember how?). Next, open the Edit menu and choose Copy. (If you prefer, you can press Ctrl+C instead of opening the menu.)

After you make the copy, nothing appears to have happened. But secretly, behind the scenes, WordPerfect for Windows made a copy of the high-lighted text and put it on the clipboard (an invisible storage area for text you're copying or moving).

In order to place the copy in the document (whether it's this document or another document), you have to use the Paste command, also in the Edit menu. Before you select Paste, however, position the cursor at the point that you want the copied text to be inserted. After you select Paste, the text is put at the cursor position.

> If you're having a fine time copying a text block and pasting copies of it here and there, you can use the Repeat command, also in the Edit menu, to repeat your last action. A little popup box appears, asking how many times you would like to repeat the action. Coming up with a reason why you might use this feature could be a little difficult, but it's just nice to know that it's an option.

Let's Put It Over There

Moving text isn't really moving text. What you're doing is cutting text from one place and putting it in another. It goes like this:

1. Highlight the text that you want to move.

2. Open the Edit menu.

3. Choose Cut.

4. Move the cursor to the place you want to place the text.

5. Open the Edit menu.

6. Choose Paste.

Pretty simple, eh? If you decide that you really don't like what you just did, you can always resort to Undo to dig you out.

Saving, Deleting, and Printing Blocks

Okay, we're cheating, lumping stuff like this all together in a single section. You don't want to read basically the same instructions over and over again, do you? Not when you could be taking a Coke break. Not when the Bulls are playing. Not when you've got one-hundred-and-one more interesting things to do.

Stack 'Em Up

Accumulating blocks? You bet. You can save the blocks you really like, the ones you'd like to use as samples in your resume. How? Like this:

1. Select the block you want to save.

2. Open the File menu.

3. Choose the Save As command. The Save dialog box pops up (see fig. 9.3).

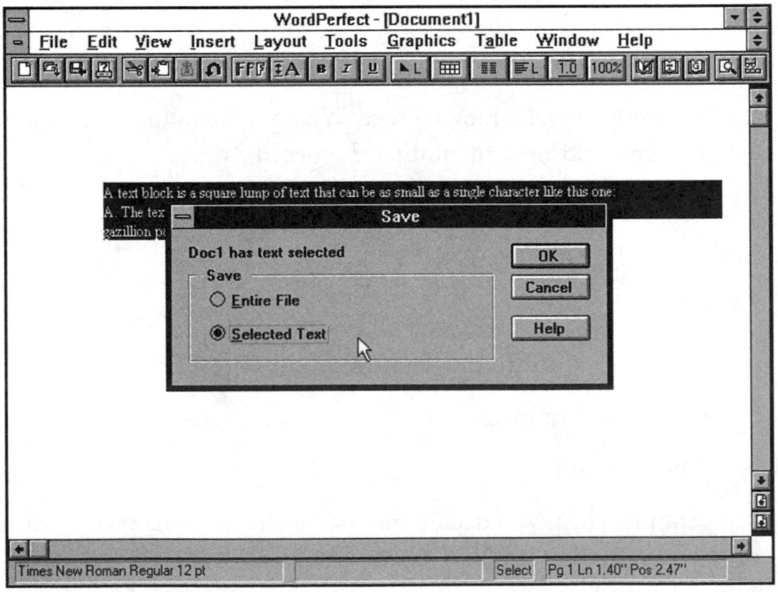

Figure 9.3

Saving innocent text blocks.

4. Make sure the Selected Text button is selected.

5. Click OK. The traditional Save As dialog box appears, with its traditional Filename: line.

6. Enter a name for the block (how about *NewKids?*).

7. Press Enter or click OK.

After the block is saved as a file, you can use the block in a file by opening the block file, copying the block, and pasting it in the other document. Who says the cool things in life have to be complicated?

Throw Away Blocks

It happens. That text block just doesn't make any sense. You wish you hadn't written it. You are suddenly overcome with this murderous urge to delete it before anyone else sees it and makes fun of you. (Boy, can I sympathize.)

1. Mark your text.

2. Open the Edit menu.

3. Choose Cut.

That's it. No, really. Sure it's part of a Cut and Paste operation, but in this case, you just don't ever Paste. The file floats around in file Purgatory forever and ever. Sound cruel? Not as cruel as your officemate getting ahold of that embarrassing memo.

Let's See It

There may be times when you want to print a text block. You might be worried that a certain paragraph is too catty for the company newsletter, so you print it out and have a cohort read it. Or perhaps you just want to prove to your boss that you really have been working today.

When you need to print a text block, follow these steps:

1. Highlight the block.

2. Open the File menu.

3. Select Print. The Print dialog box appears. In the Print Selection options (left side), notice that option 4, Selected Text, is marked (see fig. 9.4). Guess why? You're printing a text block!

4. Set any other necessary print options.

Figure 9.4
Printing blocks.

5. Click Print or press Enter.

The text block prints just the way you want it to. Such a good, good program.

They're Out To Get Us

There's really not too much that can go wrong with text blocks. They're simple, they're friendly, and they're sugar-free. WordPerfect for Windows really knows its stuff when it comes to working with blocks of text and shouldn't give you any trouble no matter what you're attempting.

There is the human error factor, however.

It's entirely possible to highlight the wrong block. You can copy the wrong block. You can put it in the wrong place. You can accidentally delete a block that you meant to keep. You can keep a block you meant to delete.

You get the idea.

If you delete a block you meant to keep, press Esc. The Undelete box appears, giving you the option of looking at your last several deletions and restoring the one you want (see fig. 9.5). Not too tough.

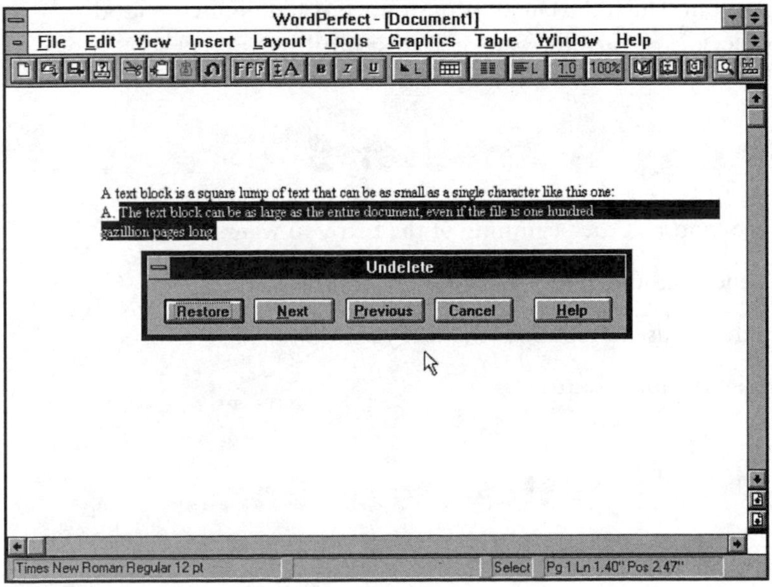

Figure 9.5
Undeleting a text block.

If you accidentally mark the wrong block, unmark it by pressing Esc.

If you copy a block to the wrong place, open the Edit menu and choose the Undo command. WordPerfect for Windows sucks that block right back up onto the invisible clipboard and waits for you to place it again.

Demon-Strations

Mark It with a B

1. Position the cursor in the paragraph you want to mark.
2. Open the Edit menu.
3. Choose the Select command.
4. Choose Paragraph.

The paragraph in which the cursor is positioned is highlighted. Good job—that block is marked forever (or at least until you press Esc).

Mark It with Another B

1. Put the mouse at the beginning of the text you want to mark.
2. Press and hold the mouse button.
3. Drag the mouse to highlight the text you want.
4. Release the mouse button.

And Put It in the Oven For...

1. Mark the block.
2. Open the Edit menu.

3. Choose Copy.

4. Move the cursor to the point in your document where you want the copy to be placed.

5. Open the Edit menu.

6. Choose Paste.

There it is. Aren't you excited?

Baby and Me

1. Mark the block.

2. Open the File menu.

3. Choose Save As.

4. Make sure Selected Text is chosen.

5. Click OK.

6. Type a name for the block in the Filename: line.

7. Press Enter or click OK.

Summary

This chapter has introduced you to one of the most important concepts in WordPerfect for Windows editing: the text block. Can you build a castle? A bridge? Will you leave your Legos behind forever? The concept of text blocks is an easy one: just mark what you want to work with before you begin to work. The next encounter takes you further into the realm of editing by introducing text searches.

Exorcises

1. A text block is _____

    a. The sentence of text preceding the cursor position.

    b. Whatever you mark as a block.

    c. Thirteen words in the middle of the document.

2. Explain two ways you can mark a block of text.

3. True or false: You cannot save a single paragraph out as a file.

4. Explain how to copy a block of text.

5. True or false: Moving is not really *moving*; it's cutting and pasting text.

Oh, *There* You Are! Finding and Replacing Text

Goal

To show you a quick-and-painless editing trick that can save you from reading through that document (again).

What You Will Need

An error-ripe document and the ability to admit your mistakes.

Terms of Enfearment

search	search and replace
case-sensitive	extended search
matches	repeat searches

Briefing

You've just finished a 20-page document, the result of your research on Tasmanian wallabies. After completing the paper and preparing to submit it to the sponsoring committee, you realize with horror that you've made a rank mistake: you accidentally used the order of the species (Marsupialia) when you should have used the class (Mammalia).

They are going to laugh at you, you know.

Glancing nervously at the clock, you begin the long task of searching line by line through the bone-dry document, looking for Marsupialia so you can replace it with Mammalia.

How much would it be worth to you to find an easier way? At least a bag of M&Ms, right?

Lost and Found

WordPerfect for Windows has something that—we admit it—just about every word processor worth its salt has: a search and replace feature. But this is one of the primo features of electronic text editing, one of those gotta-have-it features that make all the hassle worth it.

With search and replace (or just search), you can easily find words that you know are in there somewhere. If you're working on a single-page memo and you realize that you've misspelled your boss's name, it's one thing. But if you're working on a hundred-page manuscript, getting to and fixing those errors is going to be a Big Deal.

Organizing the Search Party

WordPerfect for Windows gives you the option of choosing just a search (like when you need to find the place you talked about the dietary consideration of wallabies) or choosing a search and replace (where you find one word or phrase and replace it with another).

When you're ready to start a search, position the cursor at the point at which you want to begin the search. (In most cases, it's best to put the cursor at the beginning of the document.)

Then open the Edit menu and choose Find (see fig. 10.1). If you prefer, you can start the search by pressing F2.

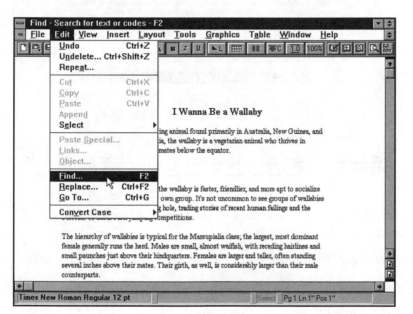

Figure 10.1
Starting out on the search.

After you select Find , the Find Text dialog box appears, as shown in figure 10.2.

In the Find: box, type the word (or phrase) you're looking for. By the way, what are you looking for?

We're All Searching for Something

Happiness. A good pizza. Shoes that fit.

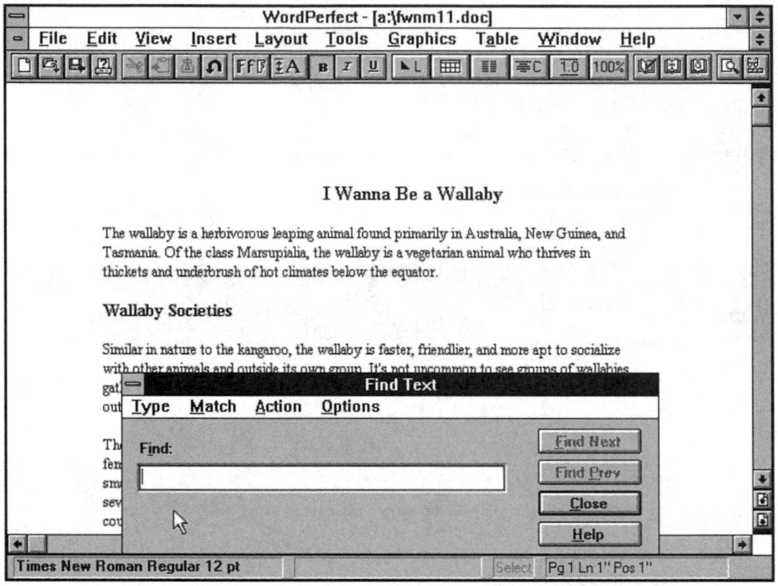

Figure 10.2
Anybody see a class of wallabies?

WordPerfect gives you a lot of latitude when it comes to the kinds of things you can search for. Here are the rules:

- You can search for a single word or a phrase (up to 80 characters total).

- The phrases can, of course, include spaces.

- You can search for numbers if you want.

- You can search for a raise (but WordPerfect for Windows won't guarantee that you get one).

- You can search for codes—which are not words or numbers, but unseen codes WordPerfect for Windows uses in your document.

You type the word, phrase, or number(s) in the Find: box. Then you can use one of the search tools to make sure that you find the something you're looking for.

Flares and Flashlights

Inside that Find Text dialog box, WordPerfect for Windows provides you with a number of search tools that you may or may not find helpful, depending on what you're searching for and where you've left the cursor. These tools are tucked away neatly inside the little menus along the top of the Find Text box. This is what they do:

Type Open the Type menu to choose either the Text or Specific Codes options. This tells WordPerfect for Windows, in one case, that you're looking for text. And, in the other case—come on, stop me before I say it—you're looking for codes.

Match With the Match menu, you tell WordPerfect for Windows how close you want the found text to match the text you type in the Find: box (see fig. 10.3). You can choose Whole Word, Case, Font, or Codes (again). Choosing Whole Word is handy if, for example, you're searching for the word

if

Why? (Oh, don't be so difficult. It's just an example.) If you don't click the Find Whole Words Only box, WordPerfect will look for anything that has those two letters in sequence. So the program will jerk to a stop every time it finds things like

thrifty

swift

rifle

ifternatius

You get the picture. It's a real hassle to find things you don't want to find. Use Find Whole Words Only anytime there's a possibility that WordPerfect will land on the wrong pad.

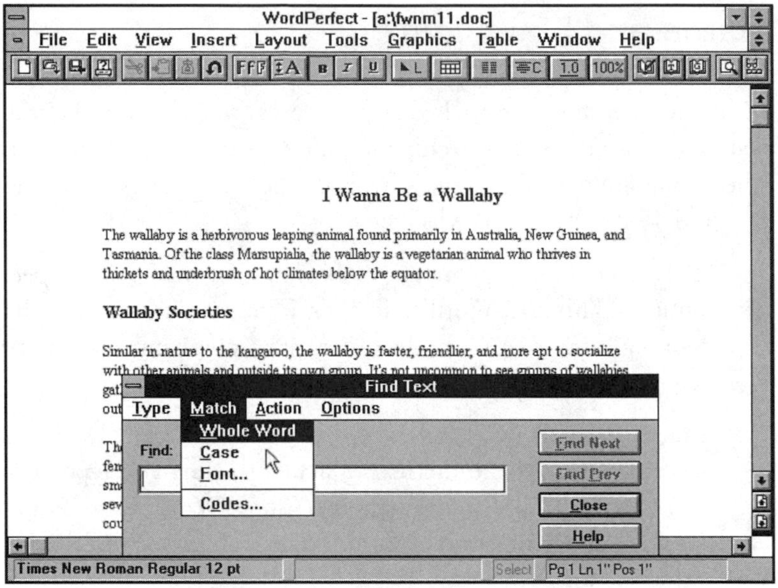

Figure 10.3
*Matchmaker,
matchmaker—poof,
I'm a match.*

If you choose Case, WordPerfect for Windows will search for words just the way you enter them. If you type KiDDo in the Find: box and choose Case from Match menu, WordPerfect will find only KiDDo— not Kiddo, kiddo, or kIddO.

If you choose Font, a little popup box displays options you can set in order to find that certain elusive font. And Codes lets you specify the codes you desperately need to locate.

Action The Action menu tells WordPerfect for Windows what you're trying to accomplish. Do you want to find a match? (The answer will be Yes about 90 percent of the time.) Do you want to position the cursor before or after the found item?

Options With the Options menu, you tell WordPerfect for Windows how you want to tackle this operation. Start at the beginning of the document? In the middle? Do you want WordPerfect for Windows to look in footers, headers, tables of content, indexes, and other stuff too?

Find **P**rev. If you click the Find Prev (short for Previous) button, WordPerfect for Windows will search backward from the cursor position. If the cursor is already at the beginning of the document (which means you just want to be difficult), WordPerfect says in its oh-so-eloquent style

Not found

Find Next If you click the Find Next button, WordPerfect for Windows tells you where your lost car keys are hiding.

Close Clicking this button says to WordPerfect for Windows "I know I pressed F2, but I forgot what I was looking for."

Help Clicking this button displays a little help box enlightening you as to the general Find process.

WordPerfect uses special codes to control formatting, font, and other specifications in your document. You can display the document with the codes intact by opening the View menu and choosing Reveal Codes. For more about this exciting topic, see Encounter 12.

There You Are!

When you've finished packing up your search tools, you can finish the process by clicking either Find Next or Find Prev. What happens?

Well, don't blink.

The cursor jumps to the space following the word or phrase you were searching for. Lightning fast. Concorde fast.

My eyes are still rolling.

What I *Meant* To Say

Sometimes you use the wrong word. In your memo, you said

> *We wanted to insure that this doesn't happen again.*

No, no, no! Your editor crumpled it up, threw it on the floor, and jumped up and down on it. How many times does she have to tell you? It's *e*, not *i* !

Okay, okay, I'll change it! You say, backing out of her office. You hurry to your desk before security arrives. Quick—you need to replace all of those insures with ensures.

Simple to do, right? Let's start with the dialog box. Press Ctrl+F2 (or open the Edit menu and select Replace). Figure 10.4 shows the dialog box that looms to greet you.

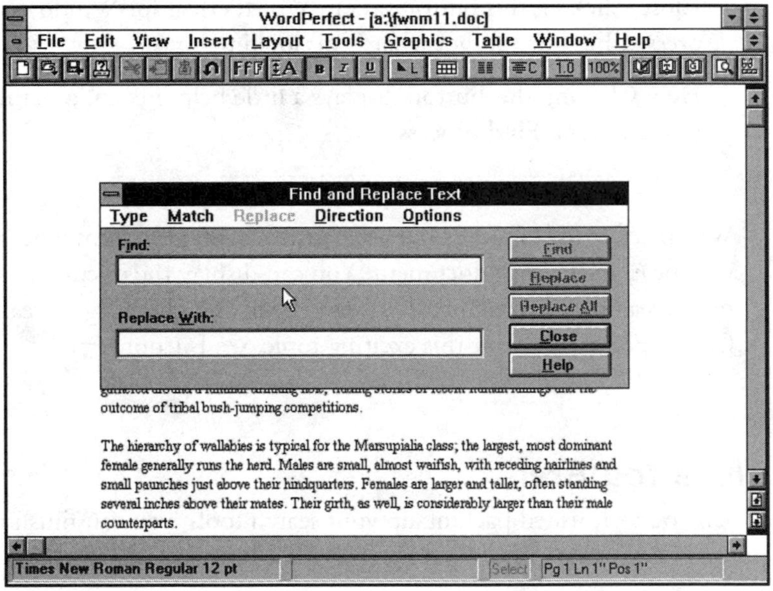

Figure 10.4
Your mission, should you decide to accept it...

Find and replace is a nice concept, don't you think? You take something away, but you make sure to plug up the hole with something else. Maybe our armed forces could use find-and-replace instead of search-and-destroy missions. Instead of search and destroying enemy weaponry, we could search for it, take it away, and leave something— like teddy bears—in its place.

Know What You're Looking for

To start the find and replace, you enter the word, phrase, or number you're searching for in the Find: box (look familiar?). Then press Tab. The text-entry box moves to the Replace With: line (see fig. 10.5).

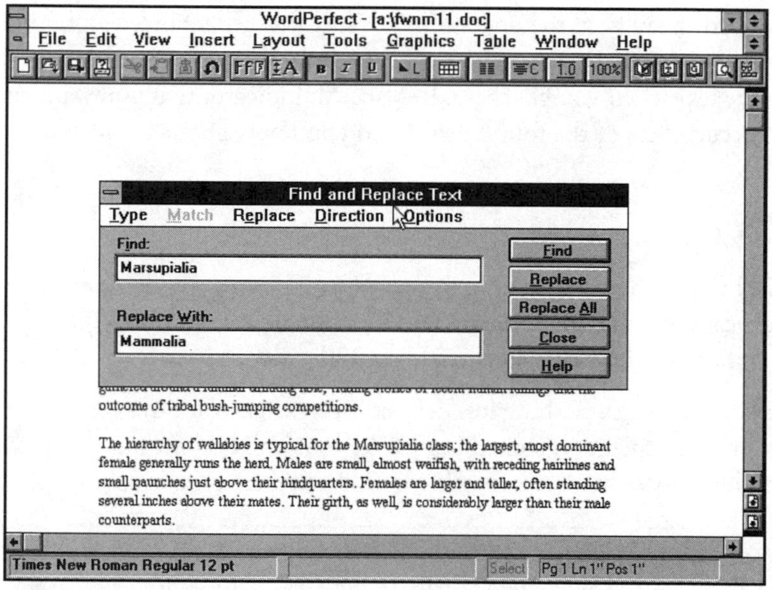

Figure 10.5
Entering what you'll put back.

Proper Etiquette

The Find and Replace Text dialog box gives you a number of menus, some similar to those in the Find Text dialog box.

> **Type** holds the same options—Text and Specific Codes—that you found in the Find box.

> **Match** is dimmed, so you can't do anything with it (except stare at it longingly).

> **Replace** lets you choose whether you want to change the case of the found text, the font, or the codes.

Direction tells WordPerfect for Windows whether you're headed north or south through your document.

Options includes the same Find options plus one: you can limit the number of changes made.

You also see a couple of new buttons. The Find button tells WordPerfect for Windows to go ahead with the operation, but just find what you're looking for (don't replace it right away). The Replace button instructs WordPerfect to replace the text when you get there. Replace All indicates that you want to replace all occurrences of the found text. (And you know about Close and Help.)

Match-Making

SNPN (Single, Non-Smoking, Proper Noun) desires companionship, modification, and enhancement from SA (Single Adjective). Enjoys cursor flashing, quick formats, and late-night file retrievals.

If you're searching for something less defined (like when you can't remember —exactly—how to spell that something you're looking for) you can use certain anything-goes characters to help you locate your Something.

You use the wildcard characters as part of the text in the Search For: box.

The anything-goes (also called *wildcard*) end (/) characters are ? and *.

The question mark can stand in for any character. Only one, though. For example, if you enter the word

ma?e

You could find

make

male

made

mane

maze

And so on. The ? is replaced with any letter.

The asterisk (*), on the other hand, means "any characters". So if you enter

m*e

You would find all the words above, plus

measure

matricide

matinee

And any other word that begins with M and ends with E.

Doing It All Over Again

You searched it once. You don't want to do it again. Isn't there a quick way to repeat the search you just entered?

F2, Enter.

What? What? (Is there an echo in here?)

After you've searched for something you particularly like, you can search for it again by pressing F2, and then pressing Enter when the dialog box appears. Simple and quick.

They're Out To Get Us

You thought you were being a model student. You wanted to make your editor happy. After hearing her rant and rave about the misuse and abuse of the word *if*, you decided to do a search and replace and plug in *whether* instead. You pressed Alt-F2, entered *if* as the Search For: text, entered *whether* as the Replace With: text, and pressed F2.

Here them playing *Taps* in the distance? That's for you.

Because every word that had the letters i and f in it now has the letters w-h-e-t-h-e-r in i-f's place. That means that what used to be

    gift

is now

    gwhethert

Hmmmm. Maybe you've created a new language. But you may not be able to communicate that to your boss.

So how do you fit it? Are you ready?

Press Ctrl+Z.

That's it. No fanfare, no hoopla. Just Undo it.

Demon-Strations

Searching in All the Right Places

1. Move the cursor to the beginning of the document.
2. Press F2.
3. Enter the text you want to search for.
4. Click whatever search options you want.
5. Click Find Next or Find Prev.

I'll Gladly Pay You Tuesday for a Hamburger Today

1. Position the cursor at the beginning of the document.
2. Open the Edit menu.
3. Select Replace (or press Ctrl+F2).
4. Type Find: text.
5. Type Replace With: text.
6. Select any necessary search options.
7. Click Find.
8. When you get to the found word (or phrase), click Replace if you want to replace it.

Summary

This encounter showed you how to use one of the streamlined, rockets-on-your-fingers editing features available in WordPerfect 6.0 for Windows: find and replace. You can now look for specific words, numbers, or phrases and, if you choose, replace those with other words, numbers, or phrases. WordPerfect for Windows also gives you the option of searching and replacing those mysterious hidden codes which you haven't yet learned about. (We'll get to it—don't worry.)

Exorcises

1. What is the difference between find and find and replace?

2. Which of the following options are part of the find process?

   a. Search Forward

   b. Find Next

   c. Find Partial Words

   d. Extended Search

3. True or False: There are two different options for code searches and no one really knows why.

4. With find and replace, you can _____

   a. Search for a word and replace it with another one.

   b. Replace all words without prompting.

   c. Search for your office partner and replace her with Cindy Crawford or Mel Gibson (whomever you'd prefer).

   d. Use wildcard characters.

5. 15-point bonus essay question: In 50 words or less, describe how WordPerfect for Windows' find and replace feature can enhance your life (include photos, if appropriate).

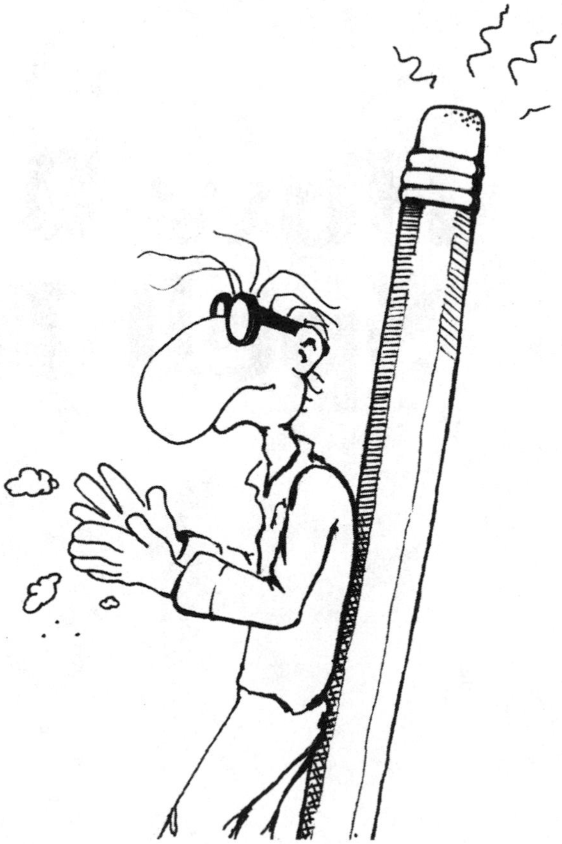

How D'You Spell That?

Goal

To help you find and use WordPerfect for Windows' built-in writing tools—the speller, the thesaurus, and the grammar-checker.

What You Will Need

A pack of gold stars, a red marker, and a Milky Way candy bar.

Terms of Enfearment

speller	thesaurus
grammar-checker	correction

Briefing

WordPerfect for Windows knows that you don't like to be sitting out here alone in the land of Dangling Participles and Erroneous Spelling. And you know that a misspelling can blow your credibility—and your document—right out of the water. You've seen that look: They are reading through your report when, suddenly, they all look up at you quizically. Carl, who was the Third Grade Spelling Champion at Saint Ignatius No. 98, says "It's s-u-p-e-r-f-l-u-o-u-s, not superfloous."

WordPerfect for Windows could have told you that.

And when you use the word *ordinarily* fourteen times in the same document, that doesn't say much for your vocabulary. You couldn't have thought up even one other word that means *ordinarily*? WordPerfect for Windows can.

The biggest error is the one that most people don't even catch. But accidentally put your report in front of someone who has a degree in English—or who has worked as an editor—and you're in trouble. There may be two or three words left in your document when she's through. If you're lucky. Grammar is a scary thing. That's why most of us ignore it.

WordPerfect for Windows will check your Ps and Qs for you.

Let's start with the obvious: Spelling.

Winner of the Speling Bea

When you're ready to run the spelling checker, open the Tools menu. Right there, at your fingertips (or at least, at the end of the mouse pointer) is the Speller command. Click it and watch the magic (see fig. 11.1).

What the heck are you supposed to do with this? Easy now. Deep breath.

> You can zip right into the Speller with a little click action by positioning the mouse pointer on the Speller button (fifth button from the right in the Button Bar) and clicking once.

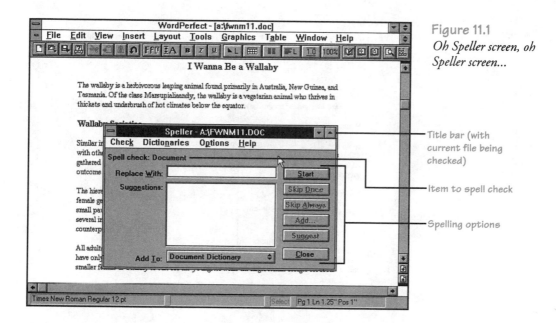

Figure 11.1
Oh Speller screen, oh Speller screen...

At the top of the Speller box, you see the title (Speller) and the name of a file (in this case, a:\fwnm11.doc). That second bit tells you the name of the file you have open (which, incidentally, is the one you are about to spell check).

The next section explains the variety of spelling options at your disposal.

Spelling M-e-n-u-s

WordPerfect for Windows is not short on features, whether you're talking about spelling or salsa. Like the Find Text dialog box in the last chapter (remember that?), the oh-so-important Speller dialog box offers you a number of features, most of which are tucked away in the menus. Here are the menu overviews:

> **Check**. The Check menu holds the commands for choosing what part of the document you want to spell check (see fig. 11.2). You can select Word, Sentence, Paragraph, Page, Document, To End of Document, Selected Text, Text Entry Box, or Number of Pages. (If you choose Number of Pages, you'll have to select the page range, too.)

Figure 11.2
Just checking.

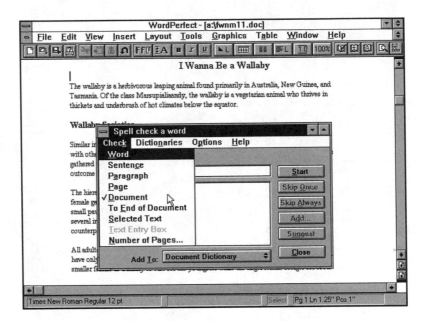

Dictionaries. The Dictionaries menu is concerned with only one thing: the dictionary you are using. WordPerfect for Windows comes with its own incredibly well-endowed dictionary, but you can also use one you create yourself (called a supplemental dictionary) that may include words that are unique to your documents (like *farlsnag* and *bitzners*).

Options. The Options menu enables you to choose the special spelling options you are interested in using. As you can see from figure 11.3, you can choose more than one option at a time. The options that are checked in the figure will find words that include numbers, duplicated words (like the the), automatically replace mistakes, and use the document dictionary.

Help. This is your standard Help menu with its ordinary—although they are better than ordinary—Help commands. If you've yelled help when you are working on documents, you won't have trouble finding your way around here.

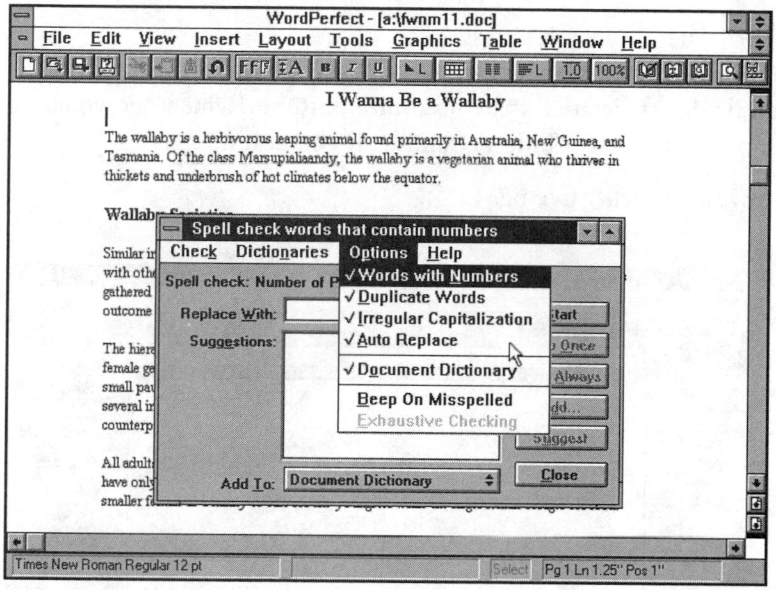

Figure 11.3
Aren't options the best thing to have?

Spelling B-u-t-t-o-n-s

And then there are the buttons, too. We've got all these to talk about:

Start. Ha! Guess this one starts the spelling routine, eh?

Skip Once. You click this button to tell WordPerfect for Windows "Oh, I know it's not spelled right, but let's pretend we didn't see it."

Skip Always. Clicking this button tells WordPerfect for Windows "You may not think it's spelled right, but it looks okay to me. Quit stopping at it every time."

Add. When you click the Add button, you tell WordPerfect you like the word so much you want to add it to the dictionary. You can click the Add To arrow (in the bottom center of the dialog box) to choose the dictionary you want to store the word in.

Suggest. Clicking the Suggest button displays a list of possible alternative words in the Suggestions box in the center of the Speller screen. They may not be what you wanted, either, but at least you had a few options.

Close. Clicking Close tells WordPerfect "I've had enough of this spellin stuff. I'm going to lunch."

BIG Spelling

Words too small for you? Having trouble squinting at that little Speller box? Oh, we can fix that. Click that there maximize button. (Remember which one it is? Go back to your Windows training, if you don't.)

Wow. Now *that's* a speller (see fig. 11.4).

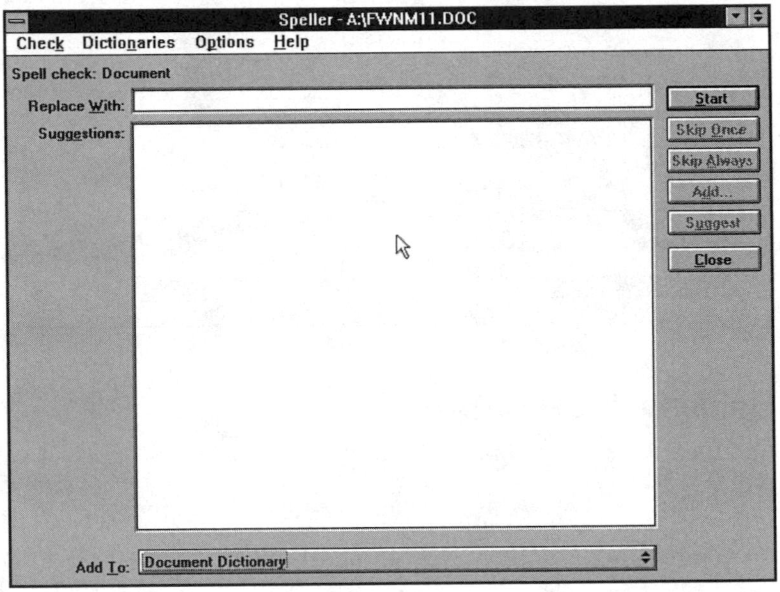

Figure 11.4
The mongo speller.

Go, Speller, Go

Assuming that everything is set up to your satisfaction, you're ready to roll (or is that drool?). To start the Speller, make your selection from the Choice menu. (Remember that? You saw it in figure 11.2.) You can spell check any of the following:

- Word
- Paragraph
- Page
- Document

- To End of Document

- Selected Text

- Text Entry Box (but this is dimmed)

- Number of Pages

After you click the one you want, WordPerfect for Windows enters your selection in the Spell check: line. This next part is really mind-boggling.

Click Start.

WordPerfect calls its Speller into action, and, when an error is found, the Speller displays a message box with a number of possible alternative words and several options (see fig. 11.5).

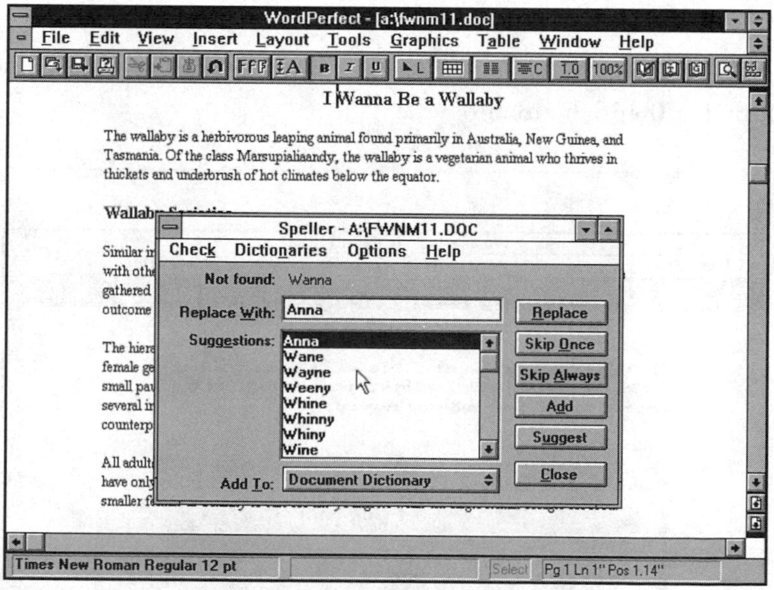

Figure 11.5
Speller in action.

The options are pretty self-explanatory: you can skip the found word this time, skip it for the whole document, add it to the dictionary, edit it, look up a similar word you specify, replace the word with one from the list, or choose a different dictionary.

If you want to choose a word from the list, click the word you want to use. The options you'll use most often are Skip, Add, and Replace.

When the Speller is finished, it tells you. Click Yes or press Enter.

What's Another Word for...

Do you ever get stuck in a word rut? That happens occasionally to the best of us—you subconsciously pick a word of the week and use it in everything from memos to letters to your son's teacher.

The Thesaurus can help you break the habit. Just click on the word you want to find an alternative to. Then open the Tools menu and select Thesaurus. The screen in figure 11.6 meets your eager eyes.

You can also start the Thesaurus by clicking the Thesaurus button in the Button Bar (fourth button from the right).

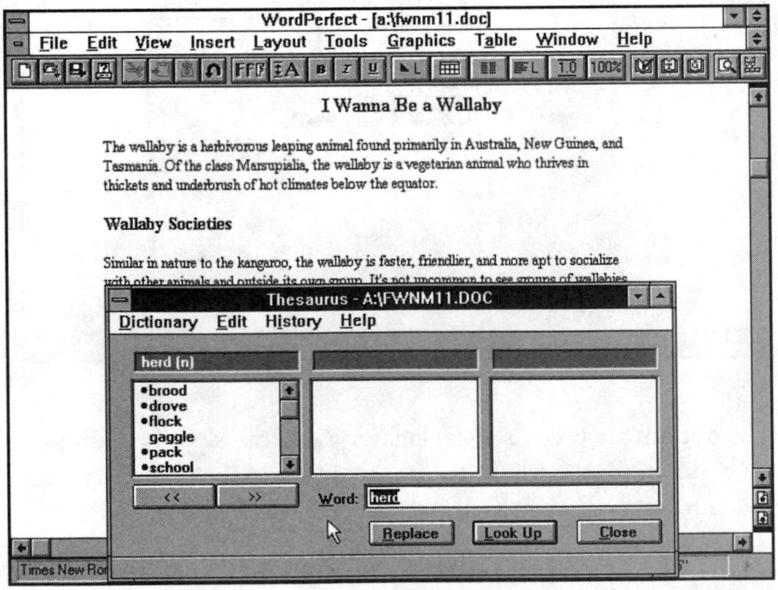

Figure 11.6
What's another word for...

You can find synonyms (different word, same meaning) and antonyms (different word, opposite meaning) with the Thesaurus. Additionally, the Thesaurus provides you with several differerent meanings (if there *are* different meanings).

WordPerfect for Windows gives you menus with all of the options you could ever want to use with the Thesaurus. Of interest (okay, maybe not) might be:

> **Dictionary**. Allows you to change the dictionary you're working with. No biggie.

> **Edit**. Lets you Cut, Copy, Paste, Select All, or Undo information in the Thesaurus.

> **History**. Displays a history of items you've looked up in the Thesaurus.

> **Help**. Your traditional help menu.

And then the Thesaurus includes these nifty buttons at no extra cost:

> **Replace**. Puts the word you chose in place of the word in the document.

> **Look Up.** Allows you to look up the meaning of an additional word. For example, suppose you placed the cursor on herd before starting the Thesaurus. WordPerfect for Windows displayed something like this:
> herd(n)
> brood
> drove
> flock
> gaggle
> pack
> school

Suppose you want to find out more about the word flock. (Don't ask.). You can click flock, then click Look Up. Another list appears, this one with flock at the top:
flock(n)
flight
gaggle
swarm

You can see how this could go on forever. If you've got the time, it can also improve (or at least expand) your vocabulary.

Close. Exits the Thesaurus without looking back.

To choose a different word, simply highlight the one you want and press R (for Replace) or click the Replace button.

I Ain't Got No Harvard Larnin'

Looking for Grammatik that "polished" sound? The grammar checker built in to WordPerfect for Windows, called Grammatik, can do a thorough check of your document and make some far-reaching suggestions.

Start Grammatik by choosing Grammatik from the Tools menu. There it is, the Grammatik screen (see fig. 11.7).

You can also start Grammatik with a click by clicking the Grammatik button in the Button Bar (third button from the right).

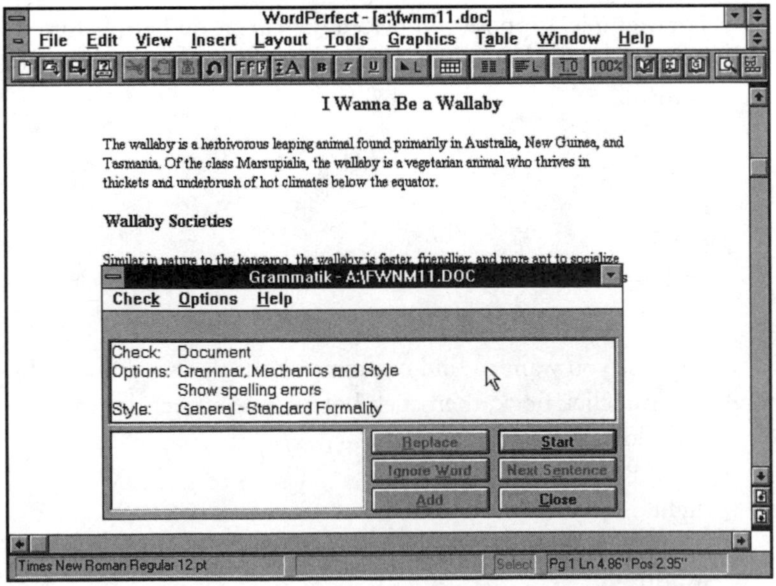

Figure 11.7
Make it sound pretty, will ya?

Grammatik really deserves a book of its own, and, if you're already dealing with WordPerfect for Windows option overload, you won't be happy to see the wealth of choices you have to make in Grammatik. You can see histories of things, fine tune writing styles, compare documents, save statistics to a file and on and on...

Facing Grammatik Menus

You'll be concerned with the things in the Options menu (see fig. 11.8). These options enable you to choose what type of checking you want done:

- Writing Style, in which your style is evaluated

- Checking Options, which lets you decide what type of errors you want Grammatik to find

- Show spelling errors, an interactive spelling check

- Grammar, Mechanics, and Style which tells Grammatik to look for errors in all three areas

- Grammar and Mechanics, in which you check only the grammar and mechanical aspects of the file

- Statistics, which prepares a statistical report of the evaluation

For our purposes, let's select Grammar and Mechanics. Grammatik goes away for a moment, and then comes back with a double screen. The top screen shows your document with the suspected error highlighted. The bottom screen shows what was found and what Grammatik thinks the problem is.

Punching Grammatik Buttons

Most of the buttons in Grammatik you'll use when you're actually using the program. But here they are (just so you'll be prepared):

Replace. Replaces the found word with one you specify.

Ignore Word. Jumps over the found word.

Add. Adds the word to the specified dictionary.

Start. The magical Go button. You use this to start Grammatik.

Next Sentence. Jumps to the next sentence.

Close. Stops Grammatik before it checks again.

Figure 11.8
*Checking everything
but the kitchen sink.*

My, Aren't We Critical?

Well, people who live in publishing houses shouldn't mince words. Grammatik wastes no time after you click that Start button. Go ahead. It won't bite.

Hmmm. Grammatik starts spitting venom at you (don't take it personally). Figure 11.9 shows an example of what Grammatik did to one of my Wallaby sentences. (I think it's a fine sentence, don't you?)

Grammatik tells you what Rule Class your error violates (this one is Long Sentence—well, excuse me) and explains why a revision would probably strengthen things. When you're ready to go on, click Resume.

The next little problem Grammatik found in my work was the phrase *some of the*, shown in figure 11.10. Too wordy, Grammatik said. Replace it with *some*.

Needless to say, I'm not going to show you any more. It's just too humiliating. I don't know what is worse—to be correct by a program, or to have the program be *right*.

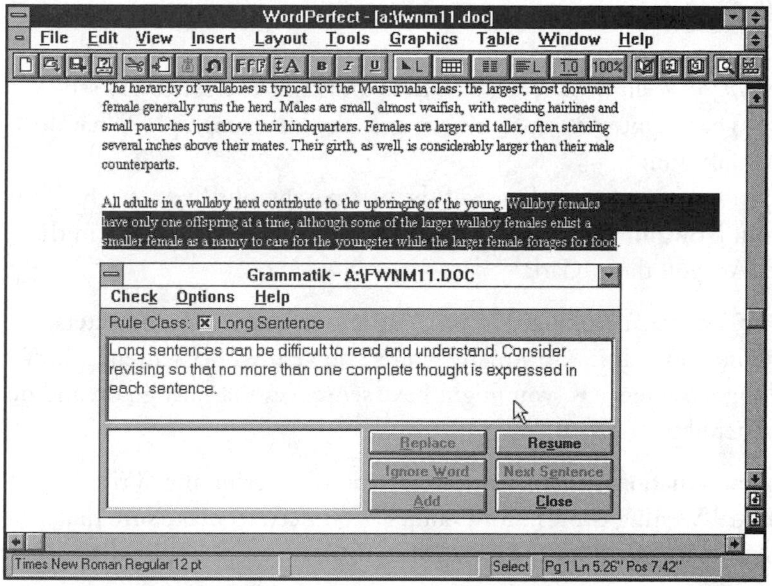

Figure 11.9
Grammatik is just jealous.

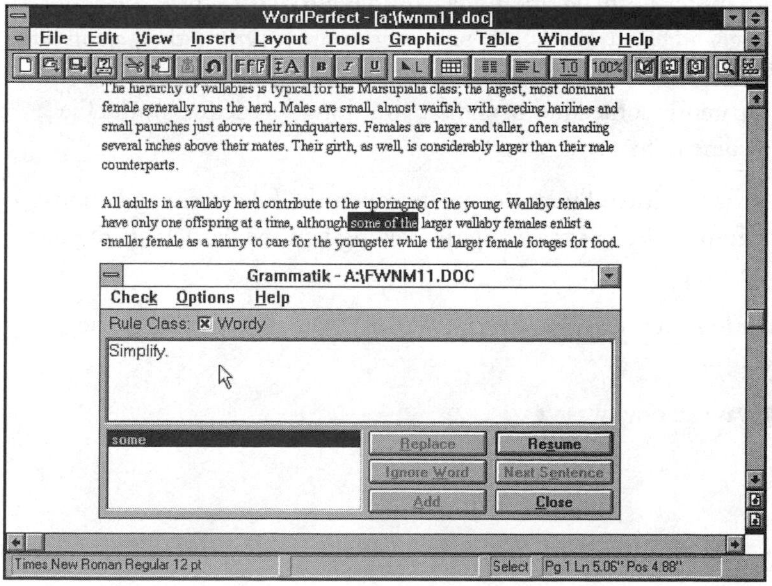

Figure 11.10
Okay, Grammatik. You win.

File Stats

Announcer: Well, we clocked that last paragraph at close to 1.4 seconds. That's quite an improvement over the last paragraph. What do you think, Jim?

Jim: Amazing, amazing. Some of the best paragraphs I've seen this season. Now, for an in-depth report, we're going down to Carl in the field. Are you there, Carl?

How's your document looking? Do you care about how many characters, words, and lines long it is, how many words you've used per sentence, how long the longest sentence is (you might have sentences that just go on and on and on, rather like this one)?

Well, in some situations, you might care. If you're entering the Writer's Digest Annual Writing contest, for example, you need to make sure that your piece isn't one word longer than 2000. If so, beeeeep! You're disqualified.

And even in more "normal" situations like trying to write a brief PR letter, trying to target an effective resume, or trying to prove wrong the person who told you "You couldn't say "This sky is falling" in less than a hundred words!" (apparently some kind of shot at your long-windedness), the file stats could come in handy.

To display the statistics of your document, open the File menu and choose Document Info. Another screen appears, telling you the particulars of your document (see fig. 11.11).

After you've looked everything over, click OK. You are returned to the document.

Well, *that* was exciting, wasn't it?

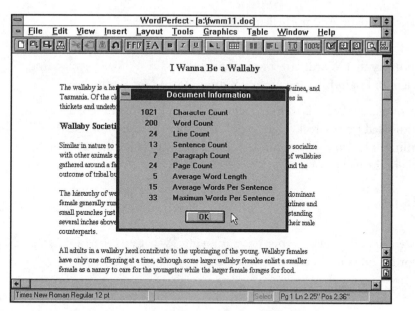

Figure 11.11
Crucial file information you may never care to see.

They're Out To Get Us

Sorry, I'm a Moron

What's the worst thing you can do when you're running the spelling checker? (Besides running over the cat's tail with your desk chair.)

Here's a candidate: Add mispelled words to the dictionary.

Oh, you're chugging right along. There are lots of words that are unique to your industry that WordPerfect keeps hanging up on. You've been adding words left and right by using option 3 in the Word Not Found box.

The front of your brain is thinking about what to have for lunch. That antipasto salad from Greek Tony's sounds really good, but you like those little mini pizzas from Pizza Hut, too. But Pizza Hut is farther and you just went there the day before...

Huh?

What?

A little voice in the back of your brain is saying "What was that? Did you see that word? Did you just add that word to the dictionary?"

Maybe you did, and maybe you didn't. You're not sure.

But you sure are hungry.

How can you look at the dictionary to see whether you've added words that shouldn't have been added? Well, first, pay closer attention to the rest of the spelling check.

Then, when the spell check is over, open the Tools menu and Speller. When the Speller box appears, open the Dictionaries menu and choose Supplementary. A popup box appears giving you a bunch of options for working with Dictionaries (see fig. 11.12).

Click the Edit button. Yet another screen appears (aren't you glad we got into this?) so that you can enter the words you're looking for. If you're not sure exactly what you messed up, you can use the other options to weed out those errors.

Then go get some lunch before you make any more goofs. Your blood sugar level must be dropping.

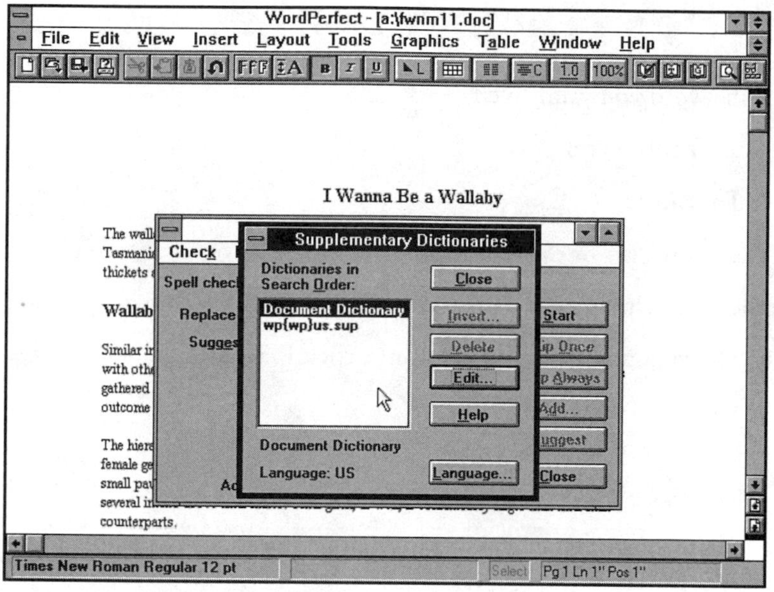

Figure 11.12
Working with dictionaries gone bad.

Demon-Strations

M-i-s-s-i-s-s-i-p-p-i

1. Move the cursor to the beginning of the document.

2. Open the Tools menu.

3. Select Speller.

4. Open the Check menu and choose Document. (Or any other option you want).

5. When a word appears in the Not found: line, choose the option you want or click a replacement word.

Azure Flash (Blue Moon)

1. Click the word you want to change.

2. Open the Tools menu.

3. Select Thesaurus.

4. Use the arrow keys or the mouse to select the word you want to use.

5. Use the Look Up button, if necessary, to find more meanings.

6. When you've found the word you want, click Replace.

Summary

Feeling a little braver now? Even if you're not a writer, editor, or grammarian, WordPerfect for Windows comes chock full of tools you can use to make yourself sound as good as possible. The Speller looks for typos (and a few other things), the Thesaurus provides you with alternative word choices, and Grammatik teaches you about your own writing and helps you fix common English mistakes.

Now go get yourself that Milky Way. You deserve it.

Exorcises

1. True or false: You must always spell check the entire document.

2. Mix and Match:

    _____ Spelling Checker   a. Finds alternative words

    _____ Thesaurus   b. Checks for typos and double words

    _____ Grammatik   c. Analyses writing strength

3. To display the Tools menu, you _____.

4. True or false: The Thesaurus shows both noun and verb forms of selected words.

5. What does Grammatik do?

   a. Make you feel bad about your writing.

   b. Evaluate your writing level and make suggestions for strengthening.

   c. Create a report of errors.

   d. Stop at each error and shout "Hey, you!"

   e. Threaten to call your high-school English teacher.

   f. Provide advice for best use of sentence length and word choice.

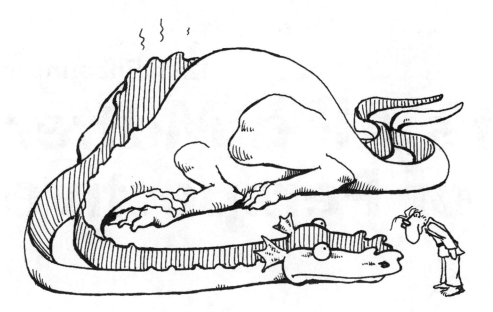

It's All a Matter of Perspective

Goal

To creatively visualize your success with WordPerfect for Windows (and learn about WordPerfect's different views).

What You Will Need

WordPerfect for Windows running (with some text displayed on the screen), some strawberry incense, and a lava lamp.

Terms of Enfearment

draft mode	graphics mode
page mode	code mode
two page mode	show mode

Briefing

Good evening, and thank you for coming. Come in and find a pillow—any one will do, just choose one that looks comfortable. Now if you'll all assume the lotus position, we'll begin our Oooommmms.

There's more than one perspective to most things in life. There's his side and her side. There's before and after. There's this and that.

WordPerfect for Windows is no exception.

You can look at text. You can look at graphics. You can look at text *and* graphics. You can see two pages. You can display hidden text. Paragraph marks. You can look at the codes only a programmer could love. By the end of this encounter, you'll be able to see your document in several new lights.

I'm in the Mode for Text

You've been looking at your document one way thus far in the book—the text way. Draft mode, it's called. Figure 12.1 shows you the way it appears on-screen, just sitting there on the screen with no respect for margins or anything.

You may be using draft or page mode as you work with WordPerfect for Windows to create those cool documents. Everything you'll use to change the way WordPerfect for Windows looks is kept right in one convenient place: the View menu (see fig. 12.2).

You don't need to know the ins and outs of every item you can add to the display, but we will show them to you. Figure 12.3 shows the page mode screen with all the hoopla turned on. Play around with the different items and decide for yourself which ones help, and which ones clutter up the screen. Sometimes, less distraction means better documents.

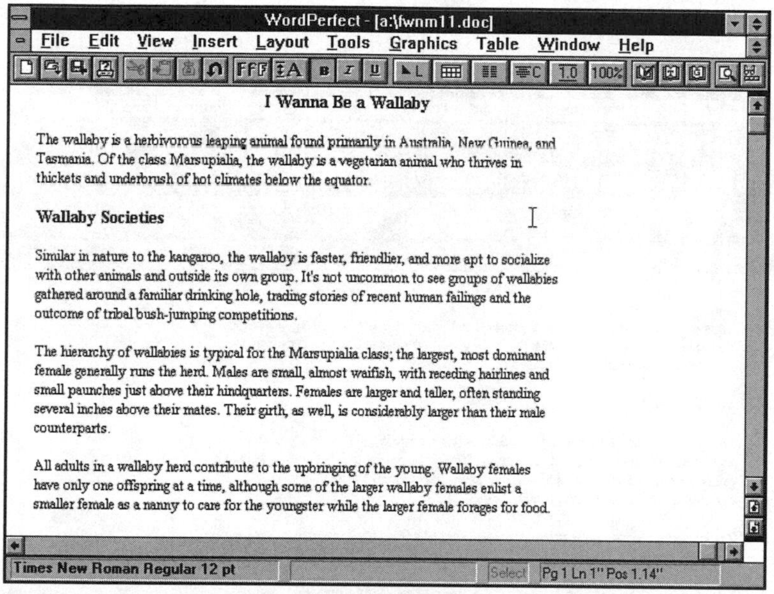

Figure 12.1
Ye ole draft mode.

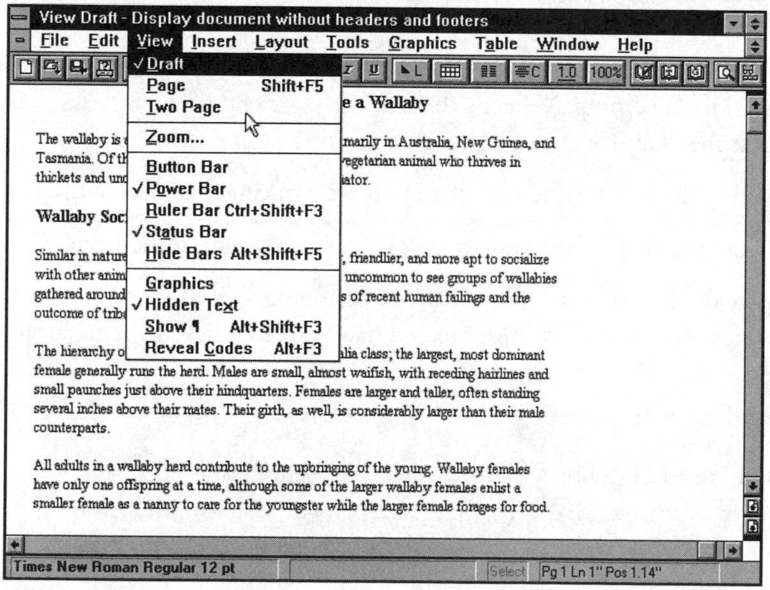

Figure 12.2
Exposing view options.

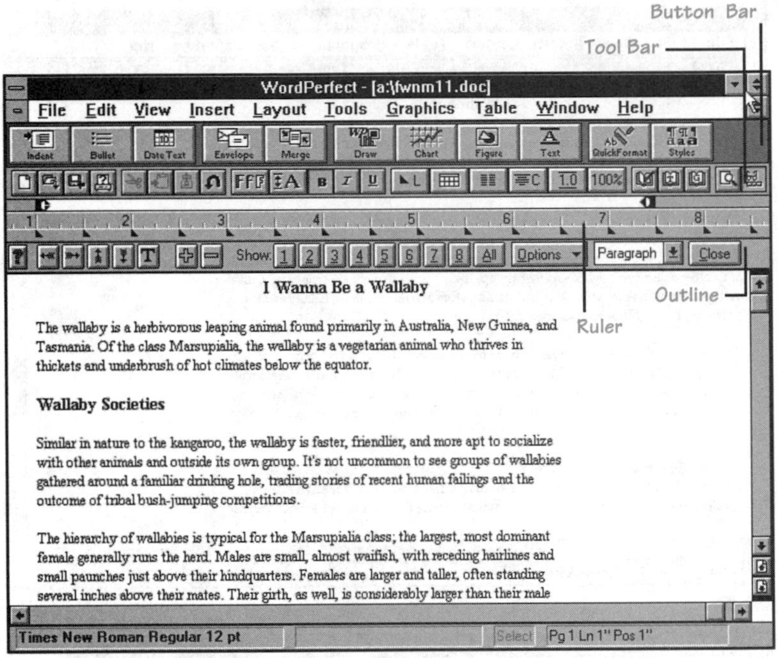

Figure 12.3
*"Enhancing" page
mode?*

Button Bar
Tool Bar
Outline
Ruler

Good grief! That's helping? Where's the text? As a general rule, you may want to limit the "helpers" you display on the screen. For example,

- Only display the Outline Bar when you are working with the outline

- Only use the ruler when you are measuring or aligning something

- Display the Button Bar only when you're adding special items to your document—charts, drawings, merged data, bulleted lists, or paragraph styles.

> You can hide all of the bars temporarily by selecting Hide Bars. A popup box warns you that everything except your text will disappear and you can return to the normal display by pressing Esc. Click OK to continue or Cancel to ... uh ... cancel.

Getting Graphics about It

Graphics mode, as you might expect, enables you to take a graphic look (that doesn't mean profanity-graphic) at your document. If you've placed art there (which we haven't covered yet and is only a nightmare on the horizon of your WordPerfect experience), you'll be able to see it in graphics mode.

To change into graphics mode, open the View menu and choose (surprise, surprise) Graphics. There it is, in figure 12.4.

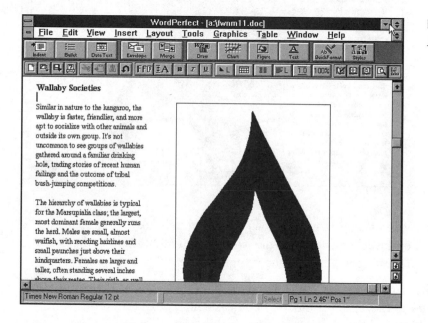

Figure 12.4
Boy, is that different.

You'll see that everything is the same, with one exception. That graphics box added (that previously was empty) now has something in it.

A Zoom with a View

What can you do in graphics mode? Everything you can do in text mode—plus one (see your graphics). You also have the luxury of zooming in on your text by using the Zoom command in the View menu. When you select Zoom, a popup menu of a bunch of view options appears (see fig. 12.5).

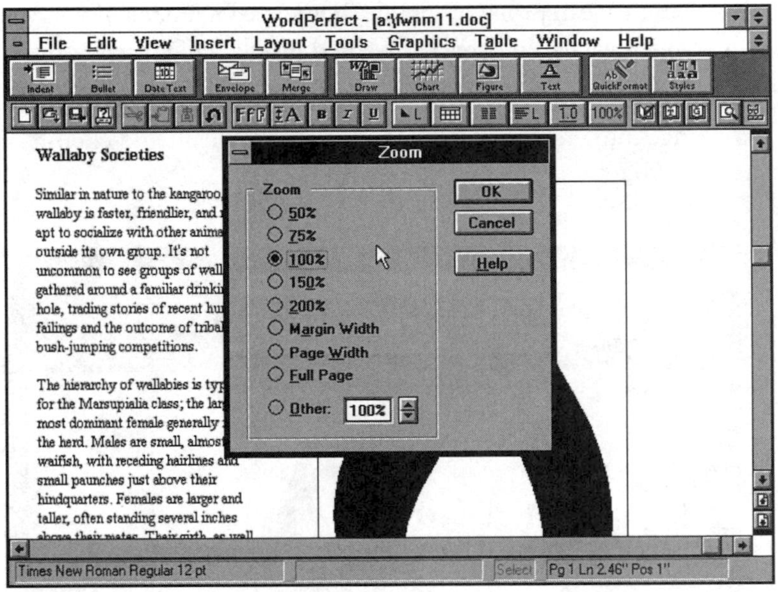

Figure 12.5

Zooming all over the place.

The view you see is Margin Width. You can zoom in to 50% (which reduces the size of the document to half the screen) or up to 200% (for when your glasses are really going bad) as shown in figure 12.6.

You have to say this for WordPerfect for Windows—the Graphics mode is superior to the "graphics modes" of other popular programs. Other word processors allow you to take a look at your document in graphics mode, but they don't allow editing. WordPerfect for Windows does. Other programs get really bogged down and work like someone poured molasses in the disk drive when operating in graphics mode; but WordPerfect for Windows zips right along, just as though you're working in page mode (which is much less draining on the memory).

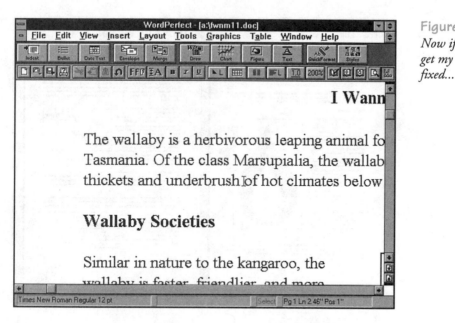

Figure 12.6
*Now if I can just
get my hearing aid
fixed...*

Two Pages a La Mode, Please

Hmmmm. Page mode and Two Page mode? Why?

Sometimes it's hard to tell what you're doing until you can back up and get a Big Picture view. Two Page mode is for that sometime. Oh, sure, you can do anything in Page mode—you can write, edit, spell-check, format, even show graphics, if you leave Graphics selected in the View menu.

But Two Page view gives you a larger slice of the Scheme of Things. You can see the way headers and footers look. You can see the way your columns fall. How does the art work look on the page? Two Page mode can show you.

Again, in Two Page mode, you can edit your document, and the changes carry through to text mode when you flip back (better have somebody spot you).

Figure 12.7
*Double your word
processing pleasure.*

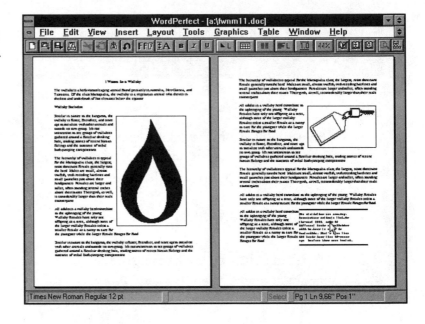

Two page mode may be a little deceiving when it comes to the old
WYSIWYG display. See that box down in the corner of figure 12.7?
Looks like it runs right up against the text, right? It doesn't. Just a little
April Fool's Joke from WordPerfect for Windows.

When you're ready to get out of Two Page mode, open the View menu and
choose Page (or another view you're interested in investigating).

The Chicken Scratch Command

Those blasted English teachers. You work all week on a paper, turn it in, and
here it comes back—all marked up with red circles, loops, and little backwards Ps.

What are those things?

Paragraph marks. And, believe it or not, people really use them. Why? To see where paragraphs begin.

To turn on paragraph marks in your document, open the View menu and choose Show &¶&. There they are, making your document darned close to illegible (see fig. 12.8). Of course, the little space markers that soak up the space between words doesn't help the readability any, either.

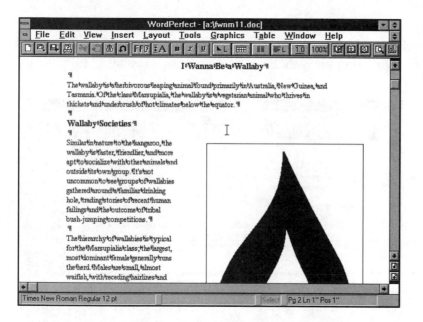

Figure 12.8
Paragraph marks and other hated symbols.

Want to get rid of them? Just repeat yourself. Open the View menu and choose Show &¶& again. Poof.

Today's View Scramble: U L B R R   E R A

The Kangaroo Rat Hops on One Foot (Secret Codes)

Shhhh. Did the Chief give you permission to read this section?

WordPerfect for Windows has many, many behind-the-scenes codes that control the way your document looks and keeps track of itself. You can display the codes in your document by using another command in the View menu: Reveal Codes.

When you select Reveal Codes, the bottom section of the screen is turned into another window. Inside of that window is the section of text at the cursor position, complete with the codes already there (see fig. 12.9).

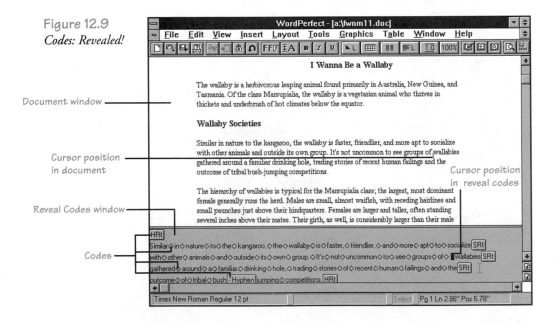

Figure 12.9
Codes: Revealed!

As you can see, the cursor is positioned in the document on the word *wallabies* in the second paragraph. In the Reveal Codes window, the cursor is placed in the same position. In the line above the paragraph in Reveal Codes, you see the code [HRt], although nothing appears there in the regular document. That code stands for hard carriage return, which means

Enter was pressed when the cursor was positioned on that line. At the end of the line in Reveal Codes, you see [SRt], which is for soft carriage return. That's what WordPerfect for Windows puts in the text when it word-wraps your text to the next line.

Neither of these codes is too exciting. Let's cursor on up to a heading and see what is happening.

Figure 12.10 shows the cursor positioned on the first character of a heading. In Reveal Codes, you can see that the heading is boldfaced. A bold code turns on the style [Bold On], and a bold code turns off the style [Bold Off]. The shape of those Bolds shows you whether the code is a beginning code or an ending code.

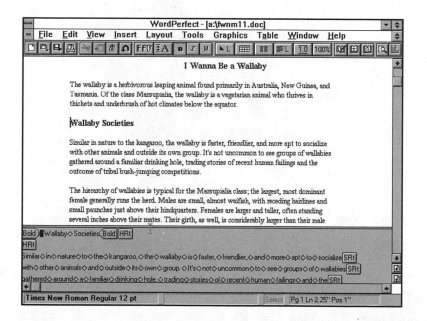

Figure 12.10
This isn't voyeurism, is it?

So what will you do with these codes? If you're like most people, probably nothing, until you hit some kind of printing glitch. Perhaps you meant to underline one word and you wound up with the second half of the document underlined. That is probably because you accidentally deleted the ending underline code. You can check by positioning the cursor at the point in the document where everything went wrong and choosing Reveal Codes.

When you're tired of looking at the world in such a complicated way, open the View menu and return to page mode.

Hint for today's View Scramble: It's where the king bellies up.

They're Out To Get Us

You'll be relieved to know that not too many things can go wrong when you're viewing WordPerfect for Windows in different modes. Possible hazards might be:

- **CSS.** Cluttered Screen Syndrome
- **ONIOOM.** Oh-No-I'm-Out-Of-Memory! crisis
- **TMV.** Too Many Views stress
- **DMV.** The Department of Motor Vehicles.

Sometimes you're so enamored with the many features of a program (after you learn how to use them) that you want to gather them all around you all the time. But sooner or later you realize that you've got a Quasi-Moto-like hump growing on your back, you squint constantly, and you breathe through your mouth. Unless you're growing hair on the back of your hands, don't worry—it's Cluttered Screen Syndrome. Don't make your eyes search for the words of your own document. Use only the special display tools you need. As your boss will tell you (although you might not agree); it's more important to get the job done than it is to look good when you do it.

You're sitting there, peacefully enough, playing around with different display modes. Then—dunh, da, DHUNNNNN!—ONIOOM, the Oh-No-I'm-Out-Of-Memory! crisis. WordPerfect's and Windows graphics mode demands that you have a good graphics card and at least 480K of RAM (available memory). If you get the error—boy, that's frustrating—exit the program and restart your computer to make sure you don't have any other programs loading, using memory you could use for graphics mode.

That is part of the problem of all the freedoms we have today. There are so many things to choose from that we don't know what to pick. When should you use what view? When is graphics appropriate? Should you edit in page view? What will your office-mate think if she looks over and sees you still using draft mode? Remember that WordPerfect for Windows offers these modes because they perform specific functions: text mode is quickest for your basic text-entry and editing procedures; graphics mode shows you art and allows you to resize and move graphics; and page mode lets you see the little extras like headers, footers, and notes. The best bet—because it's fastest—for text dealings is page or draft mode.

Nobody likes to go to the DMV. Unless you work there and you're part of the "in" crowd, you suffer from DMV stress at least once a year, when it's time for the annual license-plate-fee robbery. Oh, and remember when you have to take those driving tests? Jeez, they're the worst. Oh, great. Now you've got *me* nervous.

Demon-Strations

A Graphic a Day

1. Open the View menu.

2. Choose Graphics.

3. Add any necessary screen items (Button bar, Outline bar, etc.).

4. Do any editing you need to do (move graphics, resize things, zoom up or out).

5. Turn graphics off by opening the View menu and reselecting it.

Revealing Innermost Codes

1. Position the cursor at the point in the document you would like to display codes.

2. Open the View menu.

3. Choose Reveal Codes.

4. Move the cursor as necessary to see other parts of the document.

5. When you're finished with Reveal Codes, open the View menu and choose Reveal Codes again (or press Alt+F3).

Summary

Well, this encounter has certainly lengthened your view of things, hasn't it? You probably see WordPerfect in a completely different way. Not just a blue program with white letters, WordPerfect gives you a number of different ways to make sure the document is just the way you want it.

Oh no. You still haven't figured out today's View Scramble? The tip "Where the king bellies up" didn't help you? Well, shame on you. You're just not applying youself. The answer is "Ruler Bar" and you need to go find a copy of the latest TV Guide crossword puzzle and start practicing. You're out of shape.

Exorcises

1. How many different views does WordPerfect offer?

2. Why turn Graphics on?

3. Give two reasons why you might use Reveal Codes.

4. What is the meaning of life? (Write in and let me know, will you?)

"Well, Without It, We Couldn't Read!" (Justyifying Text)

Goal

To help you push the text around and put it where you want it.

What You Will Need

A paragraph or two of text, and nothing better to do.

Terms of Enfearment

left-justified   right-justified
centered   full-justified
ragged text

Briefing

The way your text looks is really important—second only, in fact, to your overall message. When you're sure that you've said what you set out to say and checked for typos and grammatical errors, you'll be more concerned with where the text is placed on the page. (Or maybe not.)

Typewriter flashback: Remember in the old days when you wanted to center the heading of a report you were typing? What did you do? You pressed Tab a few times, right? And then, if the last tab didn't get you close enough to the middle, you would press the spacebar to make up the difference.

Those days are gone. Good riddance.

WordPerfect for Windows gives you several different choices for the way you arrange the text in your document. When you first fire up the program and start typing, WordPerfect for Windows assumes you want *left-justification*, which means that the text lines up along the left edge, but does not line up along the right.

Jargon alert: When text doesn't line up along one edge or another, we call that text ragged (pronounced rag-ged) text.

You can also choose to align text along the right margin, creating what's known as right-justified text. Text that lines up on both ends (besides being anal-retentive) is called full-justified (or sometimes just justified) text. And, text that is centered between the margins is—you are following this, right?—centered text.

Words to the Left of Me

For many people, left-justification, the default setting of WordPerfect for Windows, is the text alignment of choice. Your everyday memo expects to be left-justified. Reports seem, somehow, more personable with that ragged right edge.

Some people disagree, however, preferring that straight-laced look of full-justified text.

When might you want to use left-justified text?

- You're writing something you want someone to read (not that I'm biased or anything).

- You don't want a lot of unnecessary spaces between words in your document.

- You're writing a memo, letter, or report.

- When your boss tells you to.

Figure 13.1 shows the Wallaby document in its original state: left-justified.

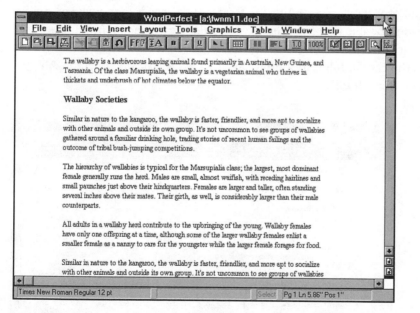

Figure 13.1
The left-justified document.

You Don't Have To Justify Yourself

Justification, or full-justification, lines the text up along both margins. The only problem with justified text is that in order to get the text justified, WordPerfect has to plug in little spaces between the words to stretch them all the way to the right margin. Looks a little contrived.

And yet there are times when you really need to use justified text. Some of those might be:

- You're working with columns and you want to give the page a uniform, less cluttered look.

- You just can't stand those little ragged creatures hanging out by the right margin.

- Something inside you relaxes when your desk is straight, your pens are lined up, and your text is justified.

- When you boss tells you to.

WordPerfect for Windows gives you two different options for justifying your text. You can choose Full, which spreads just the text paragraphs to the right margin, or you can choose All, which spreads the heads (and widows), too. You won't be able to see the change in regular text mode; in order to see full justification, you have to go to Page mode (remember how?). Figure 13.2 shows the page in full justification, and 13.3 shows the document in All (strange effect, huh?).

Figure 13.2
A full job of justification.

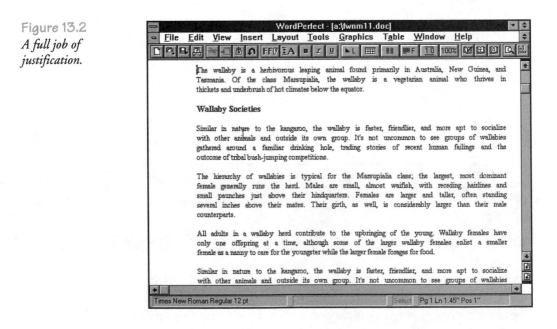

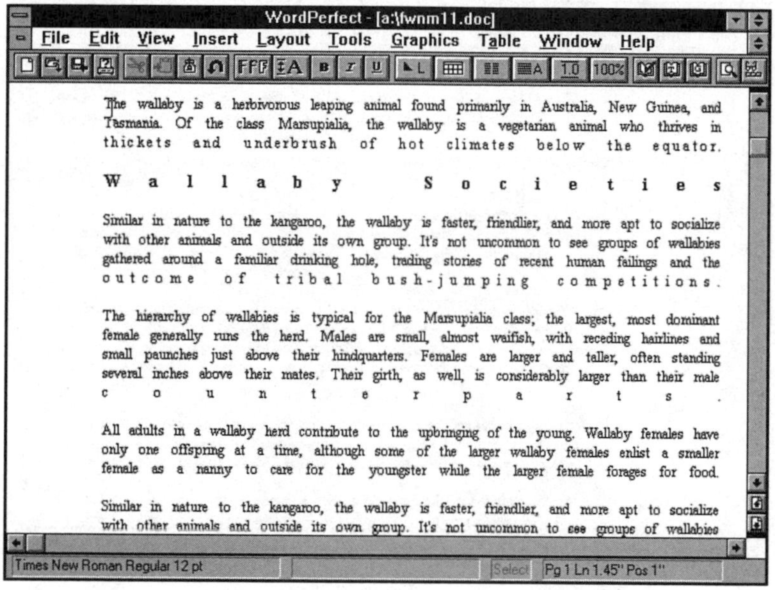

Figure 13.3
*A little overboard,
don't you think?*

Words to the Right of Me

Aligning your text along the right margin is a dramatic effect. It makes a bold statement to the world: "I'm a non-conformist."

But you may not want to be that bold.

Take a look at the Wallaby document, shown in figure 13.4. This one is right-aligned. Having trouble thinking of times when you would want to use right-alignment? Here are a few possibilities:

- You're working on an unusual project—like advertising copy, in which the layout of the text can be nontraditional.

- You want to wake up the people in your managers' meeting.

- You want to place the text against a photo or graphic element, which will be placed on the right side of the page.

- Your boss told you to.

- You want to show the world how your recent political views have swung from the left to the right.

Figure 13.4
Swinging to the right.

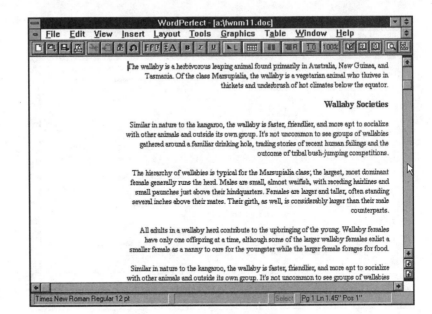

Figure 13.4
Swinging to the right.

Here I Am—Stuck in the Middle with You

And then there are those among us who are the middle-of-the-road drivers, who hate to make a commitment to either side. We like our text centered and medium well, thank you very much.

Chances are, you'll use centered text sparingly, more often than not for headings and such. Rarely, if ever, will you need to center an entire document (or large portion of text, for that matter). Reasons you might center text include:

- Adding the title for your report.
- Adding the subtitle for your report.
- Adding the headings for the sections of your report (but don't you think they would look better flush left? Hint, hint, nudge, nudge.)
- You think it looks cute.

■ You're working on a stunning piece of advertising copy, rather poetic in nature, and you want to showcase your perfect prose.

Figure 13.5 shows you an example of centered text. In the next section, we show you how to do all of these things.

Figure 13.5
Text center stage.

Going through the Change

WordPerfect for Windows makes it easy for you to arrange the text. You can do it two different ways:

■ You can use the Justification command in the Layout menu.

■ You can click the Justification button in the toolbar (eighth from the right) and select the alignment you want.

Changing the Whole Shebang

Remember those mysterious codes we talked about in the last encounter? It's those codes that control how your document places text on the page. When you want to choose a different alignment, if you want the whole document to be affected, move the pointer to the beginning of the document. Then, do this:

1. Open the Layout menu.

2. Choose the Justification command (click on it or press J). A small popup menu appears, listing these options:

   Left

   Right

   Center

   Full

   All

3. Choose the justification you want by clicking on it or by typing the underlined letter (see fig. 13.6)

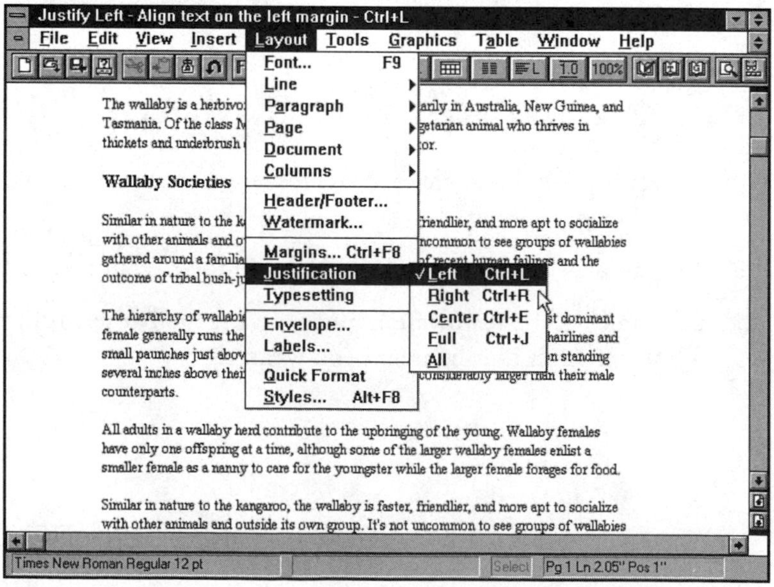

Figure 13.6

Choosing justification.

The change on-screen is immediate. Does it look awful? Open the Edit menu and choose Undo, quick, before it sticks.

If you want to see the code that you and WordPerfect have just inserted, press Alt+F3 to reveal the codes.

Quick-Change Artist, Huh?

WordPerfect for Windows lets you take a shortcut to justifying yourself. No more explaining. No more reaching into menus you would rather avoid. Just point and click.

The recipient of your click is a small tool in the toolbar. It's the eighth one from the right. When you click the justification tool, a small pop-up box appears (see fig. 13.7).

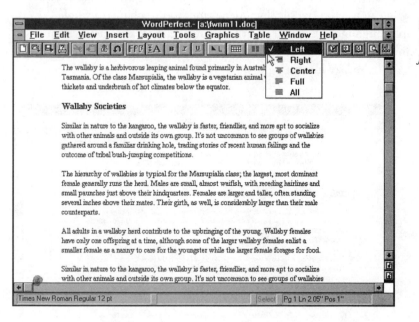

Figure 13.7
Changing alignment fast.

Hopefully, you placed the cursor first, because after you choose the justification, WordPerfect for Windows is going to put it to good use. When you plop that baby in there, everything after the cursor point changes to reflect your choice.

Changes on a Smaller Scale

Depending on the nature of your documents, you may want to use the different justification options for different items. You might, for example, want to center the primary heading in a section by left-justifying lower headings. Or you might want to center your lead paragraph but have the rest done in full justification.

Whatever.

To change the justification of the current paragraph, you

1. Highlight the paragraph you want to change. (This could be a simple one-line heading, as shown in figure 13.8.)

2. Open the Layout menu and choose the Line command. A set of options appears, as shown in figure 13.9.

3. Click the style you want; then click OK.

There you have it—the line is centered, as shown in figure 13.10. If you prefer, you can use the "whole document" method to change a single paragraph. Highlight what you want to change, choose the Justification command, and select the option you want. (Or just click the button in the toolbar, if you're lazy like me.)

Figure 13.8

On your mark, get set...

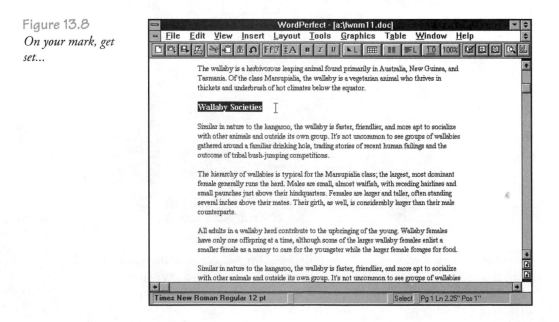

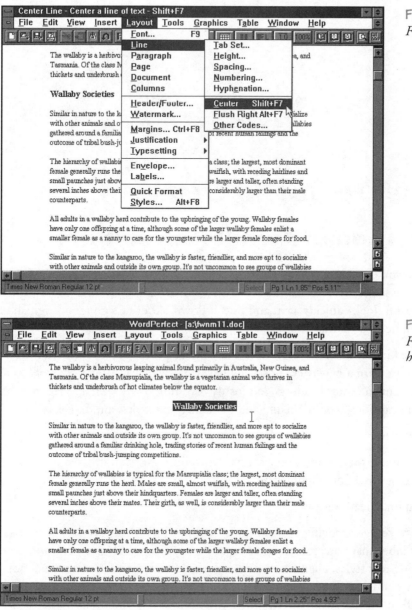

Figure 13.9
Format!

Figure 13.10
Formatting a heading.

They're Out To Get Us

This Looks Awful! (Doesn't it?)

Have you ever seen a four-year-old open birthday presents? He grabs one, rips the paper off, looks at the toy, puts it down. Grabs another one, rips the paper off, looks quickly at it, and puts it down. After he's gone through all of them, he says "Is there more?"

We're kind of like that, even from our vantage points of Absolute Maturity. After we learn a new trick, or several new tricks, we want to try them all. You want to center headings, left justify text, full justify text, and right-justify captions. You're mixing and matching text styles, and boy is it fun.

It's also ugly.

Fonts make that temptation even harder to fight. We can mix ten or twenty different typefaces, alignments, and...

Hold on. Breath deeply.

Before you go sprucing up your document until it's all spruce and no trunk, remember that your primary goal is (or perhaps, should be) to communicate. Mixing text styles, alignments, and a myriad of other special effects will only overwhelm your readers and confuse them. Choose one basic text style and justification and stick with it, unless you need to do something special with headings or captions or whatnot.

The urge to Go Creative is extremely strong. And you *should* cut loose, where your situation allows. But you'll produce better documents if you remember to Go Creative Sensibly.

Caffeine-Free Text

Is your text jumping around the document like it's pumped full of Maxwell House? When you try to change the format of a single paragraph, does the entire document just move to the right or the middle?

Could be a couple of things.

Remember how WordPerfect for Windows takes care of font and formatting issues? By inserting those mysterious little codes. Most things in WordPerfect for Windows are actually controlled by two codes—an On code and an Off code. When you make a word boldface, for example, WordPerfect puts a code that says "Bold on" before for the word and "Bold off" after.

The formatting commands in WordPerfect for Windows are single-shot commands. If you don't highlight the text, which tells WordPerfect for Windows where the beginning and end of the block is, WordPerfect will think you want to attach that code to the entire document—at least until you enter another format code somewhere else.

To make sure that you get the format on just the paragraph you want, highlight the paragraph first.

Demon-Strations

Justifying Your Document

1. Move the text pointer to the beginning of the document.
2. Open the Layout menu.
3. Choose Justification.
4. From the popup box, choose the type of justification you want.

Justifying a Line or Two

1. Highlight the area you want to change.

2. Position the mouse pointer over the justification button in the toolbar.

3. Press and hold the mouse button.

4. Click the setting you want.

Summary

The way you choose to align the text in your document may be a personal-preference issue or it may be a mandate set down from higher-ups. No matter who is responsible for the decision, WordPerfect for Windows makes it easy for you to position your text pretty much any way you want it. You can choose from left-justified, right-justified, full-justified, and centered text. The next encounter follows up on the formatting theme by showing you how to work with margins and page features.

Exorcises

1. Mix and match:

   _____ Centered   a. Aligns along left margin

   _____ Full   b. Aligns along right margin

   _____ Left   c. Aligns to both margins

   _____ Right   d. Aligns in center

2. What does All do?

3. When might you use full justified text?

4. Which of the justification styles is used most often?

5. For best results, _____

    a. Use full-justification in your documents

    b. Center memos

    c. Use at least three different types of alignment in each document

    d. Before you swim, wait at least 30 minutes after eating

    e. Use one basic justification style with a secondary style for headings

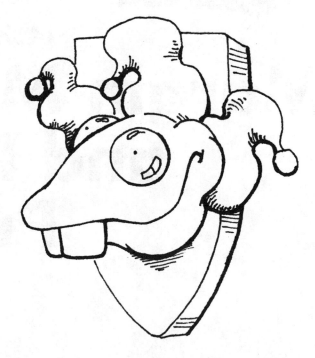

14th Encounter

Margin Mania and Page Presto

Goal

To cover all those annoying but necessary (and one or two unnecessary) things that you'll have to face sooner or later.

What You Will Need

Dry twigs, a can of Beanie Weanies, and four Twinkies.

Terms of Enfearment

margins	indents
hanging indents	page breaks
columns	

Briefing

Ohhhh, we're getting right down to the wire here. This encounter covers some of the last few basics you need in order to squelch those WordPerfect fears once and for all. You've heard of margins, right? (Not the little green men from Outer Space the FBI won't tell us about.) In this encounter, you learn to put 'em in, take 'em out, and move 'em all around. There are also some page items we need to cover—things that don't fit neatly anywhere else. Things like page breaks and columns and jumping around in the document (two, three).

All of that, jam-packed into this encounter.

Lucky you.

My Favorite Margins

The word *margin* is the technical term for the white space that surrounds your text. You can't type there. You can't print there. The margins are there to protect your text just in case you drop the page on the floor, kind of like a little pillow-action.

Your page has four margins, one on each edge of the page. These margins are named for the edge they occupy: top, left, right, and bottom.

Simple so far, eh?

WordPerfect for Windows lets you change the space used for each of those margins. You can move things way in, like setting a 3-inch left margin (but why?), or you can move things way out (but best advice is to not set margins any smaller than WordPerfect's preset 1-inch).

Setting margins is a simple business. (Hear the 50's sitcom music in the background?):

1. Open the Layout menu.
2. Choose Margins.

The Margins dialog box appears, as shown in figure 14.1. So far, so good.

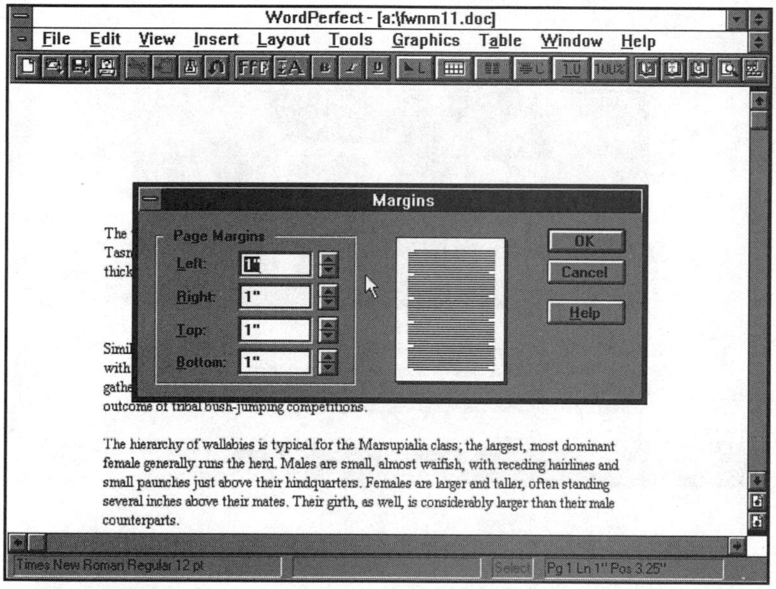

Figure 14.1
*Enjoying yourself?
Marginally.*

To make your changes, just click on the arrows beside the margin box you want (Left, Right, Top, or Bottom). The preview in the center of the Margins box changes to show your changes.

A Stroll around the Block

Aw, c'mon. Let's try it out.

Move that mouse pointer up to the Page Margins settings. Click the arrow pointing up beside Left:. Click it again. Go a little crazy clicking that button.

What happened? Each time you clicked, the margin increased by .10. And the preview changed to show what you were doing (see fig. 14.2).

Figure 14.2
See the amazing results—instantly!

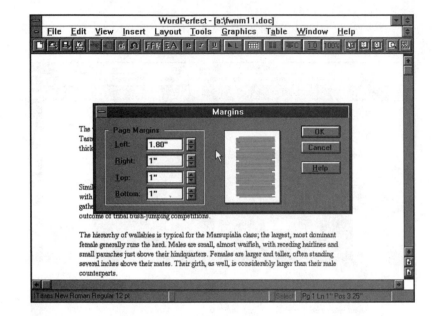

If you want to change the margin for a few paragraphs, highlight the text that you want to change before you open the Layout menu and select the Margins command.

Please Release Me! (Margins)

Sometimes you don't want margins. Oh sure, they look nice. But you've just got to fit two hundred words on that page, even if it kills you. And that means stripping out the margins.

You can do this with relatively little discomfort by opening the Layout menu, choosing Paragraph, and selecting Margin Release. From the cursor position on, your document is marginless.

Indent!

Then there will be those times when you want to indent (or outdent) selected paragraphs. Remember those awful research papers in high school in which you had to have a certain number of quotes, a certain number of footnotes, and a certain number of resources? Those quote paragraphs—called pull-quotes—had to be indented from both the right and left margins.

Ready? It's so complicated you won't believe it. Here are the steps:

1. Click at the beginning of the paragraph you want to indent.

2. Press F7.

Whoa—that whole paragraph moved in! Did you see it? Figure 14.3 shows the results.

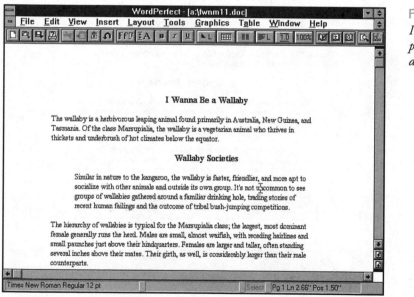

Figure 14.3
Indent your paragraph doe-si-doe.

Indent, Indent! (Double Indent)

Not enough for you? Need to indent the next paragraph even more than the first? (Indenting is habit forming, you know.) Double indenting indents on both edges. Here is the trick:

1. Position the cursor.

2. Press Ctrl+Shift+F7.

Don't blink—there it goes (see fig. 14.4). The text moves inward from both edges. Amazing.

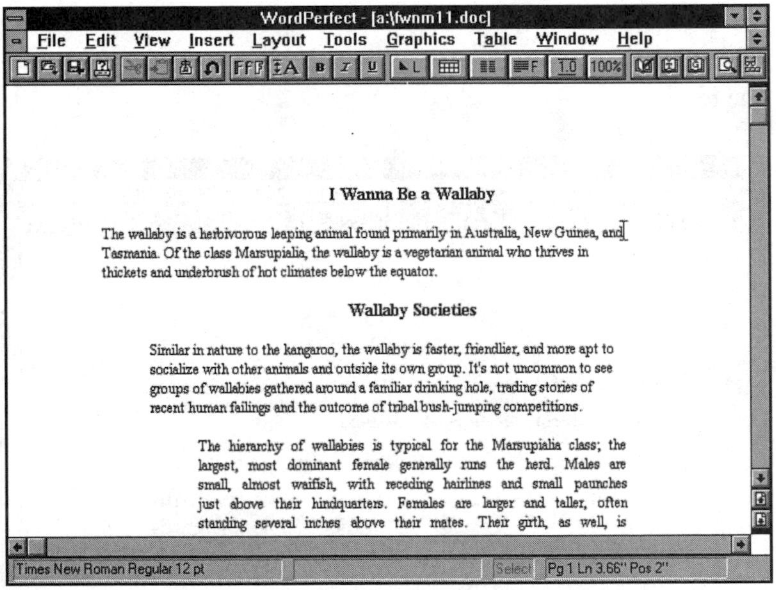

Figure 14.4
*Double-indenting
your pleasure.*

There is a button in the Button Bar specifically for indents. It's called the Indent button. Click it and amaze you friends.

There's Gonna' Be a Hangin'

Ever hear the phrase "hanging indent?" Until just a few years ago, this didn't exist, as far as I'm concerned. Now, because we are expected to do fancy-schmancy things like bulleted lists and numbered steps, we've got to have hanging indents. The little numbers have to line up. The words all have to start at the same place. The wrap-around lines have to come back to the same place.

Sigh. Give me a little whining room.

Oh, hanging indents are useful. Attractive, even.

Not to mention easy to add.

You can add a hanging indent one of two ways:

- You can place the cursor at the beginning of the text and press Ctrl+F7

- You can click the Bullet button in the Button Bar

Either way, your text comes out looking like it's ready to be hung with a bullet, number, or some other symbol. Figure 14.5 shows the hanging text.

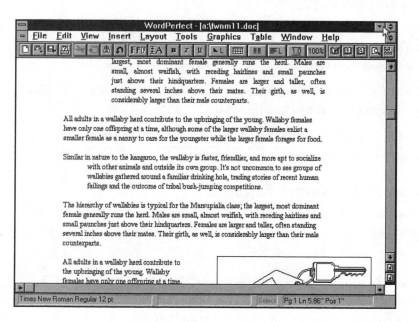

Figure 14.5
Hanging text, Tex.

Worrying about Page Stuff

As your documents get longer and longer, you'll start to worry about Page Stuff. You've got only three paragraphs on this first page, but you really want to start a new section after that point. How do you make WordPerfect move the rest of the text to the next page? And then how to do you get to the other pages once you get the text there? Finally, can any sane person put text in columns or is that a feat better left to daredevils?

We'll have all this—and more—when we return.

Breaking Pages

It's a familiar story: The two paragraphs have been together since their creation. Because of Paragraph Spacing and a few other saucy options, they've grown apart.

They need to break away.

When you want to give your paragraphs a helping hand and insert that page break, it's a simple task. Position the point at the point in your document after which you want the page break to be added.

Then press Ctrl+Enter. A line appears at the cursor position, and the cursor moves down to the next line (see fig. 14.6).

If you want to delete a page break (is reconcilliation on the horizon?), just press the backspace key until the line disappears.

Moving to Different Pages

So you've been typing happily away for hours and you've created pages and pages and pages of text. Hmmmm. Page 4? How do you get back to page 2?

Easy.

Open the Edit menu, and drag the pointer all the way down to one of the last options, Go to. This displays the Go to box shown in figure 14.7. Just type the number of the page you want to see and press Enter.

Then—zap!—you're there.

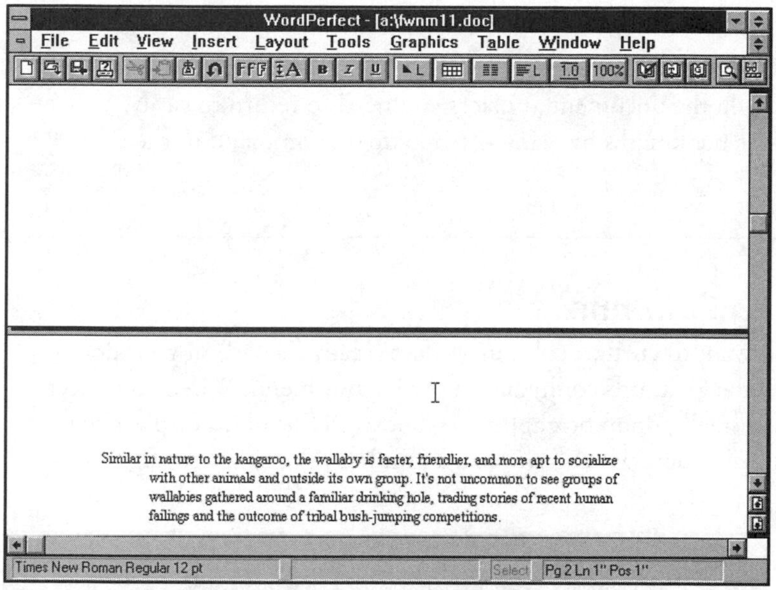
WordPerfect - [a:\fwnm11.doc]
File Edit View Insert Layout Tools Graphics Table Window Help
Similar in nature to the kangaroo, the wallaby is faster, friendlier, and more apt to socialize with other animals and outside its own group. It's not uncommon to see groups of wallabies gathered around a familiar drinking hole, trading stories of recent human failings and the outcome of tribal bush-jumping competitions.
Times New Roman Regular 12 pt
Select
Pg 2 Ln 1" Pos 1"

Figure 14.6
Breaking up isn't hard to do.

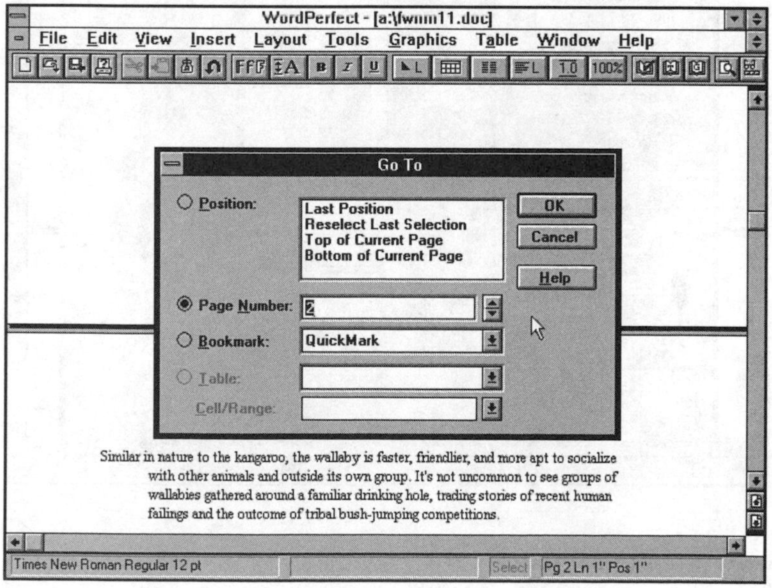
WordPerfect - [a:\fwnm11.doc]
File Edit View Insert Layout Tools Graphics Table Window Help
Go To
Position:
Last Position
Reselect Last Selection
Top of Current Page
Bottom of Current Page
OK
Cancel
Help
Page Number: 2
Bookmark: QuickMark
Table:
Cell/Range:
Similar in nature to the kangaroo, the wallaby is faster, friendlier, and more apt to socialize with other animals and outside its own group. It's not uncommon to see groups of wallabies gathered around a familiar drinking hole, trading stories of recent human failings and the outcome of tribal bush-jumping competitions.
Times New Roman Regular 12 pt
Select
Pg 2 Ln 1" Pos 1"

Figure 14.7
Are you flying first class or coach?

WordPerfect has a feature known as bookmarks that helps you insert little tags in the document at places you need to return to easily. You can create bookmarks by using the Bookmark command in the Edit menu.

Creating Columns

When you want to create a columnar effect (Hail, Caesar!) in your documents, use the Columns command in the Layout menu. When you select Columns, a small popup box appears. Choose Define. This displays the Columns dialog box, which gives you a number of options (see fig. 14.8).

Figure 14.8
Options for building columns.

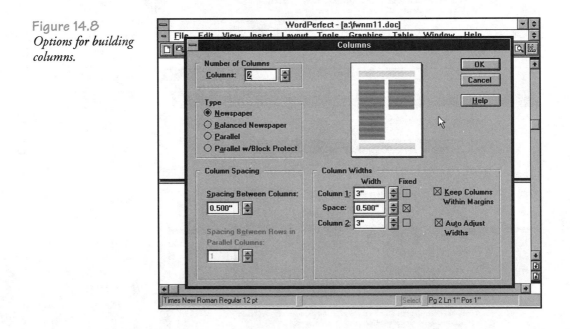

The easy way out is to let WordPerfect for Windows set the width and style of your columns for you. You may want to do this, at least the first time or two you attempt this column thing.

There are four different types of columns you can choose:

- **Newspaper columns.** With these guys, the text runs down the page, hits the bottom, and starts back up at the top.

- **Balanced newspaper.** These columns are the same as the standard newspaper, except that WordPerfect makes sure they are the same length.

- **Parallel columns.** In these columns, the text is aligned so that the next item in the left column doesn't begin until the last item in the right column finished. This is good for two column tables.

- **Parallel columns with block sunscreen protector.** This keeps your columns from suffering from ultraviolet rays and keeps them together on a page.

Next, enter the number of columns you want on the page. (WordPerfect will limit you to 24 columns, which is so ridiculous it's not worth talking about.) To change the number of columns, press 2 to select Number of Columns. Then type the number of columns you want.

You can change the spacing between the columns or the line spacing between the rows, but why mess with perfection?

Click OK or press Enter, and you've got columns (see fig. 14.9).

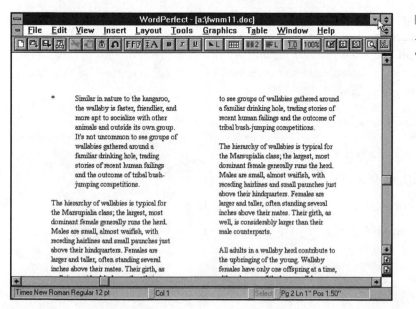

Figure 14.9
In the blink of an eye—columns.

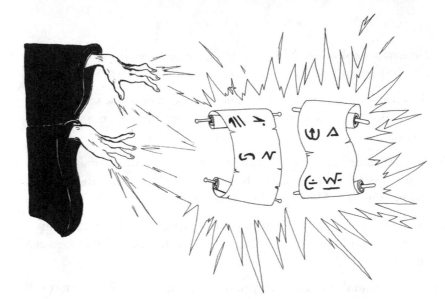

They're Out To Get Us

My Margins Are a Mess

What can go wrong with such things as margins, page breaks, and columns? Nothing truly major, certainly.

Maybe you've messed with your margins so much that everything is all moved around and you're sick of it. You don't like them now any better than you did when you started, and yet you don't remember what the default values are, so you can't even start over. Well, here they are (one less thing to gripe about):

Document Margins

Left Margin:	1"
Right Margin:	1"
Top Margin:	1"
Bottom Margin:	1" (seeing a pattern, here?)

Ugly Columns

Whoa...hold on there. You went through the motions of setting up columns just the way the book told you to. But you pressed Enter, eager to see the screen divide itself up and align, and now you're really sorry.

How do you get your single-column document back again?

Position the cursor at the point in your document where the columns begin. Then press Alt-F3. Remember what that does? It opens the small screen at the bottom where you can see the codes Wordperfect uses to control font and format. Notice, in figure 14.10, that the code

```
[Col Def]
```

is inserted at the beginning of the line where the columns start. (That's short for Column Definition.)

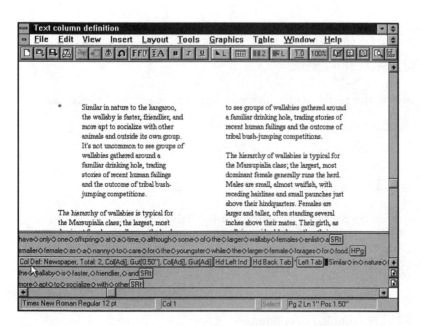

Figure 14.10
Removing unwanted columns.

To change your document from columns back to regular text, press backspace once and delete that code. Your document realigns itself immediately.

Demon-Strations

A Margin for Your Thoughts

1. Move the cursor to the point you want to change the margin. If you want to change a few paragraphs, highlight the text you want to change.

2. Open the Layout menu.

3. Choose Margins.

4. Click on the arrows beside the Page Margin values to set the new margins. The preview box shows you what is happening.

5. Click OK or press Enter.

A Good Page Break Is Worth a Thousand Words

1. Position the cursor after which you want the page break added.

2. Press Ctrl+Enter.

Columnizing

1. Position the cursor at the point you want the columns to begin.

2. Open the Layout menu.

3. Choose Columns.

4. Choose Define.

5. Specify the number of columns.

6. Select the column type.

7. Change any other necessary settings.

8. Click OK or press Enter.

Summary

This encounter has provided a three-pronged approach to finishing off the details of document basics. You've learned to set and modify document and paragraph margins, insert and delete page breaks, move to different pages, and create columns. The next encounter starts Part Four by showing you how to add some important little extras to your WordPerfect documents.

Exorcises

1. The first step in setting paragraph margins is _____

    a. Opening the Layout menu.

    b. Pressing Shift-F8.

    c. Highlighting text.

2. True or false: Paragraph margins override document margins.

3. Explain the two steps involved in setting a page break.

4. Put the following in order:

    _____ Specify the number of columns.

    _____ Select Define.

    _____ Click OK or press Enter.

    _____ Position the cursor.

    _____ Choose Columns.

    _____ Open the Layout menu.

    _____ Set other options.

15th Encounter

Headsies, Feetsies, and Other Miscellaneous Bits

Goal

To inspire you into adding those extra-special somethings that help your documents look like you know what you're talking about.

What You Will Need

Some amount of text that will qualify as a document and time to play.

Terms of Enfearment

header	footer
footnote	endnote
comment	watermark

Briefing

Unless you've been instructed to do so, adding headers, footers, and other miscellania is an optional issue. Most of us shy away from it. Why, you ask? It just *sounds* complicated, like something better left to the WordPerfect for Windows Wizards. (Say *that* three times fast.) Something else you don't need to stress about.

In the early days of word processing, adding headers and footers was a big deal. You had to know the codes. You had to get the spacing right. You had to help the program calculate how much room to leave between the edge of the page and the beginning of the text.

Just thinking about it can give you hives.

In today's WordPerfect for Windows, the process is so automated that you'll never even break out in a sweat. A couple of commands, a few words, and you're in business.

Discovering Document Poles: Headers and Footers

At the far north end of the document page, above the first line of text, we have a blank space where a header could be. What *is* a header? A line of text that contains information that you want printed at the top of every page (or on alternating pages) in your document.

> You can add two headers—Header A and Header B—and two footers—Footer A and Footer B in the document. You can enter different headers and footers on each page, if you prefer.

Not all documents need headers, and not all documents don't. Think about what your particular document might need up there, to help readers remember what they're reading and who wrote it. You might include things like the following:

- The name of the book you're writing
- Your department name
- The fact that you're due for a raise
- Your company's name
- The date
- The chapter title
- The page number
- The section title

A footer is text at the bottom of your document, providing the same basic information. People come up with all kinds of things for headers and footers. For example:

> I Wanna Be a Wallaby   Page 3

could be the header, and

> Murray December 1993

might be the footer.

Experiment. You'll get the idea,

Heads I Win

When you're ready to add a header to your document, just open the Layout menu and choose Header/Footer. The dialog box shown in figure 15.1 appears.

To add the header, click on Header A (or press A). The item is highlighted. Click Create.

The header toolbar appears just above your document. The cursor blinks, ready for you to type the header. A set of buttons stretches across the header toolbar. Want to know what they mean? Oh, sure you do:

?. Means "Help, I don't know what I'm doing."

Number. Will add a page, section, chapter, or volume number for you automatically. (Nice program.)

Line. Lets you choose whether you add a separator line below the header. Displays the Create Graphic Line dialog box so you can create the line you want.

Placement. Allows you to choose whether to put the header (or footer) on odd, even, or all pages. (If the documents you write are like mine, *all* the pages are odd.)

Distance. Lets you control the amount of space between the header (or the footer) and the text.

Close. Tells WordPerfect for Windows "Let me outta' here!"

Now you can type your header as you would any text (see fig. 15.2). When you're finished, click Close.

Figure 15.1

Head and feet box.

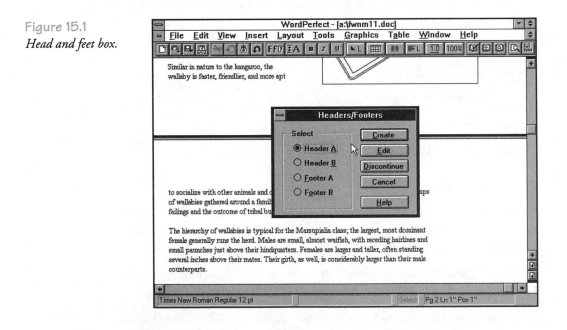

Go ahead and be creative—you can use any of the special effects in your headers and footers that you use in your document. Change the font and size, make the thing boldface or italic, whatever. Knock yourself out.

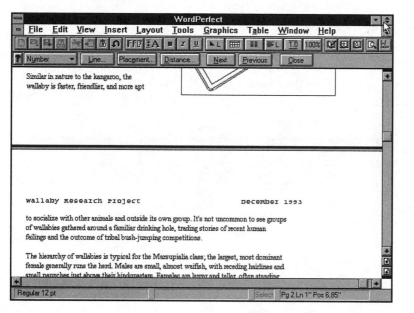

Figure 15.2
Heads up.

Tails You Lose

Adding a footer south of the border is no harder than anything else. Again, open the Layout menu and choose Header/Footer. The same dialog box appears. Select Footer A. Click Create or press Enter.

Same screen, right? Type your text, add any styles you want, and click the Close button. WordPerfect for Windows returns you to your document. Things looks the same, right?

> What the heck's a watermark? A watermark allows you to add text or art behind document text. Select a watermark as you would a header or footer, and when the watermark screen appears, type the text or place the image (use the Graphic menu's Figure command) in the screen.

There They Are!

If you want to see the header and footer at the same time and make sure that you really did enter them, change to Two Page mode by opening the View menu and choosing Two Page mode. There they are—right where you left them (see fig. 15.3).

Figure 15.3
Displaying headers and footers.

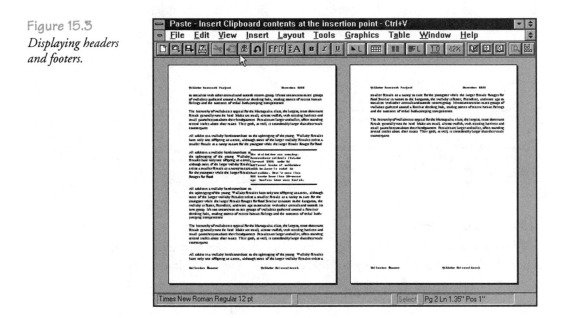

If you want to edit the header or footer you've added, you can do so easily by opening the Layout menu, choosing Header/Footer, clicking the header or footer you want to edit, clicking OK, and then selecting the Edit button. Then, when the item is displayed on the screen, edit it as you would any other text and click Close when you're done.

But I Just Want a Page Number!

Well, here is one feature that the users of WordPerfect for Windows can thumb their noses about: they've got an easy way to add page numbers. WordPerfect for DOS is clumsy (that's a nice word) when it comes to page numbers. By comparison, WordPerfect for Windows is slick.

When you want to add a page number (header or footer), just do this:

1. Open the Layout menu and choose Header/Footer.

2. Choose whichever one you want.

3. When the header (or footer) toolbar appears, click Numbers.

4. Select Page Numbers. WordPerfect for Windows sticks that fellow right in there for you at the cursor position (see fig. 15.4).

What could be easier?

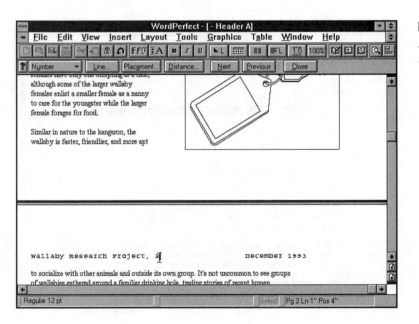

Figure 15.4
Putting in a page number.

Dr. Scholl's Footnotes

Aren't you impressed with yourself when you have an excuse to use footnotes? They look so—scholarly. With WordPerfect, adding, keeping track of, and printing footnotes is a snap. Here is how:

1. Position the cursor at the point you want to add the footnote.

2. Open the Insert menu.

3. Choose Footnote. A small popup box appears, giving you several additional options (see fig. 15.5).

4. Select Create. The Footnote toolbar appears. The display moves to the bottom of the screen, where a 1 is already entered (if this is your first footnote).

5. Type your text and press F7. The footnote is added.

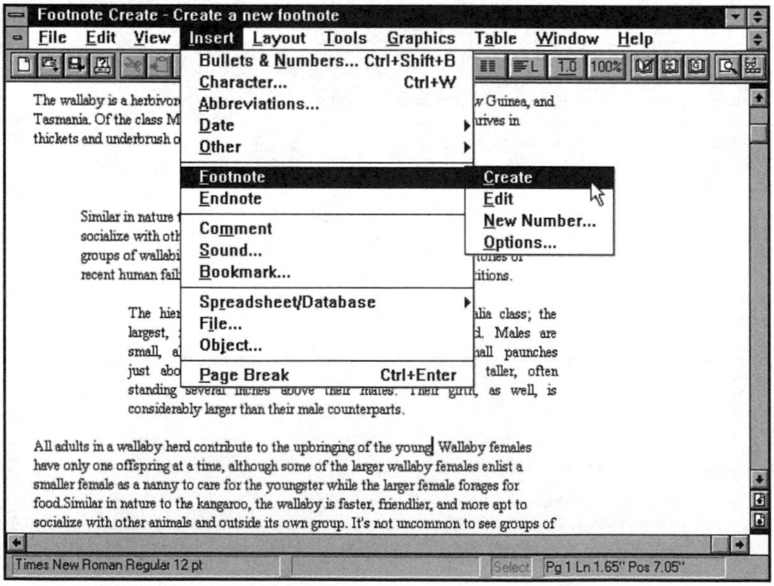

Figure 15.5

Footnote possibilities.

Again, in order to see the footnote in your document, you have to use Two Page mode or display the document in Full Page view. A footnote is always placed at the bottom of the current page (see fig. 15.6).

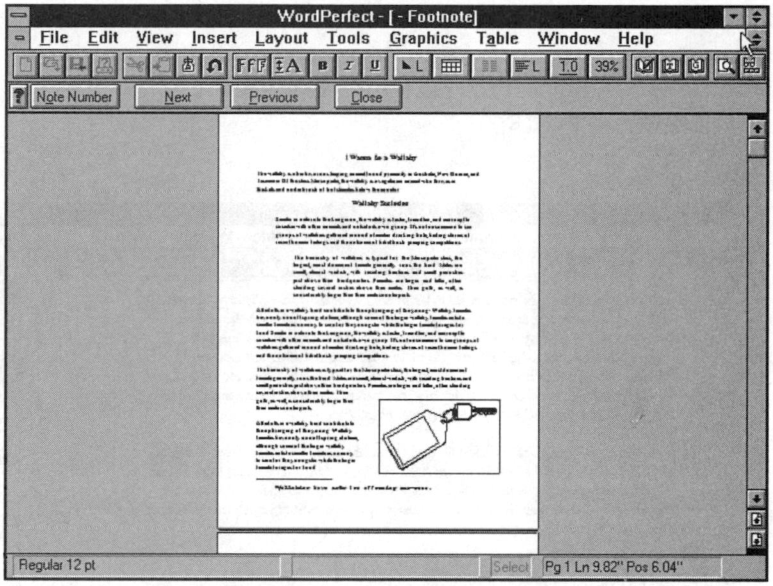

Figure 15.6
Aren't we smart?

If you add another footnote on the page, WordPerfect automatically numbers it for you. If you place it in front of the first footnote, WordPerfect renumbers the other footnotes so they are in order.

> You can edit footnotes easily. Just select Footnote, Edit, and type the number of the footnote you want to change. After you press Enter, WordPerfect for Windows displays the footnote, ready for you to edit.

The End of Everything: Endnotes

Endnotes are similar to footnotes, except that they have more to do with "end" than "feet." The endnote isn't put at the foot of the page; instead, all of the notes are placed at the end of the document. In every other way, endnotes are the same as footnotes.

When you want to enter an endnote, first position the cursor at the point you want WordPerfect for Windows to enter the number. Next, open the

Insert menu, select Endnote, and choose Create. Type the endnote and click Close. Like a footnote, WordPerfect adds the note to the document (you can see the endnote number, but not the note itself). To see the note, go to the end of the document (see fig. 15.7).

Figure 15.7

Endnotes appear at the end of the document.

They're Out To Get Us

It's possible to go a little crazy with all of the notes that you can add in your document. There are headers, footers, footnotes, endnotes, and comments. Remember to use these items sparingly and resist the temptation to assault your audience with a barrage of information—however useful it might seem to you.

When Is a Footnote an Endnote?

You've finished your document, added the footer, put in all the notes, and you're ready to print, you think. Better take a look at it in Full Page mode first.

What does Full Page mode reveal? The footer replaced the footer at the bottom of the page (see fig. 15.10).

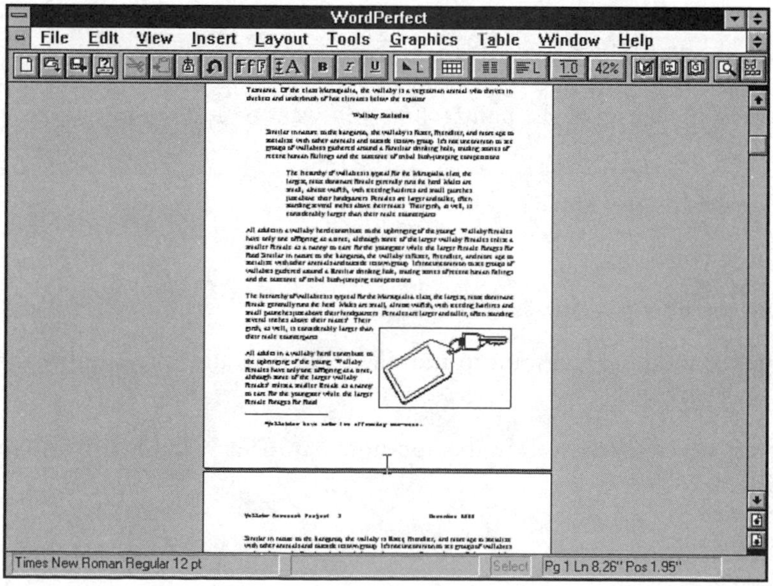

Figure 15.8
Conflicting feet.

One way around this is to make the footnote an endnote. Or, if the footnote is more important than the footer, let the footnote override the footer.

Demon-Strations

Put a Head on That, Will Ya?

1. Open the Layout menu.

2. Choose Headers/Footers.

3. Select Header A.

4. Click Create.

5. Click the necessary options in the header toolbar.

6. Click the Close button.

A Footnote by Any Other Name

1. Position the cursor at the point where you want to add the footnote number.

2. Open the Insert menu.

3. Choose Footnote.

4. From the popup menu, select Create.

5. Type the footnote you want to add. (WordPerfect adds the number for you.)

6. Set any necessary options in the Footnote bar. Click Close when you're finished.

Summary

This encounter enables you to add the finishing touches to your document. Headers, footers, footnotes, and endnotes can help you provide your reader with information about the document you've created. The next encounter looks at yet another high-end feature that gives most of us the heebie-jeebies: adding art.

Exorcises

1. What's the difference between a header and a footer?

2. What's the difference between a footer and a footnote?

3. What's the point of asking all these questions?

4. Does anybody know all the words to the Carol Burnett theme song?

5. Name four items you might want to include in a header.

Getting to the Art of the Matter

Goal

To help you face the epitome of word processing terror: Graphics Dread.

What You Will Need

Some reason to learn how to incorporate graphics, nerves of steel, and the ability to leap small doghouses.

Terms of Enfearment

graphics box	clip art
figure box	table box
text box	WP Draw
custom art	custom charts

Briefing

Adding graphics is the task most people love to hate about WordPerfect. But when it comes right down to it, the process just isn't that difficult. WordPerfect for Windows lets you add art two different ways:

- You can plug the art right into the document.
- You can create a box to hold the art you add.

Additionally, you can add lines and borders, and fill the graphics boxes you create with shading. Let's start with the easy stuff first.

> WordPerfect for Windows comes with 17 pieces of art that you can use in your own documents, so if you don't have something of your own to play with, you can use a WordPerfect clip art file.

Ready-To-Go Graphics

When you want to put a piece of art in your document without first creating a graphics box, open the Graphics menu and choose Figure. The Insert Image dialog box appears, as shown in figure 16.1. If you know the name of the art file you want to use, type it in the Filename: box. If you don't know the name or location of the file, you can use the File List or QuickLFinder to find it.

> WordPerfect's clip art files are stored in the C:\WPWIN60\GRAPHICS subdirectory. This directory comes up already chosen when you choose Graphics Figure.

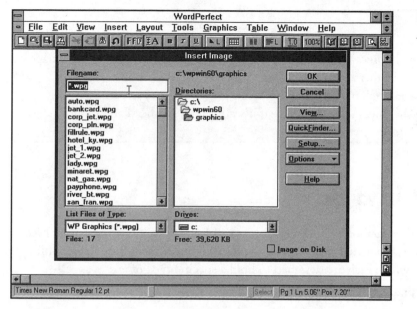

Figure 16.1
Finding the art.

After you select the file and click OK or press Enter, WordPerfect pulls the art into your document, moving the text over. The graphics isn't placed exactly at the cursor position, but it's close enough to be warm (see fig. 16.2).

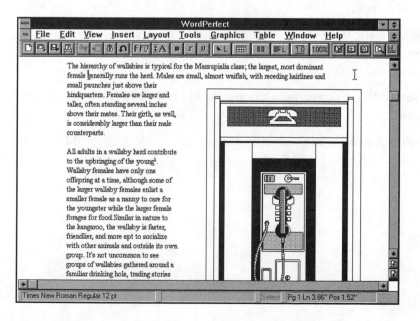

Figure 16.2
Box or art?

If you don't see an image in the box, open the View menu and make sure Graphics is selected. If it's not, your art won't display. If the image still isn't there, don't panic—it could be that your monitor doesn't have enough memory to display the graphic on the screen. Try printing the document, and then, if it's not there, go ahead and panic.

Art in a Box

The other method of adding graphics involves first creating a graphics box. WordPerfect actually allows you to create eight different kinds of graphics boxes, which each are designed to hold a specific type of art:

- **Figure box.** Stores clip art, drawings, and charts.
- **Text box.** Contains quotes, sidebars, and margin notes.
- **User box.** A borderless box that stores art images.
- **Table box.** Holds tabular information, spreadsheets, or text.
- **Equation box.** A borderless box that allows you to display equations in correct form.
- **Watermark Image box.** Remember the watermark on high-quality paper? A watermark image box places graphics (or text) behind document text.
- **Button box.** You can use art or text in a button box, which acts as an icon.
- **Inline Equation box.** A borderless box that enables you to add equations within text.

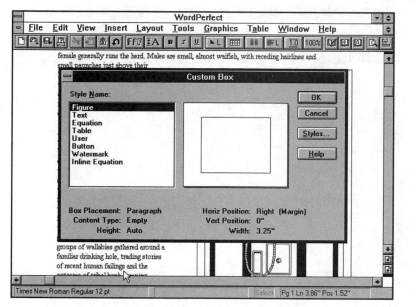

Figure 16.3
*Graphics custom
box options.*

To add the graphics box, follow these steps:

1. Position the cursor where you want the box to be added.

2. Open the Graphics menu.

3. Choose Custom Boxes. A dialog box appears, as shown in figure 16.3.

4. Select the type of box you want by clicking on it. The Preview screen shows what you've selected.

5. Choose the Create option. Now—take a deep breath—the rather frightening Graphics bar appears, as shown in figure 16.4.

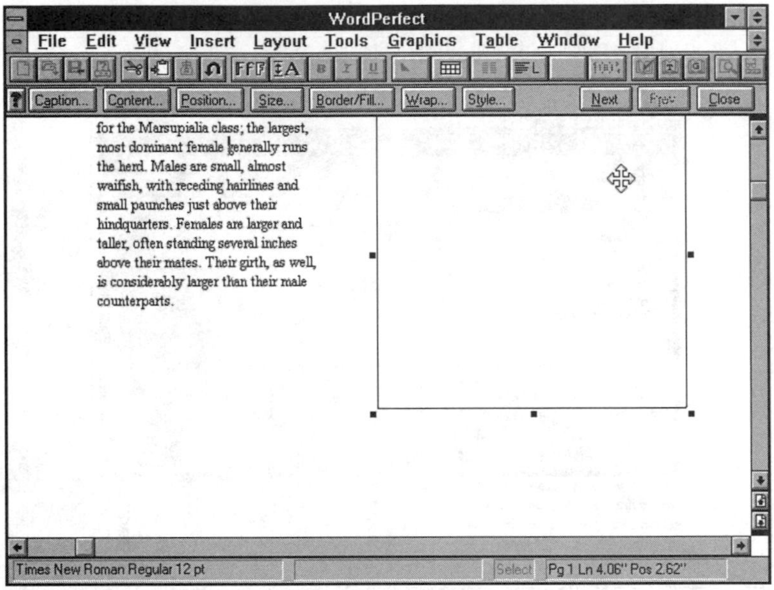

Figure 16.4
The Graphics bar has more options than you really want to deal with.

6. Here is what you do with the options:

   Caption. Add a caption to the image.

   Content. Choose what will be displayed in the box.

   Position. Choose where the box will be placed.

   Size. Select the size of the box.

   Border/Fill. Control other art elements.

   Attach To. Lets you attach the art to surrounding document items.

   Wrap. Control the placement of text around the image.

   Style. Choose the type of graphics box you want to create.

7. After entering all of the options, click Close.

WordPerfect for Windows then moves your text along the left side of the screen and places the graphics box on the right.

What I *Meant* To Do...

Don't like it? Too big? In the wrong place?

Don't sweat it.

You can edit the graphics you add to your WordPerfect document—if you don't expect too much of the word editing. Editing in this sense is not changing the look of the image, moving this person over here and this person over there. Editing when it comes to graphics means deleting. Or resizing. Rotating. Or changing the caption.

When you want to edit an image, first click on the graphics box, and then open the Graphics menu and choose Edit Box. Or press Shift+F11. Oh no. We've seen this before. This is the same as the graphics box toolbar. Make any necessary changes and click Close.

Artistic Endeavors

One of the beautiful things about working with WordPerfect for Windows is the closeness it shares with other Windows products. Right here, inside WordPerfect, you have quick access to other cousins in the WordPerfect family. For your artistic interests, you might want to create custom artwork or charts with WordPerfect Draw.

Drawing Your Own Stuff

If you want to create your own artwork, first display the Button Bar (remember how? Open the View menu and choose Button Bar). Then click the WP Draw button (in the center of the bar).

After a moment, the WP Draw screen appears (see fig. 16.5). Pretty cool, huh?

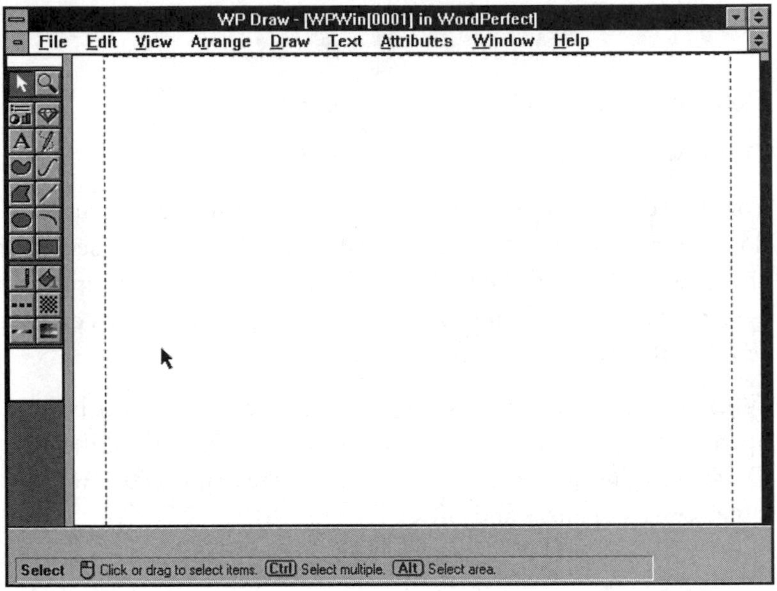

Figure 16.5
*WordPerfect
Draw—built right
in so you can add
your own genius.*

You can create whatever works in the WP Draw screen, and then copy it right to your WordPerfect for Windows document. Don't forget to save the file in WP Draw first, though. (Use the Save command in the File menu.) Notice the art-deco whozits in figure 16.6. (And to think I got kicked out of art class...)

Not-So-Original Art

Oh, you know those professional documents. They don't want our creativity. Not really. Oh, sure, they say they do. What they want is sweat. Grunt work. Statistics.

Charts. They want charts.

Okay, so it's not the most creative work in the world. Perot didn't do too badly with his. But nothing can be too interesting when you're showing the same thing over and over and over.

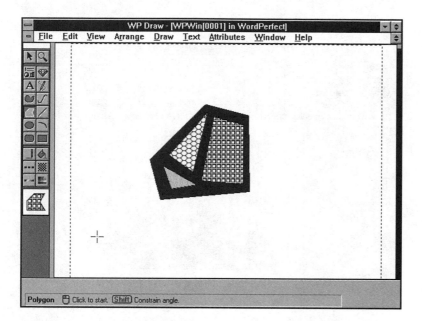

Figure 16.6
An art-deco whozits.

WordPerfect Draw offers an alternative. You can add charts to your documents (and it's easy to do, also, because it's right here in WordPerfect for Windows), and you can also free up a little room for creativity.

Just don't tell the boss.

When you're ready to create a chart with WordPerfect Draw, click the Chart button in the Button Bar (right beside the Draw button). One whopper of a screen appears, showing you lots of chart stuff that will blow your socks off (see fig. 16.7).

The process isn't as difficult as it looks. Just enter your own labels, data, and legend items in the window at the top of the screen, and when you click the Update button, WordPerfect Draw updates the displayed chart. You can select any number of chart types (just take a look at the tool bar along the left side of the screen) and come up with a huge range of enhancements.

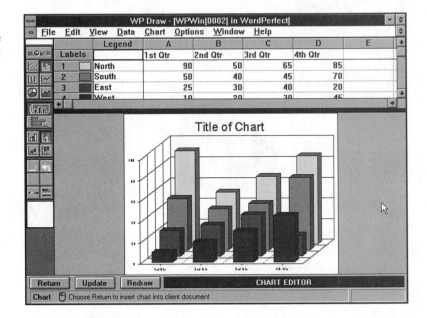

Again, you can copy the chart right into WordPerfect for Windows (or you can save it out as a file and use Graphics Figure to retrieve it). Just remember to save the file (that's the Save command in the File menu).

Play around with it some day when you've got time to experiment. Don't try to create that first chart under the gun.

They're Out To Get Us

There are a number of things that can go wrong when you're working with graphics. Luckily, catastrophic things like explosions and black-outs are rare.

Not enough memory to display graphics.

Make sure Graphics is checked in the View menu. If you still don't see the art, try printing the document.

You're having trouble positioning the graphics where you want them.

Open the Graphics menu and choose Edit Box. Adjust the Position settings. If that still doesn't help, try changing the size or position of the graphic.

You can't fit all the text on the page now that you've got the art placed.

If it just won't all go on the same page, try reducing the size of the text. More text will fit into the same amount of space, and if you only reduce the text one point size or two, the readability of the text shouldn't suffer.

You just can't leave the art alone.

This is known as Chronic Graphics Adjustment Syndrome, a problem that occurs when you just can't leave sleeping dogs lie and insist on fixing things that aren't broken. Have your officemate watch for that far-away, glazed look and repeat to yourself "I can overcome. I can overcome."

You're seeing graphics boxes before your eyes.

A new disorder, known as *box-sighted-ness,* that is prevalent among WordPerfect users. Blink several times in quick succession. If that doesn't help, you can send away for special 3-D glasses that can keep the condition from worsening.

Demon-Strations

Quick Clips

1. Position the cursor where you want the art to appear.

2. Open the Graphics menu.

3. Choose Figure.

4. Choose the file you want.

5. Click OK.

Shadow Boxing

1. Put the cursor where you want the art.

2. Open the Graphics menu.

3. Choose Custom Box.

4. Select Create.

5. When the Graphics box toolbar appears, select any necessary options.

6. Click Close.

Summary

This encounter shed some light on one of those horrid things most new WordPerfect for Windows users have nightmares about: graphics. You can add to your document's eye-appeal dramatically by putting in your own art, whether that art is just a company logo, a drawn image, or clip art. And it's not as hard as it looks. The next encounter finished off the book by explaining... (gulp)... merging documents.

Exorcises

1. True or false: You have to get clip art files before you can use WordPerfect's graphics features.

2. Name the two methods of adding art.

3. Put the following steps in order:

_____ Select Create

_____ Put the cursor where you want the art

_____ Choose the art file you want to add

_____ Add a caption, if necessary

_____ Call your mother

_____ Open the Graphics menu

_____ Choose the box style

_____ Choose the Custom Box command

_____ Click Close

_____ Use the toolbar

4. True or false: Once you position the art in the box, you cannot edit it.

5. What other program lets you add custom art and charts?

17th Encounter

All Files
Merge Right

Goal

To provide you with some emergency information just in case you are ever faced with—horror of horrors!—mail merging.

What You Will Need

Nerves of steel, a hard hat, and a sack lunch.

Terms of Enfearment

mail merging	merge printing
form	data
field	record

Briefing

The concept of *mail-merging*, also called *merge printing* by those not in-the-know, may be entirely new to you. If so, you may be, understandably, quaking (or quacking) in your boots by the end of this encounter.

Merging two documents is just what it sounds like: the process of taking this document and mixing it—like shuffling a deck of cards—into that document. The information in document 2 is used to plug holes in document 1.

Why would you be interested in such a thing? Well, remember those awful letters you get every month that sound like the following:

Congratulations [Mr./Mrs./Ms.] *Your last name*,

You have been entered in our drawing and are guaranteed one of the following prizes:

- An outdated Sony walkman

- A 27-inch Toshiba color television

- A mink coat (with the mink still in it)

All you have to do, [*Your first name*], is call our 1-800 number between the hours of 8 and 5 to collect your prize.

Even those obnoxious letters had to be written somewhere. And the idea—being able to send out a form letter with the right names and information printed within the body of the letter—can be quite a boon for businesses.

Another common use of the mail merge feature is producing mailing labels. That is something that makes even a die-hard WP enthusiast cringe. Oh, sure, it's easy to set up. But after you do, when you start to print, will your printer cooperate?

A Whole Lot of Merging Going On

Mail merging is really a simple concept. You create a letter with fill-in-the-blank spaces where the names should be. Then you create another file to store only the names. Then, through the miracle of mail merging, WordPerfect takes the names and plugs them into the blanks of the letter.

A lot better than creating one hundred copies of the same letter and entering the right names in each one, right?

Each of these fill-in-the-blank spaces is called a field. You can create fields to store different kinds of information, not just names. For example, you might include the following fields in a form letter about a new product your company is introducing:

Firstname
Lastname
Title
Company
Address
City
State
ZIP

Seems like a lot of information, but take a look at the letter shown in figure 17.1. In that letter, all these things are included as a matter of course. You probably type them so much you don't even notice.

If you wanted to send this letter to one hundred clients, you'd have your hands full erasing the names and addresses and typing in new ones one hundred times. (Each letter, in mail-merge terms, is called a *record.*) Instead of all that hassle, WordPerfect gives you the option of making that letter a form into which all the information can be plugged automatically.

Ready to try it?

Figure 17.1

Frank's pushing his fuschia fenders.

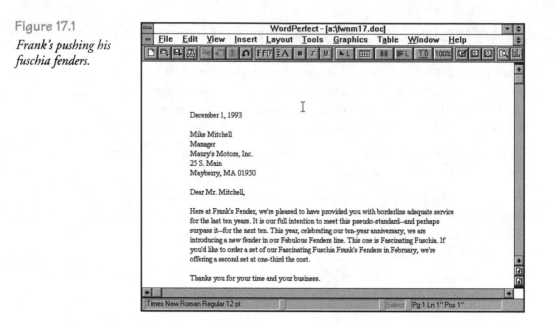

The Letter: Only a Shell

When you're ready to start your letter, open the Tools menu and select Merge. A popup Merge form appears, as shown in figure 17.2.

The Merge form gives you three options. You can click Data to start your data file (notice the nifty little picture), Form to start the form (that's the letter part), or Merge to put them both together (which we're not ready to do yet).

Let's start with the form.

Starting with the Form

When you click the Form button, the Create Form File dialog box appears (see fig. 17.3). It's asking you for the name of the data file you're going to use, but you don't have a data file yet. Click None for now (we can go back and change it). Then click OK.

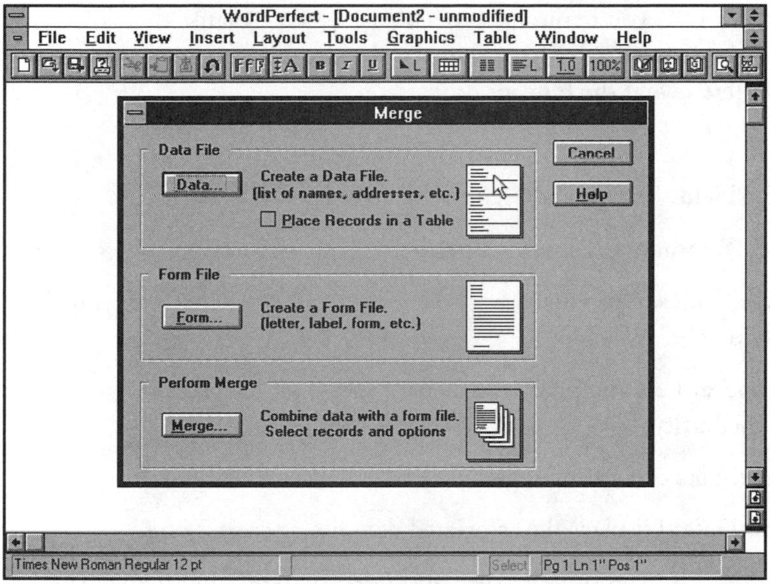

Figure 17.2
*Selecting the
necessary options.*

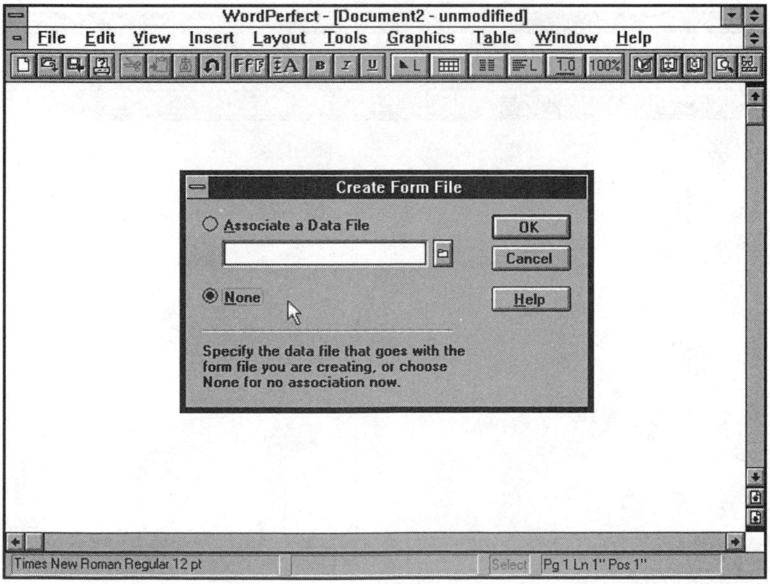

Figure 17.3
*Starting the data
form.*

After you click OK, you're dumped to a blank screen—blank, that is, except for the Merge bar (see fig. 17.4). (There is a bar for everything in this program.) Here's what the buttons do:

? Help!

Insert Field. Lets you add data fields to the form.

Date. Automatically inserts the date.

Merge Codes. Lets you control the merge codes—something you *don't* want to do!

Keyboard. Lets you pause the merge process for keyboard input (another rarity).

Merge. Puts everything together.

Go to Data. Displays the associated data file or creates one.

Options. Displays or hides the data codes, markers, and merge bar.

Figure 17.4
Checking out the merge bar.

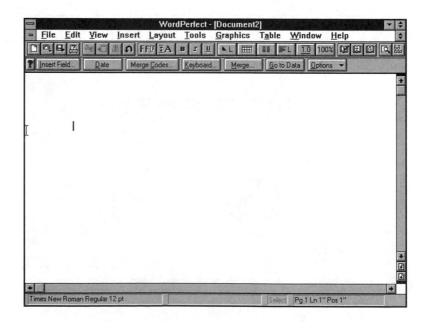

Ready? Click Insert Field. WordPerfect for Windows says, "Sorry, but there aren't any fields—oh, wait a minute..." and displays the Select Field Name box after you click OK (see fig. 17.5). Type something, like Firstname, and click Insert.

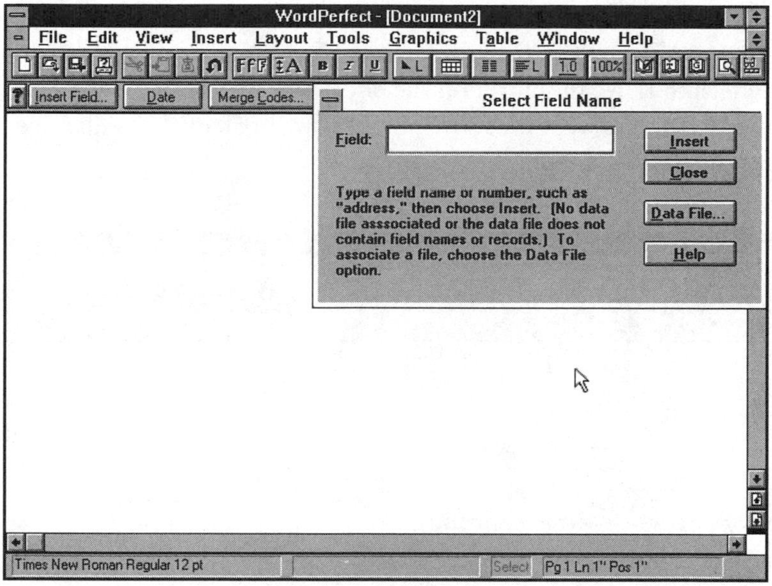

Figure 17.5
Adding a field name.

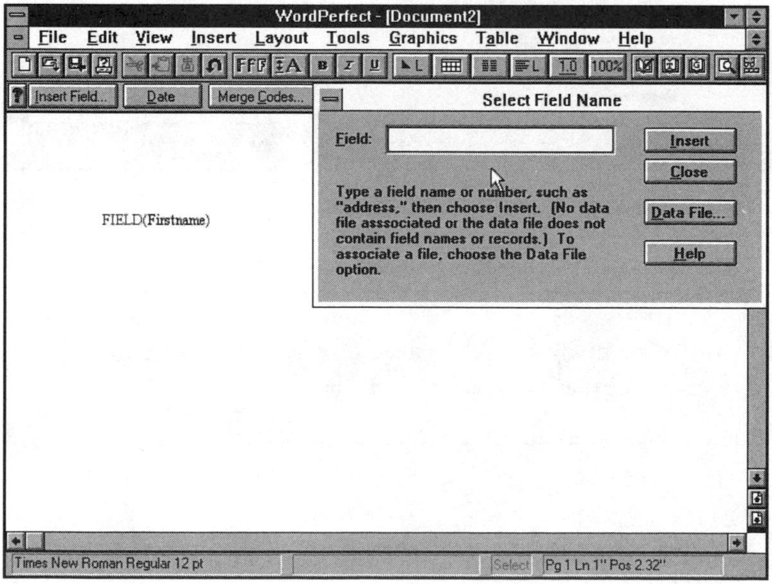

Figure 17.6
Whew. Finally.

Isn't that neat? WordPerfect for Windows did just what we expected it to. Now you can continue adding fields—the Select Field Name box will stay on the screen—and move the cursor on the document by pressing Enter as usual. Figure 17.7 shows what the form looks like when all of the fields have been entered.

Figure 17.7

Just what the mail carriers want—more form letters to deliver.

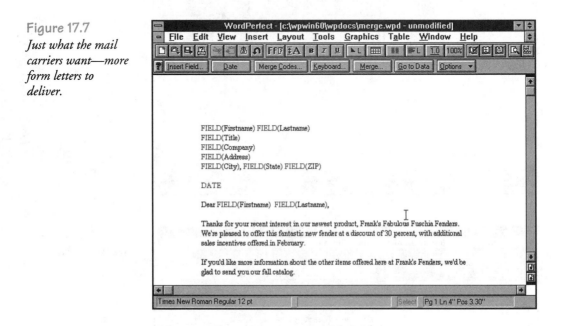

When you're finished with the form, save the file.

If you want to create mailing labels instead of a data form, just enter the fields as you want them to appear on the label.

The Data, Looking for a Home

Now for the other part. We're going to make the data file. Click the Go to Data button to display the Associate window (see fig. 17.8). Then click Create.

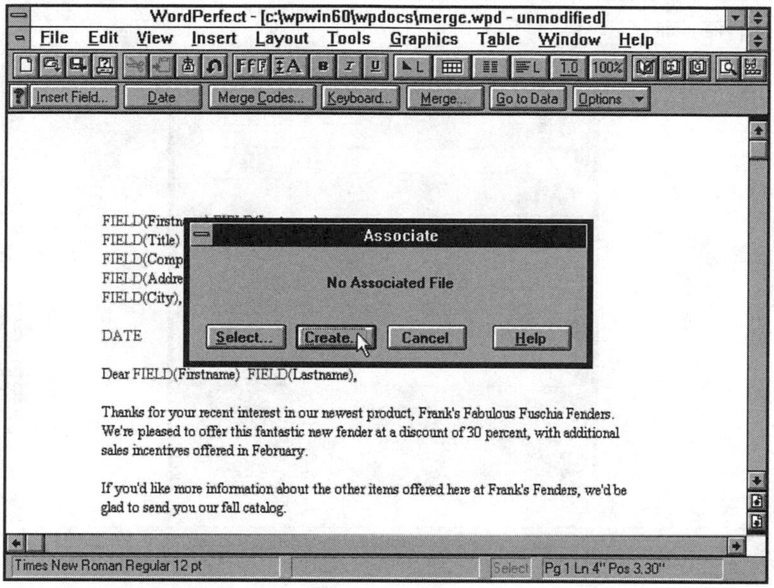

Figure 17.8
*The Associate
window.*

After a second, a new bar appears and is covered up by the Create Data File dialog box (see fig. 17.9). Here you will enter the basic fields and then the data. First enter the field names exactly as you created them in the data form. After you click OK, WordPerfect for Windows enters the field names at the top of the data file and displays the Quick Data Entry form (see fig. 17.10).

After you're finished entering your data, click Close. WordPerfect for Windows pours the data into the data form, as shown in figure 17.11. Ready to save the file? Let's merge this puppy.

Mail-Merge Matchmaking

Okay, let's sit back and survey our work.

What do we have? One form, saved in a document file. One data file, saved as a document.

What do you think we do with them?

Ready, set, shuffle!

Figure 17.9
*You have created ...
by the Create Data
File dialog box.*

Figure 17.10
*Quick Data Entry.
Really, it is.*

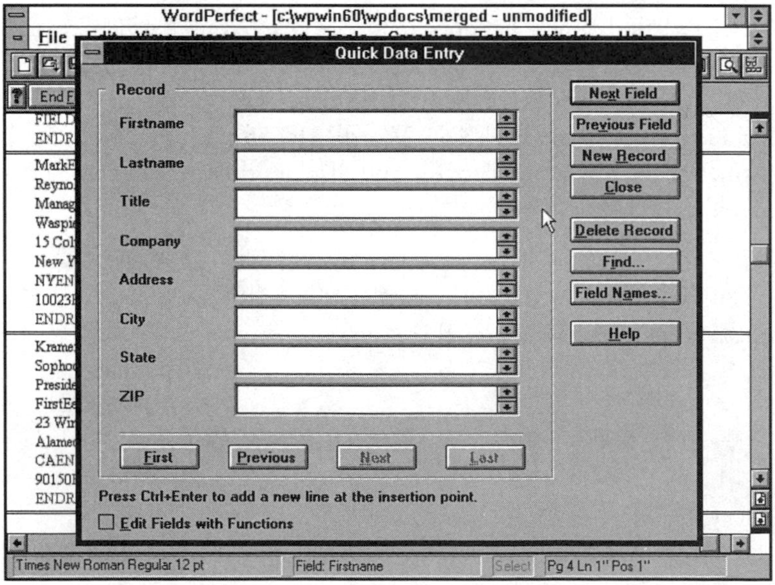

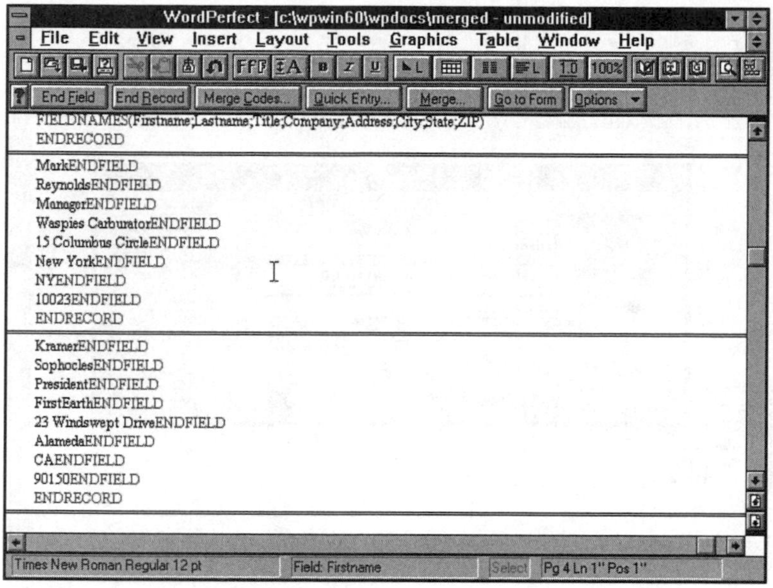

Figure 17.11
*Data in the data
form.*

The actual process of merging the form file and data file is a simple one. Click the Merge button. The Merge dialog box appears again. Click the Merge button, and the Perform Merge dialog box appears (see fig. 17.12). Make sure the right file names are entered for the form and the data file. Then click OK.

After a moment, WordPerfect for Windows displays the merged document in a document window. Check out figure 17.13. This may seem like a lot of work for two or three letters, but if you're dealing in the hundreds, it's a real lifesaver.

Now go ahead and save your file. Then walk around the office primping and patting yourself on the back (those two things are hard to do at the same time). You deserve the recognition: you faced a worthy foe and lived to tell about it.

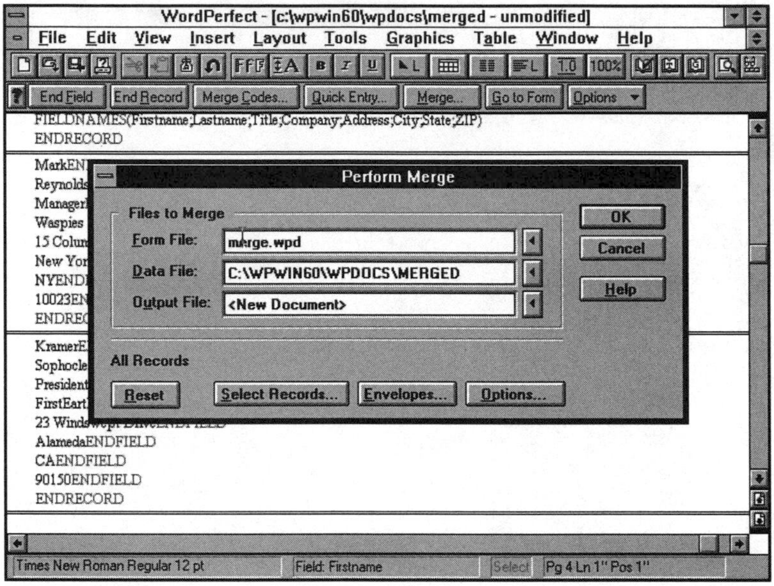

Figure 17.12
A whole lot of mergin' goin' on.

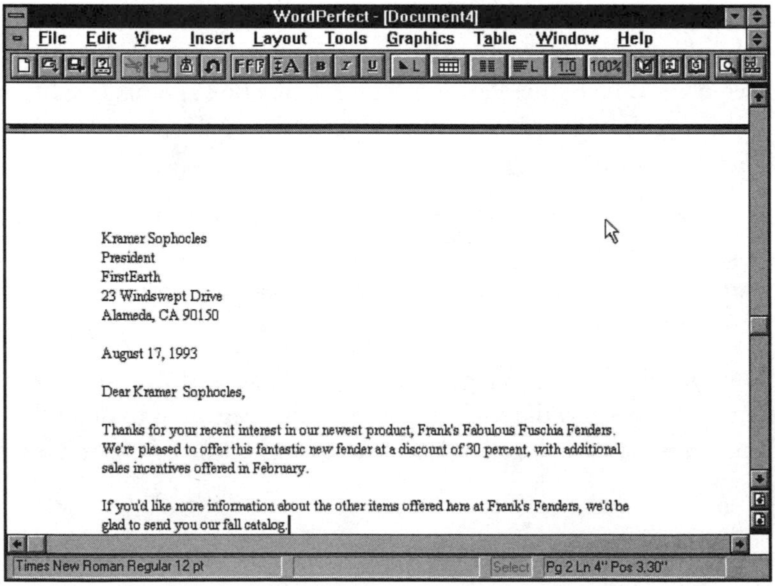

Figure 17.13
Congratulations. The merged document.

They're Out To Get Us

What's that? It *didn't* work? Oh, come on. Did you follow our flawless direction? Did your eye wander from the page—if only for an instant?

Oh, we're just kidding you.

Of course it didn't work. Most complicated things don't—the first time. (If your first merge print was wonderful, consider yourself lucky: the WordPerfect gods smiled on you today.)

The most obvious problem in a mail merge occurs when one of two things happens:

- The filenames you enter on the data form are different from those on the form letter.

- The fields in the data form are placed in an order that is different from the data form.

Keep trying; you'll get it. There are only so many things that can go wrong.

Demon-Strations

Forming a Form

1. Start with a new document.

2. Open the Tools menu.

3. Choose Merge.

4. Choose Form.

5. Click Insert Field.

6. Click OK.

7. Enter the first field name, click OK.

8. Continue entering all necessary field names.

9. Save the file.

10. When you're done, click Go to Data.

Doing Data

1. After clicking Go to Data, enter a name in the Associate box.

2. Enter the field names; then click OK.

3. Use the Quick Data Entry form to enter data.

4. When you're finished, click Close. WordPerfect for Windows places the data on the data form.

5. Remember to save the file when you're finished entering data.

Summary

This encounter brings you right up close to the biggest of all WordPerfect for Windows evils—mail merging—and then whisks you away again (kind of like a ride at Disney World). With the completion of this encounter, you've mastered all basic WordPerfect fears and should be starting to emerge as a WordPerfect-confident (or at least non-bumbling) user.

This encounter also brings your initial experience with *Fear WordPerfect for Windows No More* to a close. Those little beasts weren't so bad, after all, were they?

But—

[cue ominous music]
what will happen when—gasp—they introduce WordPerfect 7.0?

Dunh-duh-*DAAHHHHH*!

Exorcises

1. True or false: Mail merging is something you use only to produce mailing labels.

2. What is a field?

3. Match the following:

   _____ Where you enter fields   a. The data file

   _____ Where you enter data   b. The data form

4. How many ways can you output the merged file?

5. Don't you think that mail merging is the coolest thing ever?

Exorcise Answers

You're not cheating, are you? Oh, come on—you really couldn't come up with those answers by looking them up in the chapter?

Well, shame on you. You realize you're wracking up bad karma, right?

1st Encounter

1. 6.0 (You're looking this up?)

2. Menus (or Tupperware—whichever's handiest)

3. Falsetto. But it makes a lot more sense.

4. c

5. For letters, for memos, and for reports. (Also, newsletters, books, brochures, or anything with words that you print.) And the documentation really holds down the papers on your desk, too.

2nd Encounter

1. Oh, pretty much.

2. A cold boot freezes your foot and a warm boot doesn't.

3. A kind of program that helps you move in and out of other programs.

4. "I Left My Heart in San Fransisco."

5. By using the mouse (point at the menu and click) or by using the keyboard (press the Alt key and the highlighted letter in the menu name).

3rd Encounter

1. Dairy, meat—oh, wait. QWERTY, cursor keys, numeric keypad, and special keys.

2. Duh. Move the cursor.

3. c

4. "Do it!" or "Go!" or "Get up off the couch, you!"

5. Point, click, double-click, and drag.

4th Encounter

1. __2__ Words

   __C__ Pages

   __A__ Lines

   __A__ Paragraphs

   __2__ Characters

   __C__ Screenfuls

2. Bars you can display along the bottom edge and right edge of the screen to help you scroll through a longer document using the mouse.

3. That would be true.

4. c

5. a (but I wish it was d)

5th Encounter

1. c

2. Times Roman and Courier

3. Typeface, size, and style

4. Bold, italic, underline, and normal

5. Highlight it.

6th Encounter

1. Left, Right, Center, and Decimal

2. To line things up.

3. brussel sprout

4. b

5. That's a big negatory, good buddy.

7th Encounter

1. Monospaced characters all take up the same amount of space, and proportional characters are assigned the amount of space necessary for the letter.

2. b

3. b

4. You can see how the headsies and feetsies look together.

5. I've sworn off vitamins. A good Big Mac for breakfast really gets me going.

8th Encounter

1. Save and Save As. Save As lets you save the file under a different name.

2. Dream on.

3. Nope. WordPerfect loves everybody's files.

4. Open takes longer but they both do basically the same thing.

5. Sorry Charlie. No cookie.

9th Encounter

1. b

2. Use the mouse to highlight it, use Select, or write its phone number on the bathroom wall.

3. Wrong-o, bucky.

4. Select it, open the Edit menu and choose Copy.

5. How right you are.

10th Encounter

1. Find just finds, and find and replace puts something else in place of the something found.

2. b

3. Well, *someone* probably knows why.

4. Everything except c.

5. Oh come on. You're cheating on a bonus question?

11th Encounter

1. False.

2. __b__ Speller Checker

   __a__ Thesaurus

   __c__ Grammatik

3. Press Alt+T or click the durned thing.

4. True-a-mundo.

5. b and f

12th Encounter

1. Four: Draft, Page, Two Page, and Reveal Codes

2. So you can see the art you create and import.

3. (a)To see the secrets of your document; (b)To delete codes that grew there accidentally.

4. I'm not sure, but it has something to do with Big Bird, knee X rays, and painted rocks.

13th Encounter

1. __d__ Centered

   __c__ Full

   __a__ Left

   __b__ Right

2. Spreads out all lines, including headings and leftovers.

3. When you're using columns, or when you're feeling really defensive.

4. Left, your left, your left...

5. e (and d, too)

14th Encounter

1. a

2. False.

3. Position the cursor and press Ctrl+Enter.

4. Gosh, I hate these, don't you? The first is Position the cursor, and the last is click OK. Do what you want in the middle.

15th Encounter

1. A header is at the top; and a footer's at the bottom of the page.

2. A footer is something that prints on every page that has no ties in the text; a footnote is a note placed at the bottom of the page that clarifies a point in text.

3. Got me.

4. Send them to Kelly Dobbs, c/o Brady Books.

5. Company name, date, your name, and the document title.

16th Encounter

1. False. WordPerfect comes with 17 graphics files.

2. You can add graphics free-form or bring it into a graphics box.

3. Why, oh *why*, did I write this question in the first place? Here are the numbers 4, 1, 6, 7, 8, 2, 5, 3, 9 (if you win the lottery, let me know).

4. False.

5. WordPerfect Draw.

17th Encounter

1. False.

2. A place in Indiana where they grow lots of corn.

3. b and then a

4. To a new (or the current) document, to the printer, to a file, or to another document you specify.

5. No. Those little sports socks are the coolest thing ever.

Index

Fear No... More

A New Computer Book Series for the Absolute Beginner

Never before has mastering a computer been so practical, fun, simple, and completely panic-free. Filled with off-beat characters, practical "demon-strations," and skill-building "excorcises," FEAR...NO MORE focuses exclusively on the needs of the first-time computer user.

Now Available

FEAR MACS NO MORE
ISBN 1-56686-082-2
$15.95

- Developed by award-winning author Danny Goodman!

- Illustrated in 2-color!

FEAR EXCEL NO MORE
Version 4.0 for the Mac
ISBN 1-56686-083-0
$15.95

FEAR WINDOWS NO MORE
ISBN 1-56686-081-4
$15.95

- Makes learning the computer fun and challenging!

- Available for Mac & Windows

FEAR EXCEL NO MORE
Version 4.0 for Windows
ISBN 1-56686-084-9
$15.95

ISBN	Qty	Title	Price
1-56686-082-2		Fear Macs No More	$15.95
1-56686-081-4		Fear Windows No More	$15.95
1-56686-083-0		Fear Excel No More for the Mac	$15.95
1-56686-084-9		Fear Excel No More for Windows	$15.95

Send to: **Brady/Fear Titles**
Prentice Hall Computer Publishing
201 W. 103rd Street
Indianapolis, IN 46290
or toll free: 1-800-428-5331

Subtotal _____
State sales tax _____
Shipping & Handling ($2.50/title) _____
TOTAL _____

☐ Check ☐ VISA ☐ MasterCard ☐ American Express

Acct. # _____ Signature _____

Ship to: Name _____ Company _____

Address _____

City _____ State_____ Zip_____